John Karlsrud – with his insider knowledge – asks and answers the right questions: Why does the UN act the ways it does, and how do those ways of operating become established policy norms? This is an accessible and valuable book.

Roger Mac Ginty, *Professor of Peace and Conflict Studies, University of Manchester, UK*

Out of new conceptual space, Karlsrud adapts the 'linked ecologies' framework to provide fresh analytical thinking on norm arbitrage as a policy practice with real impact.

Diane Stone, *University of Warwick, UK and Centenary Professor, University of Canberra, Australia*

John Karlsrud provides a valuable new perspective for understanding and explaining the dynamics of UN peacekeeping missions. Norm Change in International Relations should be read by anyone wishing to understand the evolution of UN peacekeeping practices and how norm change is enacted within international organizations.

André Broome, *Director of the Centre for the Study of Globalisation and Regionalisation, University of Warwick, UK*

Where do new peacekeeping norms come from? John Karlsrud's incisive book shows how senior mission leaders in the field and broader epistemic communities that advocate on peacekeeping issues bring their ideas to the competitive arena of the United Nations, and why certain ideas, including the 'responsibility to protect' and the need for 'integrated missions', won out in the battle for normative supremacy.

Paul D. Williams, *Elliott School of International Affairs, the George Washington University, USA*

Norm Change in International Relations

In recent decades there have been several constructivist scholars who have looked at how norms change in international relations. However, few have taken a closer look at the particular strategies employed to further change or looked at the common factors in play in these processes. This book seeks to further the debates by looking at both agency and structure in tandem.

It focuses on the practices of linked ecologies (formal or informal alliances), undertaken by individuals who are the constitutive parts of norm change processes and who have moved between international organizations, academic institutions, think tanks, non-governmental organizations (NGOs), and member states. The book sheds new light on how norm change comes about, focusing on the practices of individual actors as well as collective ones. The book draws attention to the role of practices in UN peacekeeping missions, how these may create a bottom-up influence on norm change in UN peacekeeping, and the complex interplay between government and UN officials, applied and academic researchers, and civil society activists forming linked ecologies in processes of norm change. With this contribution, the study further expands the understanding of which actors have agency and what sources of authority they draw on in norm change processes in international organizations.

A significant contribution to the study of international organizations and UN peacekeeping, as well as to the broader questions of global norms in international relations (IR), this work will be of interest to students and scholars of international relations alike.

John Karlsrud is a senior research fellow at the Norwegian Institute of International Affairs (NUPI).

Routledge Research on the United Nations

1 **Chairing Multilateral Negotiations**
The case of the United Nations
Spyros Blavoukos and Dimitris Bourantonis

2 **Individual Agency and Policy Change at the United Nations**
The people of the United Nations
Ingvild Bode

3 **Reforming UN Decision-Making Procedures**
Promoting a deliberative system for global peace and security
Daniel Niemetz Martin

4 **The UN International Criminal Tribunals**
Transition without justice?
Klaus Bachmann and Aleksandar Fatić

5 **Norm Change in International Relations**
Linked ecologies in UN peacekeeping operations
John Karlsrud

Norm Change in International Relations

Linked ecologies in UN peacekeeping operations

John Karlsrud

LONDON AND NEW YORK

First published 2016
by Routledge

2 Park Square, Milton Park, Abingdon, Oxfordshire OX14 4RN
711 Third Avenue, New York, NY 10017

Routledge is an imprint of the Taylor & Francis Group, an informa business

First issued in paperback 2018

Copyright © 2016 John Karlsrud

The right of John Karlsrud to be identified as author of this work has been
asserted by him in accordance with sections 77 and 78 of the Copyright,
Designs and Patents Act 1988.

All rights reserved. No part of this book may be reprinted or reproduced or
utilised in any form or by any electronic, mechanical, or other means, now
known or hereafter invented, including photocopying and recording, or in
any information storage or retrieval system, without permission in writing
from the publishers.

Notice:
Product or corporate names may be trademarks or registered trademarks,
and are used only for identification and explanation without intent to
infringe.

British Library Cataloguing in Publication Data
A catalogue record for this book is available from the British Library

Library of Congress Cataloging-in-Publication Data
Names: Karlsrud, John, author.
Title: Norm change in international relations : linked ecologies in UN
    peacekeeping operations / John Karlsrud.
Description: Milton Park, Abingdon, Oxon ; New York, NY : Routledge,
    2016. | Includes bibliographical references and index.
Identifiers: LCCN 2015028344 | ISBN 9781138942707 (hardback) |
    ISBN 9781315672984 (ebook)
Subjects: LCSH: United Nations—Peacekeeping forces. | Peacekeeping
    forces. | International relations—Philosophy. | International relations—
    Social aspects.
Classification: LCC JZ6374 .K37 2016 | DDC 341.5/84—dc23
LC record available at http://lccn.loc.gov/2015028344

ISBN: 978-1-138-94270-7 (hbk)
ISBN: 978-1-138-32026-0 (pbk)

Typeset in Times New Roman
by Apex CoVantage, LLC

For Gabriel and Ive with love

Contents

Figures	xi
Preface and acknowledgments	xiii
Acronyms and abbreviations	xvii

1 Linked ecologies in United Nations peacekeeping   1

Introduction 1
Norm change in UN peacekeeping after the Cold War 2
Aims and questions of the book 7
Methodology 9
Outline of the book and short introduction to the case studies 12

2 Theorizing linked ecologies in norm change processes   18

Basic norms and norms in international relations 18
From bureaucracies to professions 24
Using practice theory and the sociology of professions
    to augment constructivist theorizing of norm change
    in international organizations 26
Informal alliances for norm change as social practices 28
The United Nations as a competitive arena for informal
    policy alliances 35
Conclusions 37

**3 SRSGs as norm arbitrators? Understanding
bottom-up authority in UN peacekeeping**   43

Introduction 43
Giving meaning to peacekeeping norms through actions:
    a bottom-up, practice-driven approach? 44
Côte d'Ivoire – what does "robust peacekeeping" really mean? 45
Afghanistan – upholding the principle of impartiality or
    undermining the operation? 52

x *Contents*

SRSG autonomy – the composition of authority in peacekeeping 56
Autonomous behavior of IOs – the role of SRSG norm arbitration 61
Conclusions 63

4 Linked ecologies and Responsibility to Protect   72
Introduction 72
The evolution of R2P – from concept to principle? 73
*Viewing the R2P process in terms of a constructivist/sociology of
    professions framework 76*
Advancing the principle inside and outside the UN 85
Conclusions 86

5 Linked ecologies and revolving doors for
   norm change in peacekeeping operations   94
Introduction 94
Evolution of the integrated missions concept 95
Linked ecologies and revolving doors 103
Conclusions 111

6 The United Nations as a competitive arena
   for norm change   116
Introduction 116
Building policy alliances for norm change: Norway 117
Two understandings of the UN as an arena 118
Infusing the UN with intellectuals – strategic planning at the UN 120
Think tanks and policy formulation in member states 127
Linked ecologies: contributions to norm change 135
Conclusions 137

7 Linked ecologies in international relations   142
Introduction 142
Main findings of the book 143
Final observations and recommendations 148

Index   151

Figures

1.1	Basic norms, norms/conventions, and practices in UN peacekeeping	8
2.1	Linked ecologies in UN peacekeeping	34
5.1	Organization of leadership tasks in integrated missions	96
5.2	Relationships between key actors in the integrated missions process	107
7.1	Grundnorms, norms/conventions, and practices in UN peacekeeping	144

Preface and acknowledgments

This book has two origins. While working for the UN peacekeeping mission in Chad and the Central African Republic (MINURCAT), I found myself struggling with a puzzle – the more I got to know the key principles or norms guiding peacekeeping, the more I came to realize that these norms did not constitute a harmonious set of principles, but could even be directly at odds with each other in given situations. I was struck by how my boss, Victor Angelo, the UN special representative of the secretary-general (SRSG) and head of MINURCAT, continuously had to carefully consider how to respond to emerging situations, weighing the various norms guiding peacekeeping missions against each other. In doing this, he was relying on experience from a long career as a UN official and the inculcated norms that follow, consulting headquarters in New York, but he was also asking for input from the staff around him.

The peacekeeping mission I was working for, MINURCAT, had been mandated to help the government of Chad protect vulnerable populations and humanitarians in the eastern part of the country and also to provide institutional support to strengthen the rule of law and facilitate intercommunity dialogue at the local level. In this mandate there was a potential conflict between giving support to the government to enable it to expand and (re-)establish authority, while at the same time remaining an impartial mediator at the local level. Although the mission did not have a political mandate to mediate between the government and the rebels who were vying for power (which made it somewhat of an outlier in terms of peacekeeping missions), there was strong tension between the mandates we were given – a tension that in my view is common to all peacekeeping missions today. This tension emerges from the fact that while peacekeeping missions today are supposed to be impartial, maintain consent of the main parties, and use as little force as possible, they are also supposed to extend state authority and protect civilians against harm, even when the perpetrator is the state itself. These core and conflictual norms of peacekeeping have developed since the beginning of the UN itself, a point to which I return in the following.

A second feature of day-to-day operations was the continuous contact with researchers from think tanks and academia, the media, and others specifically interested in the mission, and often in the topic of peacekeeping as such. I was one of Victor Angelo's special assistants, tasked with keeping him abreast of a

xiv *Preface and acknowledgments*

range of issues, and I accompanied him on his travels to the field to visit refugee camps and met with government officials, humanitarians, and other UN officials, as well as joined him for meetings in the UN Security Council, with member state officials in various capitals, and with researchers, activists, and others interested in the situation in Chad and the Central African Republic. I found that all these actors, including donor and embassy staffers, journalists, and researchers from think tanks and academic institutions, most often had clear opinions about peacekeeping operations and what purpose they should serve and were advancing particular agendas aimed at changing peacekeeping practices in the field and at headquarters.

In 2010, I wanted to study this interaction between UN peacekeeping professionals and researchers, academics, and member state officials and the impact this interaction could have on the norms guiding UN peacekeeping. I took up a job as a research fellow at the Norwegian Institute of International Affairs (NUPI) and started to work on a PhD on this theme at the University of Warwick. I also had previously worked on peacekeeping-related issues at another think tank in Norway, the Fafo Institute for Applied International Studies (FAFO-AIS). My previous experience also included two years at the United Nations Development Programme (UNDP) in New York and one year as a military liaison officer for NATO (North Atlantic Treaty Organisation) in Bosnia and Herzegovina.

These various classes of actors, which I in this book call 'ecologies,' interacted closely with UN peacekeepers and appeared to play an important part in the constant balancing between and redefinition of the core norms guiding peacekeeping. However, this interaction – which unfolds on a daily basis in the field, at UN headquarters in New York, and in various capitals around the world among ministry officials, think tank and academic scholars, and others – seemed to me reflected to only a limited degree in the literature on peacekeeping and on norm change in international organizations more generally. This book is the final result of my PhD and examines this phenomenon and its possible implications for understanding norm change in peacekeeping and international organizations (IOs) in general.

The book could not have been completed without the unending support, critical comments, and constructive suggestions of my supervisor at the University of Warwick, Prof. Leonard Seabrooke. I would also like to thank colleagues at the Norwegian Institute of International Affairs for discussions and constructive criticism, in particular Ole Jacob Sending, who has helped with thoughtful advice on innumerable occasions, and Morten S. Andersen, Marina Caparini, Cedric de Coning, Karsten Friis, Heidi Kjærnet, Iver Neumann, Randi Solhjell, and Lotte Vermeij, for sharing ideas and giving input and feedback as the project has developed. I would also like to extend my heartfelt thanks to those who agreed to be interviewed for this project and all those who have given me pointers and guidance regarding literature and persons to meet and interview. I am indebted to many people who have at various stages shared their ideas, comments, and inputs with me, including Simon Adams, Victor Angelo, Henk-Jan Brinkman, Christopher Coleman, Jan Egeland, Espen Barth Eide, Kai Eide, Katharina Glaab, David S. Guttormsen, Anja Kaspersen, Philip Kalantzis-Cope, Kai Michael Kenkel,

Preface and acknowledgments xv

Randolph Kent, Robert Kirkpatrick, Jostein Leiro, Connie Peck, Giulia Piccolino, Ramesh Thakur, Jakob Townsend, Eleni Tsingou, Catherine Weaver, and Thomas G. Weiss. Special thanks also to Benjamin de Carvalho, who helped me with the initial proposal and introduced me to NUPI, and Arthur A. Schulte, who has helped me from the very initial stages of writing a proposal and finding my way through the vast amounts of literature, to voluntarily reading through the entire thesis during the final rewriting stage. I am also thankful to Ingrid Aune, who gave me numerous valuable comments at the final stage, and Susan Høivik, who read through the entire manuscript and helped improve my rather poor English. Chris Wilson has been a great dialogue partner and has helped out with ideas and support throughout the process. Ståle Ulriksen and Vegard Valther Hansen gave me an initial workspace at NUPI which over time developed to my current position as a research fellow, and for this I am very grateful. Astrid Hornslien has been a source of unending support and encouragement during the final stages of this book.

I have benefited immensely from the input and feedback received at various conferences and workshops. I would also like to thank editors and peer reviewers at various journals where material in this book has been previously published and for which permissions have been obtained for republishing material in this book. Chapter 3 is an extended version of "SRSGs as Norm Arbitrators? Understanding Bottom-Up Authority in UN Peacekeeping," which first appeared in *Global Governance* 19 (2013). A shorter version of chapter 4 appeared as "Responsibility to Protect and Theorising Normative Change in International Organisations: From Weber to the Sociology of Professions" in *Global Responsibility to Protect* 5 (2013). Chapter 5 draws empirical material from the article "Multiple Actors and Centres of Agency? Examining the UN as Competitive Arena for Normative Change," published in *Journal of International Organization Studies* 4 (2014). Chapter 6, "UN as a Competitive Arena for Linked Ecologies: The Case of UN Peacekeeping," is here in its third incarnation and draws from the article in *Journal of International Organization Studies* mentioned earlier and "UN as a Competitive Arena for Linked Ecologies: The Case of UN Peacekeeping," published in *Political Perspectives* 7 (2013).

I am particularly grateful to Victor Angelo, the former UN SRSG in Chad. His advice and comments on early drafts of my PhD proposal, as well as unwavering support in a very difficult time for me personally, were very helpful for me. The time I spent in New York, working for the UNDP, and in Chad with the UN peacekeeping mission MINURCAT, gave me insights into internal UN working processes and gave me the opportunity to meet and become friends with the many dedicated staff, both in the field and at headquarters, who on a daily basis work to improve the lives of people living in countries experiencing conflict and crises. This thesis would not have seen the light of day without them.

Oslo, June 2015

Acronyms and abbreviations

ACCORD	African Centre for the Constructive Resolution of Disputes
APSTA	African Peace Support Trainers' Association
AIPR	ASEAN Institute for Peace and Reconciliation
ASEAN	Association of Southeast Asian Nations
ASF	African Standby Force
ASG	assistant secretary-general
AU	African Union
BiH	Bosnia-Herzegovina
*BRICS	Brazil, Russia, India, China, and South Africa
C34	UN General Assembly Special Committee on Peacekeeping Operations
CAP	Consolidated Appeals Process
CEBRI	Centro Brasileiro de Relações Internacionais
CIC	Center on International Cooperation (New York University)
CSO	civil society organization
CUNY	City University of New York
DDR	disarmament, demobilization, and reintegration
DPKO	Department of Peacekeeping Operations
DPA	Department of Political Affairs
DRC	Democratic Republic of the Congo
DSRSG	deputy special representative of the secretary-general
ECPR	European Consortium for Political Research
EOSG	Executive Office of the Secretary-General
FAFO-AIS	Fafo Institute for Applied International Studies
FARC	Revolutionary Armed Forces of Columbia
FARDC	Forces Armées de la République Démocratique du Congo
FDSCI	Forces de défense et de sécurité de Côte d'Ivoire
FRCI	Forces républicaines de Côte d'Ivoire
FUNAG	Fundação Alexandre de Gusmão
GAPCon	Group of Analysis on International Conflict Prevention
GCR2P	Global Centre for the Responsibility to Protect
HC	humanitarian coordinator
HRL	human rights law

xviii *Acronyms and abbreviations*

IASC	Inter-agency Standing Committee
ICISS	International Commission on Intervention and State Sovereignty
ICRtoP	International Coalition for Responsibility to Protect
ICRC	International Committee of the Red Cross
IDPs	internally displaced persons
IDRC	International Development Research Centre
IHL	international humanitarian law
IM	integrated missions
INGO	international non-governmental organization
IO	international organization
IPI	International Peace Institute (previously International Peace Academy, IPA)
IPRI	Instituto de Pesquisa de Relações Internacionais
IPSS	Institute for Peace and Security Studies, Addis Ababa University
IR	international relations
ISAF	International Security Assistance Force
ISS	Institute for Security Studies
LoA	logic of appropriateness
LRA	Lord's Resistance Army
MFA	Ministry of Foreign Affairs
MINURCAT	United Nations Mission in the Central African Republic and Chad
MINUSMA	United Nations Multidimensional Integrated Stabilization Mission in Mali
MINUSTAH	United Nations Stabilization Mission in Haiti
MONUC	United Nations Organization Mission in the Democratic Republic of the Congo
MONUSCO	United Nations Organization Stabilization Mission in the Democratic Republic of the Congo
MSF	Médecins Sans Frontières
NAM	Non-Aligned Movement
NATO	North Atlantic Treaty Organisation
NGO	non-governmental organization
NUPI	Norwegian Institute of International Affairs
OAS	Organization of American States
OAU	Organization of African Unity
OCHA	Office for the Coordination of Humanitarian Affairs
OECD	Organisation for Economic Co-operation and Development
ONUC	Organisation des Nations Unies au Congo
ONUCI/ UNOCI	United Nations Operation in Côte d'Ivoire
OO	Office of Operations
OSCE	Organization for Security and Co-operation in Europe
PA theory	principal-agent theory
PBPS	Policy and Best Practices Service

Acronyms and abbreviations xix

PKO	peacekeeping operation
PoC	Protection of Civilians
PR	permanent representative (ASEAN)
R2P	Responsibility to Protect
R2P-CS	Responsibility to Protect – Engaging Civil Society
RC	resident coordinator
REC	Regional Economic Communities
RUF	Revolutionary United Front
RwP	Responsibility while Protecting
SG	secretary-general
SMG	Senior Management Group
SOP	standard operating procedure
SPU	Strategic Planning Unit
SRSG	special representative of the secretary-general
SSR	security sector reform
ToR	Terms of Reference
UNAMA	United Nations Assistance Mission in Afghanistan
UNAMID	The African Union – United Nations Mission in Darfur
UNCT	United Nations Country Team
UNDP	United Nations Development Programme
UNDSS	UN Department of Safety and Security
UNEF	United Nations Emergency Force
UNGA	United Nations General Assembly
UNHCR	United Nations High Commissioner for Refugees
UNICEF	United Nations Children's Fund
UNMISS	United Nations Mission in the Republic of South Sudan
UNPROFOR	United Nations Protection Force
UNSC	United Nations Security Council
UN SCR	United Nations Security Council Resolution
UNSG	United Nations secretary-general
UNTSO	United Nations Truce Supervision Organization
UNU	United Nations University
USG	under-secretary-general
WFP	World Food Programme

1 Linked ecologies in United Nations peacekeeping

Introduction

During the two past decades there have been several constructivist scholars who have looked at how norms change in international relations, for example, highlighting the role of epistemic communities and activists and the role of agents (outside of states) versus process and structure. However, only few scholars have looked closer at the particular strategies that are employed to further change and some of the common factors that have been in play in these processes. This book continues this endeavor looking at both agency and structure in tandem. It posits that while parsimony may be reached by focusing on either structure or agency, what is between is the most interesting. The book focuses on the practices and processes of linked ecologies – formal or informal alliances – performed by individuals who are the constitutive parts of norm change processes and who have moved between international organizations, academic institutions, think tanks, non-governmental organizations (NGOs), and member states. By focusing on these individuals and the processes they have been part of, we can learn more about how informal alliances are shaped and how norms have been formed and changed in international relations.

The book looks at norm change processes for UN peacekeeping, an area where there have been significant new norms that have been developed over the last two decades or so, providing a particularly rich case to study. Furthermore, the book analyses tension and conflict between some of the basic norms guiding peacekeeping, most crucially between sovereignty, on the one hand, and core humanitarian principles and human rights on the other. This tension is reproduced at the norms and guidelines level, and as a result UN peacekeepers are constantly facing dilemmas where several norms apply and clash. The book argues that there are multiple sources of agenda and agency within the UN, resulting in diverging and conflicting norm pressures and practices, particularly between headquarters and the field, but also between the Security Council, the General Assembly, and the Secretariat of the Secretary-General.

The book's main aim in concentrating on linked ecologies in norm change is four-fold: First, the book can enrich the literature on agency by focusing on the working level. Linked ecologies are constituted of working-level individuals who form informal and formal policy alliances on particular issues. By focusing on

2   *Linked ecologies in UN peacekeeping*

these individuals and the processes they have been part of, we can learn more about how informal alliances are shaped and how norms have been formed and changed. Second, the book contributes to the unpacking of agency in norm change processes by showing how informal and formal policy alliances are formed, often pivoting around individuals moving back and forth through revolving doors between the UN, think tanks, and member states. Working-level officials in various 'ecologies' such as international organizations, member states, think tanks, and academia have formed informal policy alliances to establish new norms, principles, and concepts such as 'responsibility to protect' and 'integrated missions,' effectively constituting and driving norm change in the international system. The book understands these processes as collective practices and by this further expands the understanding of which actors have agency and what sources of authority they draw on in norm change processes in international organizations.

Third, the book also expands the theoretical understanding of these processes using the sociology of professions and practice theory to advance constructivist theorizing of norm change in international organizations. In the empirical chapters it looks at two decisive ways in which linked ecologies can have an impact on norm change. In the first case study on the role of UN special representatives of the secretary-general (SRSGs), the relative autonomy of an SRSG is scrutinized, and a typology of the sources of authority that the SRSG draws upon is presented. Here I argue that individuals such as SRSGs can draw upon a 'revolving door' authority, as they have built up relationships and support over a lengthy career within several ecologies. In the second and third empirical chapters, two distinct norm change processes are examined – the Responsibility to Protect and the Integrated Missions processes – and the linked ecologies concept is used to unpack the constitutive members and drivers of these processes.

Fourth, I argue that the UN can be seen as a competitive arena where informal policy alliances, or 'linked ecologies,' put forward ideas on how to solve policy issues. In a broad sense, the UN is an arena where informal alliances are formed around issues of common concern; with the financial support of donor states and the knowledge production of think tanks, academia, and the working level of the UN, ownership among member states is built in consultative processes. As such, the book provides further empirical support for the use of the 'linked ecologies' concept to better understand norm change processes (see also Stone 2013, Seabrooke and Tsingou 2009, 2015, Seabrooke and Nilsson 2015).

Norm change in UN peacekeeping after the Cold War

UN peacekeeping is not mentioned in the UN Charter. Nevertheless, peacekeeping is today one of the most recognized tools of the world organization and is used to help states overcome conflict, re-establish order, and open up space for peacebuilding and development. In the years following the signing of the UN Charter on June 26, 1945, a few missions were mandated. The still-existing UN Truce Supervision Organization (UNTSO) is often cited as the first peacekeeping operation (Bellamy et al. 2010, 83). It was followed by several other observation missions in

Linked ecologies in UN peacekeeping 3

the 1950s, including missions to India/Pakistan (Kashmir) in 1949 (until today), Israel/Egypt (1956–67), and several other countries. During the Cold War, most of the missions the UN deployed were observer missions, with the notable exceptions of the UN operation in Congo (ONUC, 1960–4), which had an executive mandate to restore order and assist the Congolese government (ibid.), and the UN force in Korea, mandated to defend South Korea (ibid.). ONUC is of particular interest, as it has been widely seen as a predecessor to today's multi-dimensional missions. However, just as the case with contemporary multi-dimensional missions, it was also criticized for being too intrusive and costly. Due to the difficulty of finding consensus between the veto powers of the UN Security Council during the Cold War, few new missions were deployed until the end of the 1980s.

The end of the Cold War saw a surge in the deployment of UN peace operations.[1] These operations took place in a range of new theaters previously inaccessible due to the standoff between the United States and the Soviet Union in the Security Council and the vetoes that prevented intervention in proxy wars. The change in the 1990s saw a thaw in the standoff and increasing consensus allowing UN peace operations to be authorized. The interventions in internal conflicts were given more expansive mandates and varying degrees of civilian authority in addition to supervising elections, starting with Namibia in 1989 and Cambodia in 1993 (Chesterman 2004).

In 1992, UN Secretary-General Boutros Boutros-Ghali was tasked by the Security Council to reflect on the role of the UN with regard to preventive diplomacy, peace-making, and peacekeeping (Boutros-Ghali 1992). To this he added 'peace-building' – which he defined as "action to identify and support structures which will tend to strengthen and solidify peace in order to avoid a relapse into conflict" (Boutros-Ghali 1992, 2). The inability of the UN to perform according to expectations in the former Yugoslavia and in Rwanda halted the expansive rhetoric of Boutros-Ghali, who issued a 'conservative supplement' to his program for peace-building in 1995 (Boutros-Ghali 1995). Here he acknowledged the failures of Somalia and Srebrenica in Bosnia-Herzegovina; he also warned against resource constraints due to the rapid expansion of missions and tasks and lack of coordination between various UN entities taking on the longer-term tasks of rebuilding war-torn societies.

Since the end of the Cold War, the nature of the conflicts that the UN has engaged in has thus changed significantly. The international system is composed primarily of states and international organizations (IOs); traditionally, mediation and peace efforts had been between states. While the UN is a statist organization originally set up to deal with peace and security between states, after the Cold War it has dealt almost exclusively with internal conflicts. Second, not only has the UN been tasked with operating in several new crises, but the mandates of its peace operations have been significantly expanded – something Boutros-Ghali referred to as "multifunctional peace-keeping operations," now known as 'multi-dimensional' peacekeeping operations:

> The United Nations found itself asked to undertake an unprecedented variety of functions: the supervision of cease-fires, the regroupment and demobilization

4 Linked ecologies in UN peacekeeping

of forces, their reintegration into civilian life and the destruction of their weapons; the design and implementation of de-mining programmes; the return of refugees and displaced persons; the provision of humanitarian assistance; the supervision of existing administrative structures; the establishment of new police forces; the verification of respect for human rights; the design and supervision of constitutional, judicial and electoral reforms; the observation, supervision and even organization and conduct of elections; and the coordination of support for economic rehabilitation and reconstruction.

(Boutros-Ghali 1995, 6)

In 1993, John Ruggie warned that the UN had entered "a vaguely defined no-man's land lying somewhere between traditional peacekeeping and enforcement – for which it lacks any traditional guiding operational concept" (Ruggie 1993, 26). There was an urgent need to match the changing environment and expanding scope now facing UN peacekeeping operations with appropriate and applicable normative guidance, not only on the strategic level, but also in terms of guidelines, best practice, and lessons learned reports.

However, the exponential increase and conceptual refocusing of peacekeeping missions after the Cold War was not paralleled by an increase in the necessary resources. Not until 1995 was the first Lessons Learned Unit of Department of Peacekeeping Operations established, and it had only two positions – head of unit and research assistant (Benner and Rotmann 2008), seconded by member states. The situation improved only slowly, and the UN peacekeeping doctrine (Capstone Doctrine) was finalized as late as 2008 (UN 2008). The production of official policy and guidance for peacekeeping thus lagged behind the actual practices of peacekeeping in the field – a situation that, I argue, continues today. Practices in the field have relied on various forms of guidance, such as reports, memos, and other written material issued by the secretary-general or his Secretariat, the mandates of the UN Security Council, norms inculcated through experience working in the organization, and other relevant experience of senior decision-makers such as the special representative of the secretary-general.

This book aims to investigate change in the core norms guiding UN peacekeeping. Norms are generally defined as "a standard of appropriate behavior for actors with a given identity" (Finnemore and Sikkink 1998, 891). In 1995, Secretary-General Boutros-Ghali highlighted three important and traditional principles or norms that guide peacekeeping: "the consent of the parties, impartiality and the non-use of force except in self-defence" (1995, 9). However, all of these principles were established for inter-state conflicts, so the UN faced major challenges when deploying to intra-state conflicts, particularly in 'humanitarian interventions' where one or more of the parties would come in direct conflict with the peacekeeping forces – as amply demonstrated by the failures of Somalia and Bosnia-Herzegovina (BiH). The UN mission in BiH, UNPROFOR, had extra tasks added under a Chapter VII mandate – the mission was to protect civilian populations in designated safe areas – but, without the commensurate military

Linked ecologies in UN peacekeeping 5

capabilities to execute the task, the consequences were catastrophic. It became clear that the expansion of mandated tasks and the deployment of forces to internal conflicts put the UN between a rock and a hard place: "Existing peace-keeping operations were given *additional mandates that* required the use of force and therefore *could not be combined* with existing mandates requiring the consent of the parties, impartiality and the non-use of force" (Boutros-Ghali 1995, para 35, emphasis added).

The normative dilemma entailed in applying traditional principles of 'first-generation' peacekeeping to peace operations dealing with internal conflicts, actively engaging armed non-state actors, has continued to trouble UN peace operations. While advisory and UN reform documents on peacekeeping have lauded the core principles listed earlier, reality and practices on the ground have changed significantly. The *Report of the Panel on United Nations Peace Operations* (known as the 'Brahimi Report' after the panel chair, UN Under-Secretary-General Lakhdar Brahimi) held that the traditional principles "should remain the bedrock principles of peacekeeping" but that peace operations should be sufficiently mandated with robust rules of engagement for civilian protection and have the necessary resources to react where civilians were in danger (UN 2000, ix–x).

This recurring normative dilemma has led the UN Security Council in recent years to provide most missions with explicit 'protection mandates,' aimed at protecting civilian populations from harm, as exemplified in South Sudan (UNMISS), Darfur (UNAMID), and Chad (MINURCAT). In Haiti, MINUSTAH engaged in direct battle with criminal gangs, killing several gang members as well as leading "to the injury of dozens of civilians, primarily women and children" (Lynch 2005). Jean-Marie Guéhenno, UN under-secretary-general for peacekeeping operations at the time, said it was

> necessary to stand up to armed groups that threaten to undermine peacekeeping missions. But he said U.N. commanders had to strike a balance between engaging in all-out warfare and resorting to the passive military posture that characterized U.N. operations in Srebrenica.
>
> (ibid.)

Other missions – including the UN stabilization mission in the Democratic Republic of Congo (MONUSCO), the UN mission in Haiti (MINUSTAH), the UN mission in Côte d'Ivoire (ONUCI), and the recently established UN mission in Mali (MINUSMA) – have been involved in direct confrontation with one or more of the parties to conflicts, resulting in instances of peace enforcement (Karlsrud 2015). In such instances, the norms of impartiality, consent of the main parties, and non-use of force and the question of whether and how they should apply are challenging. Mindful of its failures in Srebrenica and Rwanda, the UN has even used force against strategic-level actors such as the incumbent president of Côte d'Ivoire, President Gbagbo, in April 2011 (see chapter 3). The use of force in these cases has been motivated by the norm that the UN should step in to protect civilians when the host state no longer is willing or able to do so.

6 *Linked ecologies in UN peacekeeping*

The motivation for giving increasingly robust mandates to peacekeeping operations has partly been anchored in the state-centric nature of the UN and has led to a trend of mandates to support the extension of state authority. It is indeed now a staple ingredient and guiding principle of most peacekeeping operations. Johnstone argues that evolving practices of peacekeeping operations suggest a normative shift, where the protection mandates are merged "with proactive public order mandates for peace operations" (2010, 197). This also involves a dilemma – and in many instances it is hard to reconcile the mandate to strengthen state authority with being an impartial actor that has the consent of the main parties to the conflict – and in recent mandates there has been a tendency toward authorizing more offensive operations that border on peace enforcement (Karlsrud 2015). In 2014, Secretary-General Ban Ki-moon nominated a High-Level on Peace Operations, led by former president of Timor-Leste and Nobel laureate Jose Ramos-Horta. Faced with increasingly robust mandates issued to the UN peacekeeping operations in the Democratic Republic of Congo, Mali, and the Central Africa Republic, and the increasing frequency of deadly attacks against the mission in Mali in particular, the panel was tasked to give their recommendations on how the UN should navigate this new reality. In 2015, the Ramos-Horta panel noted that "the concepts, tools, mission structures and doctrine originally developed for peace implementation tasks may not be well suited for these settings" and advised that if the Security Council decides to mandate "conflict management" missions to situations where there is no peace to keep, for a limited period with focused mandates, they need to be sufficiently robust and underpinned by a long-term political strategy where the UN has a lead role in the political process (Ramos-Horta et al. 2015, 30).

As to the norm change process of UN peacekeeping, two main trends can be discerned. First, the field of peacekeeping has undergone a process of professionalization and has achieved considerable conceptual refinement and depth over the last two decades, laying claim to new substantive areas of work. Peacekeeping now includes a range of sub-fields, including security sector reform (SSR); disarmament, demobilization, and reintegration (DDR) of ex-combatants; mediation and negotiation; and constitutional and governance reform. Some of these are mainly substantive, whereas others are more process oriented, such as coordination of actors in the field and in integrated missions. The substantive deepening and expansion of peacekeeping give ample evidence of the growing professionalization and institutionalization of UN peacekeeping.

Second, there are several norms and principles – or, rather, sets of norms and principles – that guide peacekeeping concurrently. Change has been a constant feature of UN peacekeeping over the last twenty years, and frequently more than one norm will apply to a given situation, opening up for interpretation at various levels in the organization. The book explores this through the case studies at the various levels, showing how practices in the field and *linked ecologies* are crucial in driving norm change in peacekeeping. Ecologies are defined as the various environments that are involved in the development of peacekeeping norms and policies, such as member state and UN officials, academic scholars, think tank

Linked ecologies in UN peacekeeping 7

officials, and NGO activists.[2] Linked ecologies are formed when these ecologies link up with each other to form informal or formal norm or policy alliances. I will return to describe these terms more in detail in chapter 2.

This chapter proceeds in three main sections. First I detail the aims and questions of the book. Then I present some of the methodological challenges entailed in applying the theory framework to my three case studies and the challenges related to qualitative research using interviews and various forms of written material. The third section provides a chapter-by-chapter outline of the book.

Aims and questions of the book

This book aims to contribute to the understanding of how norms guide UN peacekeeping change and who the important actors are in these processes, thereby contributing to the wider literature on norm change in IOs. In terms of theory, I seek to advance an analytical framework that draws attention to the role of practices on the ground that may create a bottom-up influence on norm change in UN peacekeeping and the complex interplay between government and UN officials, applied and academic researchers, and civil society activists in processes of norm change.

I have sought to expand the understanding of norm change in international organizations with the help of empirical illustrations from UN peacekeeping and have chosen three case studies for this purpose. Sub-questions include what role UN special representatives and envoys have in terms of norm change – can they be seen as norm entrepreneurs, similar to the UN secretary-general? A related topic is how organizational change occurs in IOs, with further study of the UN in peacekeeping as a more complex organization where there may be several centers of agenda and agency.

I argue that there is tension between the basic norms guiding peacekeeping,[3] most crucially between sovereignty, on the one hand, and core humanitarian principles and human rights on the other (Wheeler 2000). Furthermore, I argue that there are multiple sources of agenda and agency within the UN, resulting in diverging and conflicting norm pressures and practices, particularly between headquarters and the field, but also between the Security Council, the General Assembly, and the Secretariat of the Secretary-General at HQ.

The book examines how peacekeeping is evolving and investigates emerging practices since the end of the Cold War. It holds that norm development and change in peacekeeping are closely related to new practices on the ground in peacekeeping operations and that such norm change originates in part with new practices of leaders of peace operations, practices later codified into doctrine and guidelines.

Using a practice-oriented approach, I show how rational and functional theories are ill-suited for explaining anomalous behavior of IOs in general and UN peacekeeping in particular. Sociological constructivism can better account for these anomalies, but it has limited explanatory power as regards accounting for the interaction between various classes of actors, or what I refer to as 'ecologies' (Abbott 2005). The book argues that in applying constructivism to the international system, the concept of choice virtually disappears, and that much of the constructivist literature relies on a Pavlovian view of socialization of norms.

With this book, I seek to remedy this shortcoming in constructivist theory by first using a practice-oriented approach to examine the practices of senior UN representatives in the field. I hold that UN special representatives in the field can be seen as norm arbitrators strengthening one norm at the expense of another and thus showing how practices can precede and be constitutive of norm change.

Second, based on the sociology of professions, I will also show how peacekeeping norms and doctrine development can be influenced through a 'revolving doors' process where key individuals move between donors, think tanks, and academic communities, supporting the formation of 'linked ecologies' or informal policy alliances to advance new norms and concepts.

Basic norms and ambiguity

The book highlights that ambiguity is deeply rooted in UN peacekeeping, as the basic norms and the norms guiding peacekeeping are not in concordance, but often are in conflict. This underscores the importance of the role of practices of professionals who have to discern and deliberate on the conflicting norms applicable to particular situations. First, then, the book argues that practices serve to inform the balance between existing norms and the development of new norms and examines UN SRSGs as actors where conflicting norm pressures meet each other in peacekeeping in the field.

Second, I see the UN as a competitive arena for norm change in both a wide and a narrow sense. In a narrow and formal sense, the UN is a competitive arena where member states meet, discuss, and agree on regimes on issues of common interest, thereby shaping, reshaping, and balancing norms guiding UN peacekeeping. However, from a more process-oriented, wider, and informal view, the UN

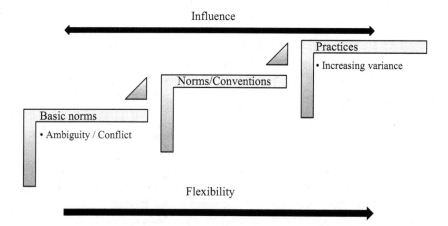

Figure 1.1 Basic norms, norms/conventions, and practices in UN peacekeeping

Linked ecologies in UN peacekeeping 9

can be seen as a competitive arena for norm change that includes actors like think tanks, academic institutions, NGOs, and private corporations (see e.g. Weiss et al. 2009). In line with Andrew Abbott, I argue that these represent various ecologies that can link up and rally around a common topic and form informal policy alliances to advance change, forming linked ecologies (Abbott 2005). These linked ecologies thus become co-constitutive actors in processes of norm change. These processes are seen as social practices in the international arena.

The empirical aim of this book is to use case studies to trace and analyze empirically the research question set out here. The main objective is to better account for the complex interrelationship between the various classes of actors that have been mentioned, with the three case studies helping shed light on the roles various classes of actors can have and why. The following offers a more detailed description of these case studies, but first a few words about the methodology.

Methodology

This book is qualitative in nature and employs an inductive approach, using case studies to draw broader conclusions and recommendations. Using case studies entails the small-n problem – the difficulty of drawing valid causal inferences from only one or very few research units (George and Bennett 2005). In this book, the challenge of small-n is to some degree mitigated by the use of several case studies.

A triangulated mixed method case approach has been applied in this project, involving three steps to fuse theory, method, and empirics – and to ensure the credibility of the empirical findings. First, participation with the UN in peacekeeping contexts, and with scholars in think tanks and academia, has made possible 'observant participation' (Czarniawska 1998, 28), a variation of ethnographic studies, permitting long-term engagement and observation, and "insider ethnography of organizations and public policy" (Mosse 2006, 936). Undertaking a similar study of knowledge networks and linked ecologies in the World Bank, Diane Stone argues that such an inquiry requires long-term engagement with participants from all the ecologies and "a considerable investment of time and resources to secure interviews, participate in conferences, or reside in Washington DC or country offices" (Stone 2013, 254). To ensure the validity of the material gathered, I have conducted a broad review of the literature as well as a number of interviews. The desk studies have provided an overview of the literature and an empirical and theory-grounded basis for analysis.

Practices are studied as empirical evidence of norm contestation and change, accentuating the interplay between material and ideational factors in norm change. The book examines practices in peacekeeping on two levels. First, the practices of SRSGs are scrutinized in chapter 3. Second, I look into the social practices of linked ecologies furthering norm change in chapters 4 and 5 on R2P (Responsibility to Protect) and the Integrated Missions concept respectively. As such, practices constitute an important methodological tool for investigating the main research question and the hypotheses of the book.

10 *Linked ecologies in UN peacekeeping*

Emanuel Adler and Vincent Pouliot define practices as "competent performances," or:

> More precisely, practices are socially meaningful patterns of action which, in being performed more or less competently, simultaneously embody, reify and act out background knowledge and discourse in and on the material world.
>
> (Adler and Pouliot 2011)

Morten S. Andersen holds that a study of practices must examine "the observable 'doings' of physical bodies and entities" (2010, 16). In this book, practices are investigated on two levels. First I examine the practices among senior leadership in the field and then the practices of individuals, institutions, and linked ecologies in processes of norm change.

Some reflections on personal experience

My professional background, described in the preface of this book, has given me the opportunity to see how decisions are made in a peacekeeping mission in the field and how the research community engages with policy-makers of member states as well as international organizations. From these experiences I have gained insights that inspired me to undertake this study and enabled me to read official statements, policy papers, and similar documents with an insider's eye. This also goes for official statements, interviews, and conversations. As for methodology, my personal experience in UN peacekeeping activities provided many opportunities for 'observant participation' in the production of justifications and narratives for changes in practices (Czarniawska 1998). My previous socialization into the culture(s) of the UN family enabled me to better understand and interpret the subtext of the information I received. It has also put me in the group of people who are part of the 'revolving doors' phenomenon, as I have spent a fair amount of time in peacekeeping, in think tanks, and in academia.

However, this personal experience has also entailed some challenges, as I have developed a very close relationship to the topic and have worked in all the ecologies the book studies. I have sought to mitigate this by selecting case studies in which I had not been involved myself and selecting interview subjects not known to me personally when I began work on this book. This provides greater distance to the subject matter, while I can still make use of my observations gathered in the different ecologies.

A note on interviews

This book draws on a range of semi-structured interviews with UN and member state policy-makers, think tank staff, and scholars in the field of peacekeeping. Interviewees were selected on the basis of their positions within peacekeeping operations, think tanks, and academic institutions. The interviewees who work with peacekeeping were selected for their central roles as those individuals who must respond to the demands of both official mandates and actual policy implementation. The think tank staff and scholars interviewed were working on peacekeeping and related issues. Information from interviews has been cross-checked with official documents, internal memos, and other types of primary literature.

The triangulation approach – use of archive material in addition to interviews with officials at different levels – should ensure the authenticity of the findings and avoid a one-sided reliance on interviews where interviewees might justify their actions and give new rationales *post facto*. As the officials interviewed come from different contexts, and it would have been difficult to repeat a standard interview format, the use of survey-style interviews was ruled out. Open-ended interviews were conducted at initial stages of the research, informing the analysis of written material. Later interviews were conducted in a semi-structured manner, with several broad questions and topics set at the opening of the interview but leaving space for the interviewee to follow his or her own impulses and share experiences and recollections. Interviews were conducted in several locations in New York, in field missions, and in various capitals and other sites around the world.

Using interview material involves some challenges. A selection bias may develop, whereby the researcher interviews only persons who confirm and support the main argument of his or her thesis (George and Bennett 2005, 22–4). This selection bias can be reinforced if the researcher follows the recommendations of interviewees for other persons to interview ('snowballing'), as it is natural that those recommended will have similar opinions. Other challenges include blurred or selective memory on the part of the interviewee, as well as problems of language and culture. Interviews with Norwegians were conducted in Norwegian, whereas I took notes in English in simultaneous translation. All other interviews were conducted in English. At the UN, as well as in many other organizations, turnover is high, resulting in short institutional memories. These challenges can be mitigated to a certain degree through triangulation with official documents, internal memos, and other written materials. It should also be noted that my access to interviewees has to a certain extent been dominated by the relatively good access I have enjoyed to Norwegian interviewees. I have sought to mitigate the potential bias this could give by seeking highly relevant sources from other parts of the world, and in particular from the South, who have shared their experiences and views. These inputs have been important when trying to understand how various countries from the South engage on issues pertinent to UN peacekeeping in chapter 6.

Most of my interviewees either asked not to be attributed as a source after an interview or agreed to an interview on the condition that the interview would be conducted on a non-attributable basis. While this contributes to a lack of transparency of the book, it has greatly helped the process of obtaining important material.

A note on the written material

This study investigates processes of norm change, and several types of material have been studied and used. As will be seen later in the study, the establishment of prescriptive policy guidance for peacekeeping is relatively new: some scattered

12 Linked ecologies in UN peacekeeping

policy documents have been issued during the last two decades, with a more coherent approach starting with the 'Brahimi Report' in 2000; the *United Nations Peacekeeping Operations: Principles and Guidelines* in 2008, also known as the Capstone Doctrine (UN 2008); and finally, the Ramos-Horta report of 2015 (Ramos-Horta et al. 2015). In addition, academic books, journal articles, and other scholarly materials have been consulted, as well as reports, policy briefs, and other material originating from think tanks and academic institutions. Finally, I have consulted news articles and online media in connection with the individual case studies.

Outline of the book and short introduction to the case studies

This book is divided into seven chapters. This introduction has given a short background on the development of peacekeeping, particularly since the end of the Cold War, introducing the puzzle I encountered when I began work on this book. I then presented the main aim and questions of the study, the research problem and the main argument, and some of the methodological challenges facing qualitative studies of norm change in international relations. In chapter 2, "Theorizing Linked Ecologies in Norm Change Processes," I develop the theory framework, drawing on the sociology of professions and practice theory. Chapters 3 to 5 are dedicated to case studies.

Two main factors have influenced the selection of cases. The engagement of Kai Eide, UN special representative of the secretary-general, with the Taliban in Afghanistan is an interesting case where there were clearly several sets of norms for peacekeeping and principles of the UN guiding action on the ground at the same time, thus putting the SRSG in a difficult position. Also SRSG Choi Young-jin in Côte d'Ivoire was faced with a dilemma and made a controversial decision. These cases can shed light on the role that SRSGs and the field level can play in norm change in the international system and are portrayed in chapter 3.

Drawing on the sociology of professions, the book will also show how peacebuilding norms and doctrine development can be influenced through a 'revolving doors' process with key donors, think tanks, and academic communities, where linked ecologies or informal policy alliances are formed to advance new norms and concepts. To exemplify this phenomenon I look more closely at the R2P and Integrated Missions processes in chapters 4 and 5.

Case study 1: SRSGs as norm arbitrators? Understanding bottom-up authority in UN peacekeeping

The third chapter thus presents the first case study, focusing on SRSGs in UN peacekeeping. The chapter looks at some potentially controversial actions of SRSGs, asking whether such actions can reveal how authority is composed in the UN system and the roles of SRSGs in the norm change processes of that system. It investigates how practices evolve on the ground and what impact these may have for norm development in the organization.

Linked ecologies in UN peacekeeping 13

The chapter studies how norms are internalized, put into practice, and codified. Using practice theory as a method to strengthen the methodological framework of constructivism, I maintain that there is a significant lag between the reality in which the UN and its senior leaders in the field are operating today and the doctrines that guide these operations. I examine how the SRSGs in Afghanistan and Côte d'Ivoire made controversial decisions and analyze why this was possible, looking at the various sources of authority an SRSG can draw upon.

From the empirical material, the chapter analyzes the sources of authority on which SRSGs may draw in arbitrating between conflicting norms guiding peacekeeping. The chapter argues that SRSGs can act as *norm arbitrators* in the UN system, generating new practices by weighing against each other the conflicting grundnorms that guide peacekeeping. SRSG Eide's engagement with Taliban and SRSG Choi's use of force in Côte d'Ivoire are instructive. They argued for their choices based on a combination of personal experience and conviction, their understanding of competing norms and principles, and the mandate of the mission. I argue that practices from the field, crystallized through the actions of SRSGs, constitute a bottom-up source of influence on norm change processes in the UN. Special representatives enjoy relative independence and physical distance from UN headquarters. Often coming from backgrounds in diplomatic careers, and enjoying relative autonomy and flexibility in interpreting what the UN is and what it stands for, they can wield influence thanks to a certain level of decentralized authority and their *personal prestige* within the UN.

Case study 2: Linked ecologies and Responsibility to Protect: the role of academic institutions and think tanks in norm change

Chapter 4 examines the Responsibility to Protect norm change process through the lens of the theory framework of the sociology of professions, asking who the main actors have been in the drive to establish the norm and what consequences this has had for understanding and theorizing norm change in international organizations. The chapter looks at how the evolving norm of R2P has a significant impact on how the UN supports and intervenes in member states and on the core principle of sovereignty in the international system. By examining the R2P concept and development process, I show how key donor states, think tanks, and academic institutions have, together with the UN, pushed for R2P, effectively driving norm change in the international system. The change is seen not solely as a top-down function of state interests, but as also a bottom-up process driven by advocacy and support from key donor states, think tanks, and academic circles. I conclude that linked ecologies were a key factor in explaining the success of establishing and getting the R2P concept adopted by member states at the General Assembly in 2005.

Applying the theory framework developed in chapter 2, I show how the sociology of professions can augment constructivist theories of norm change in

14 *Linked ecologies in UN peacekeeping*

international organizations. In the conclusion, I note the need for further exploration of this potentially fruitful collaboration between the two research streams and the need for a fundamental rethink when ascribing agency in norm change processes of international organizations.

Case study 3: Linked ecologies and revolving doors for norm change in peacekeeping operations: the development of the Integrated Missions concept

Chapter 5 focuses on to another norm change process and examines the development of the integrated missions concept and the norm debate that followed it, focusing on the period from 2003 to 2007. Although 'integrated missions' is generally considered a concept and not a norm, I show that it had staunch supporters and opponents who based their arguments on solid normative grounds. Those opposing the concept did so based on their conviction that humanitarian aid should not be politicized or securitized, which are strong norms in the humanitarian domain. Those supporting the concept wanted the UN to be able to coordinate its work in post-conflict countries across organizational silos, to improve delivery to host populations, and to avoid unintended and negative consequences from the lack of coordination. I thus argue that the process is a valid case study for the study of norm change and, further, that UN peacekeeping is characterized by a high degree of volatility and change but also relies on firm norms that guide peacekeeping operations.

The chapter analyzes the debate around the concept of integrated missions as an example of how norms, principles, and concepts are advanced in international organizations and to identify the principal actors of these processes. I show how the process was driven forward by a close-knit group of individuals from a few member states, think tanks, and the academic community, as well as the UN. Several of these individuals have been working within all these institutions, creating a 'revolving doors' effect and linking the ecologies closer together. Chapter 5 concludes that, although the integrated missions process cannot be considered a success, linked ecologies and the collective actions and processes they are involved in are decisive for understanding norm change processes.

Chapter 6, "The United Nations as a Competitive Arena for Norm Change," analyzes the implications of the empirical material on our understanding of authority and agency in international organizations. It draws on and further develops the literature on the concept of 'arena' in international relations by viewing the UN as a *competitive arena* for norm change from a constructivist point of view. Whereas neorealists see the UN mainly as an arena for competition, and rational institutionalists see the UN as an arena where the principals (states) delegate authority to the UN (agent), this book argues that informal policy alliances are created and involve a range of actors other than member states. The formation of these informal policy alliances – including think tanks, academia, civil society organizations, and other actors with vested interests – leads me to a novel and constructivist understanding of the arena concept. Here

Linked ecologies in UN peacekeeping 15

I distinguish between wide and narrow understandings of the UN as a competitive arena for norm change. In the wide sense, informal policy alliances are formed and ownership is built around a certain change agenda through the development of knowledge products, expert meetings, and regional consultations with member states. This process prepares the ground for the narrow understanding of the UN as a competitive arena where formal negotiations take place within the organization between member states and where other actors take a background, more supportive, role.

In the concluding chapter I sum up, asserting that practices in the field and by linked ecologies are important sources of agency in norm change processes in UN peacekeeping. Using theory drawn from the sociology of professions can provide a more nuanced understanding of the complex interplay involving member states, think tanks, academic institutions, and the UN with its sub-components in the norm formation for peace operations. This in turn can help us better understand how the concepts, rules, and norms of the UN are influenced through interactions among these sectors. Such interplay has two main dimensions. Actors within these ecologies can shape informal policy alliances to advance a particular issue on the international agenda. Ecological theory usually assumes a system of actors in various locations but often disregards how different sets of actors can interact between ecologies. This book builds on the insights of Andrew Abbott (1988, 2005), Leonard Seabrooke and Eleni Tsingou (2009, 2015), Diane Stone (2013), and Leonard Seabrooke and Emelie Nilsson (2015) on how different ecologies can form policy alliances, or 'linked ecologies,' often through individuals who move through 'revolving doors' between different sectors, such as donor governments, academia, and think tanks, and act as professional brokers between these ecologies (Seabrooke 2011).

Through the 'revolving door' phenomenon, ecologies link up to form informal policy alliances to achieve norm change in peacekeeping. The book examines linked ecologies established to achieve norm change in peacekeeping and the key actors in these alliances, whether they be individuals, institutions, or both. These linked ecologies and their actions are examined as social practices that advance particular sets of ideas in the international arena. Understanding the UN as a competitive arena can be helpful, including actors other than member states in informal policy alliances or linked ecologies. This enables a better understanding of how the concepts, rules, and norms of peacekeeping develop through interaction between these ecologies. Linked ecologies, understood as informal policy alliances, are often formed at the working level, a point that warrants further attention. Furthermore, several conflicting norms guide UN peacekeeping operations: change is not unilinear, but there will be a continuous waxing and waning in the relative relationship between norms. These factors should be explored further in other international organization as well. Another area for further research could be how think tanks, academia, and member state officials interact on UN peacekeeping and other issues in emerging economies. And finally, the development of UN peacekeeping as an 'issue profession' deserves further scrutiny (Seabrooke and Henriksen forthcoming 2016).

16 *Linked ecologies in UN peacekeeping*

Notes

1 In this book, 'peace operations' is used as a general term encompassing all UN missions in the area of peacekeeping and peacebuilding, including special political missions (see also Ramos-Horta et al. 2015). The Organisation for Economic Co-operation and Development (OECD) defines peacebuilding as "a broad range of measures implemented in the context of emerging, current or post-conflict situations and which are explicitly guided and motivated by a primary commitment to the prevention of violent conflict and the promotion of a lasting and sustainable peace" (Organisation for Economic Co-operation and Development's Development Assistance Committee [OECD-DAC] 2005, 1). This definition has become dominant, and in the UN there is an evolving understanding that "peacekeepers are peacebuilders" and should implement early peacebuilding tasks (UN 2012, 10).
2 See Figure 2.1.
3 I will give a more thorough introduction to the concept of basic norms or grundnorms in the next chapter.

References

Abbott, Andrew D. (1988) *The System of Professions: An Essay on the Division of Expert Labor.* Chicago: University of Chicago Press.

Abbott, Andrew D. (2005) 'Linked Ecologies: States and Universities as Environments for Professions', *Sociological Theory*, 23 (3), pp. 245–74.

Adler, Emanuel and Vincent Pouliot (2011) 'International Practices: Introduction and Framework,' in Adler, Emanuel and Vincent Pouliot eds., *International Practices.* Cambridge: Cambridge University Press, pp. 3–35.

Andersen, Morten S. (2010) *Putting Structure into Practice: The 'Practice' Turn in IR and Ontologies of Structural Inquiry.* MIMEO.

Bellamy, Alex J., Paul Williams and Stuart Griffin (2010) *Understanding Peacekeeping.* Cambridge: Polity.

Benner, Thorsten and Philipp Rotmann (2008) 'Learning to Learn? UN Peacebuilding and the Challenges of Building a Learning Organization', *Journal of Intervention and Statebuilding*, 2 (1), pp. 43–62.

Boutros-Ghali, Boutros (1992) *An Agenda for Peace: Preventive Diplomacy, Peacemaking, and Peace-Keeping: Report of the Secretary-General Pursuant to the Statement Adopted by the Summit Meeting of the Security Council on 31 January 1992.* New York: United Nations.

Boutros-Ghali, Boutros (1995) *A/RES/51/242: Supplement to An Agenda for Peace.* New York: United Nations.

Chesterman, Simon (2004) *You, the People: the United Nations, Transitional Administration, and State-Building.* Oxford: Oxford University Press.

Czarniawska, Barbara (1998) *A Narrative Approach to Organization Studies.* Thousand Oaks, CA: Sage.

Finnemore, Martha and Kathryn Sikkink (1998) 'International Norm Dynamics and Political Change', *International Organization*, 52 (4), pp. 887–917.

George, Alexander L. and Andrew Bennett (2005) *Case Studies and Theory Development in the Social Sciences.* Cambridge, MA: Belfer Center for Science and International Affairs, Harvard University.

Johnstone, Ian (2010) 'Normative Evolution at the UN: Impact on Operational Imperatives,' in Jones, Bruce D., Shepard Forman and Richard Gowan eds., *Cooperating for Peace and Security: Evolving Institutions and Arrangements in a Context of Changing U.S. Security Policy.* Cambridge: Cambridge University Press, pp. 187–214.

Linked ecologies in UN peacekeeping 17

Karlsrud, John (2015) 'The UN at War: Examining the Consequences of Peace Enforcement Mandates for the UN Peacekeeping Operations in the CAR, the DRC and Mali', *Third World Quarterly*, 36 (1), pp. 40–54.

Lynch, Colum (2005) 'U.N. Peacekeeping More Assertive, Creating Risk for Civilians', *Washington Post*, www.washingtonpost.com/wp-dyn/content/article/2005/08/14/AR2005081400946.html. Accessed September 4, 2013.

Mosse, David (2006) 'Anti-Social Anthropology: Objectivity, Objection, and the Ethnography of Public Policy and Professional Communities', *Journal of the Royal Anthropological Institute*, 12 (4), pp. 935–56.

Organisation for Economic Co-operation and Development's Development Assistance Committee (OECD-DAC) (2005) *Preventing Conflict and Building Peace: A Manual of Issues and Entry Points.* Paris: OECD DAC Network on Conflict, Peace and Development Co-operation.

Ramos-Horta, José et al. (2015) *Uniting Our Strengths for Peace – Politics, Partnership and People: Report of the High-Level Independent Panel on United Nations Peace Operations.* New York: United Nations.

Ruggie, John G. (1993) 'Wandering in the Void – Charting the UN's New Strategic Role', *Foreign Affairs*, 72 (5), pp. 26–31.

Seabrooke, Leonard (2011) 'Economists and Diplomacy: Professions and the Practice of Economic Policy', *International Journal*, 66 (3), pp. 629–42.

Seabrooke, Leonard and Lasse F. Henriksen (forthcoming 2016) 'Issue Control in Transnational Professional Networks and Organizations,' in Seabrooke, Leonard and Lasse F. Henriksen eds., *Professional Networks in Transnational Governance*. Cambridge: Cambridge University Press.

Seabrooke, Leonard and Emelie R. Nilsson (2015) 'Professional Skills in International Financial Surveillance: Assessing Change in IMF Policy Teams', *Governance*, 28 (2), pp. 267–54.

Seabrooke, Leonard and Eleni Tsingou (2009) *Revolving Doors and Linked Ecologies in the World Economy: Policy Locations and the Practice of International Financial Reform.* Warwick: University of Warwick, CSGR Working Papers.

Seabrooke, Leonard and Eleni Tsingou (2015) 'Professional Emergence on Transnational Issues: Linked Ecologies on Demographic Change', *Journal of Professions and Organization*, 2 (1), pp. 1–18.

Stone, Diane (2013) ' "Shades of Grey": The World Bank, Knowledge Networks and Linked Ecologies of Academic Engagement', *Global Networks*, 13 (2), pp. 241–60.

UN (2000) *Report of the Panel on United Nations Peace Operations.* New York: United Nations.

UN (2008) *United Nations Peacekeeping Operations: Principles and Guidelines.* New York: United Nations Department of Peacekeeping Operations and Department of Field Support.

UN (2012) *Peace: Keep It. Build It. The Contribution of United Nations Peacekeeping to Early Peacebuilding: Strategy.* New York: United Nations Department of Peacekeeping Operations and Department of Field Support.

Weiss, Thomas G., Tatiana Carayannis and Richard Jolly (2009) 'The "Third" United Nations', *Global Governance*, 15 (1), pp. 123–42.

Wheeler, Nicholas J. (2000) *Saving Strangers: Humanitarian Intervention in International Society.* Oxford: Oxford University Press.

2 Theorizing linked ecologies in norm change processes

Norm change in international organizations has been much studied over the last three decades. International organizations and institutions have both gained in prominence and number as new regimes have been established. Over a fairly short period, new treaties and institutions have come into existence – such as the Mine Ban Convention (1997), the International Criminal Court (2002), and the UN Peacebuilding Commission (2005). Existing institutions have experienced moderate to major changes. In the UN, considerable effort has been expended in getting the various parts of the organization to work more closely together, as shown by the many reform efforts under Secretary-General Kofi Annan, continued also under Ban Ki-moon.

Theories of international relations have developed concurrently with the development of international regimes, organizations, and institutions, grappling with how they are formed and who has agency and authority within and outside them to affect change. Development and change in international relations indicate the continuous process of norm change in the international system on many issues, including how member states want to deal with issues such as violent conflict between and within states, control of sea waters and the seabed, and international human rights.

Looking at UN peacekeeping, this book further explores how change in the international system comes about, who the important actors in this process are, and how they interact to achieve change. This chapter is divided into five sections. First, I present the concept of basic norms and review the international relations literature on norms, norm change, and development, ending up with constructivism. I then proceed with a critique of constructivist theory on norms, norm change, agency, and autonomy in international organizations, showing some of its shortcomings. Third, I outline the linked ecologies theory framework, which draws on constructivism, the sociology of professions, and practice theory. Fourth, I revisit the concept of 'arena' in international relations, asking whether and how it can be adapted to incorporate non-state actors. Finally, I draw a few conclusions.

Basic norms and norms in international relations

The book draws upon, but also challenges, the concept of *grundnorm*, which originated from the legal philosopher Hans Kelsen (1881–1973). Kelsen argued that, in analyzing norms, it should be possible to trace them back to what he called the

Theorizing linked ecologies   19

grundnorms upon which they rest (the terms 'basic' or 'fundamental' norms are often used in English translations). In his *Theory of Law and State* (first published in 1944), a collection of his work after arriving at Harvard from Germany during World War II and earlier writings in German, he asserted:

> A norm the validity of which cannot be derived from a superior norm we call a 'basic' norm. All norms whose validity may be traced back to one and the same basic norm form a system of norms, or an order. This basic norm constitutes, as a common source, the bond between all the different norms of which an order consists.
>
> (Kelsen 1961, 111)

His monistic theory of law, organizing norms according to their relative validity, presupposed that there would be a system of norms and a point where the regression would stop. However, he has been criticized for trying to achieve an artificial closure of a system of norms where this theoretically cannot be achieved:

> Kelsen's closure of the legal order is a sort of reference back from final causes to the first cause, from empirical determinations to the *causa sui*. Thus in an essentially non-metaphysical thinker like Kelsen the 'closure' of a system through the Grundnorm is only, so to speak, a closure of convenience. It is a little like the idea of the absolute sovereignty of the nation-state. The idea of sovereignty as 'power of powers' is a closure of convenience, no different from the *Grundnorm* conceived of as a 'norm of norms'. Nothing verifiable corresponds, nor can correspond, to these notions.
>
> (Bobbio and Zolo 1998, 358, italics in original)

I will thus use the concept of *basic norms* as an analytic rather than ontological tool. Instead of querying whether such norms actually exist, I simply postulate that some norms are more fundamental than others, and these I will call grundnorms or basic norms. Upon these basic norms, other norms rest. While practices are the everyday manifestation of these basic norms and norms, I assert that practices also can affect the relationship between norms and basic norms and introduce new norms.

States have been the focus of early studies of norms in international relations, and the state is still a core feature: "Sovereignty is usually considered the *grundnorm* of international society" (Reus-Smit 2004, 34). When Kelsen developed his theory in the inter-war years, states enjoyed a relatively strong position as regards their citizens, and he argued: "It is, in particular, wrong to maintain that the individual has a natural claim to protection for certain interests such as life, freedom and property" (Kelsen 1961, 237). After World War II, the human rights movement gained ground, and the Universal Declaration of Human Rights was adopted by the UN General Assembly on December 10, 1948 (UN 1948).

This book will use the analytical concept of basic norms to explore norm change in the international system. I argue that two fundamental norms, or basic

20 *Theorizing linked ecologies*

norms, are in tension with each other in the international system, giving rise to continuous contestation and change. These two norms are the norm of *sovereignty* and the norm of *core humanitarian principles and human rights*. As we will see, the tension between these two basic norms is played out in the Responsibility to Protect norm change process and, to a lesser degree, in the integrated missions process.

Constructivist theorizing of international organizations (IOs)

Constructivism argues that not only material, but also ideational forces, shape international relations and organizations (Wendt 1992), moving beyond the state to look at other actors that may influence change. Norms and rules shape IO behavior, and IOs shape norms. Constructivism emphasizes the importance of non-material structures on interests and "the role of practices in maintaining and transforming those structures" (Reus-Smit 2001, 212). Structuration theory is often invoked as the ontological background of constructivism (Wendt 1987, Sending 2002). Structures and agency are mutually constitutive; here agents can reproduce but also alter the structures of society (Giddens 1984). This applies to constructivism as well: "For constructivists, agents (states) and structures (global norms) are interacting; they are mutually constituted" (Checkel 1998, 328).

Norms may be formal or informal and can structure and regularize behavior. Shared norms about appropriate behavior give institutional stability in IOs. According to Martha Finnemore and Kathryn Sikkink (1998), new norms in the international system are formed by norm entrepreneurs persuading member states. Norm entrepreneurs call attention to and 'frame' issues through the application of new terms, reinterpreting issues and putting them into new contexts. As one example of such a norm entrepreneur they mention Henri Dunant, the founder of the International Committee of the Red Cross. The establishment of new norms will necessarily break with existing ones. Using the logic of appropriateness (LoA) terminology, Finnemore and Sikkink assert that "to challenge existing logics of appropriateness, activists may need to be explicitly 'inappropriate'" (ibid., 897). Explaining behavior using LoA as a theoretical framework thus also entails some difficulties, a point to which I return later. Finnemore and Sikkink argue that norm entrepreneurs use their organizational platform as well as their expert knowledge to advance a given norm vis-à-vis member states, IOs, and networks of professionals. The development of professional expertise and control of the area of peacebuilding could also be theorized through the use of Haas's concept of "epistemic communities" (Haas 1992). Epistemic communities are characterized by expert groups who, by establishing knowledge and norms, are able to shape and change state interests. However, that theory takes expert groups or epistemic communities as ontologically given, focusing rather on how these groups can have influence on states by establishing knowledge claims over a particular issue area. Ole Jacob Sending shows that the epistemic communities approach is less suited for explaining why particular groups are

Theorizing linked ecologies 21

able to assume control of a particular issue area – "defining an epistemic community as *already* recognized as being authoritative and policy relevant" (Sending 2010).

Sending (2002) has argued that sociological constructivism has relied too heavily on LoA, a concept developed by March and Olsen (1998, 951–52). They see individual behavior in organizations as structured by the norms, rules, and routines of the organization. Routines play a central role in their theoretical framework; applying this to political activity, they argue that a political community is "created by its rules, not by its intentions" (March and Olsen 1995, 38). The primacy of rules over intentions brings us back to the work of Michael Barnett and Martha Finnemore, which can be useful for an analysis of the usefulness of this theoretical approach, as they have invoked LoA as a theoretical framework. In *Rules for the World* (2004), they showed how IOs at times acted in contradiction to the intentions of the organization, secured in an interpretation of the rules guiding action of the particular issue. However, while Barnett and Finnemore argue that these actions are based on a narrow reading of the rules of the organization, they also argue that other interpretations and other rules could be available to tweak the interpretation in a quite opposite direction (2004).

In sociological constructivism, LoA provides the normative rationality of action (Risse 2000). Sending criticizes the lack of discussion of the rationality over individual action as it is presented in constructivist theory: "Most constructivists in this debate have accepted the validity of the LoA as their action-theoretical foundation without an in-depth exploration of its core theoretical building blocks" (2002, 444). He goes on to show how "LoA has a structural bias both regarding the understanding and the explanation of individual action" (2002, 445).

Two criticisms of the LoA as a theoretical framework can be launched. First, it could be argued that using the logic of appropriateness as a theoretical framework "robs actors of their actorness" (Seabrooke and Tsingou 2009, 7) by reducing the space for decision-making of the actor to the available rules of his or her organization. Sending concords with this, arguing that institutions in this sense are "the prime supplier of and partly constitutive for the very frames of understanding through which individuals come to interpret and understand the world" (2002, 451). As the LoA takes the formal and informal rules of the organization as a point of departure, it cannot account for inappropriate behavior. Individual action that breaks with established norms and induces change falls outside the theoretical grasp of LoA. Andersen argues that Barnett and Finnemore assume that norms are a contextual variable in their analysis of IOs:

> In short, how norms are formed, used, adapted, changing, constituting, influencing both IOs and other interacting partners, is not central to the analysis. Norms, in short, are not problematized, but assumed to manifest as another contextual variable, and to be used and spread. IOs, they argue, "often act as conveyor belts for the transmission of norms and models."
>
> (Andersen 2010, 9)

22 *Theorizing linked ecologies*

The role of culture and informal policy alliances

'Culture' has played a major role in constructivist explanations of action in UN peacekeeping. Scholars of constructivist theory and organizational sociology have investigated bureaucratic dysfunction within public bodies, showing that bureaucratic culture can develop and guide autonomous action in IOs (Barnett and Finnemore 1999, Barnett and Finnemore 2004, Weaver 2008, Lipson 2007, Koch 2009). In *Rules for the World* (2004), Barnett and Finnemore show that bureaucratic culture can develop and guide autonomous action in IOs and that informal rules may trump the formal ones set by member states. Barnett and Finnemore define bureaucratic culture as "the solutions that are produced by groups of people to meet specific problems they face in common. These solutions become institutionalized, remembered, and passed on as the rules, rituals and values of the group" (2004, 19). They argue that bureaucratic culture shapes the rationality of the actors in these institutions in ways that may occasionally lead to decisions that are at odds with the intentions of their creators. In line with constructivism, they argue that the "relationship between bureaucrats and rules is mutually constitutive and dynamic" (ibid., 20). This influence on the shaping of the rules of the organization also implies that bureaucrats, and ultimately IOs, are capable of autonomous action. Barnett and Finnemore focus on exposing instances of pathological behavior by IOs, like the UN's failure to act on the many and early signs of genocide about to unfold in Rwanda in 1994. They argue that the rules which had been developed over time for UN peacekeeping

> created an organizational culture where it was tolerable, even desirable, to disregard mass violations of human rights not only in Rwanda but elsewhere, most famously in Srebrenica in July 1995. Rwanda, in this respect, was not an unfortunate mistake. It was the predictable result of an organizational culture that shaped how the UN evaluated and responded to violent crises.
>
> (Barnett and Finnemore 2004, 155)

While their argument is valid and original, their theoretical framework refers only to a bureaucratic culture that has developed internally within the organization. I argue that they fail to theorize sufficiently the interaction that international organizations have with other sets of actors, like think tanks and academia. Furthermore, their use of the concept of 'culture' includes some of the core principles of peacekeeping at the time as well as now, such as the principles of impartiality and having the consent of the main parties. What became apparent in Srebrenica and Rwanda was the chasm between these traditional core principles of peacekeeping and other principles that had been steadily strengthened ever since the founding of the organization – core humanitarian principles and human rights. However, the relationship between these had not been reconciled, as the tragedies of Srebrenica and Rwanda revealed.

In *The Trouble with the Congo*, Severine Autesserre (2010) builds on the culture argument of Barnett and Finnemore and holds that the international peacebuilding

Theorizing linked ecologies   23

community has largely ignored local-level conflicts and micro-level effects of violence. Examining the period of transition in Democratic Republic of Congo (DRC) from the installation of the Transitional Government on June 30, 2003, to the inauguration of Joseph Kabila as president on December 6, 2006, Autesserre argues that this blind spot is maintained by the culture internal to and dominant in the international peacebuilding community. This culture, she explains, has four core features. First, the peacebuilding community consists of UN staff, members of the diplomatic community, and non-governmental organizations (NGOs). All of these, and in particular UN staff and diplomats, tend to focus on regional and national issues when dealing with the continued violence and atrocities in eastern DRC. Second, by labeling the situation as 'post-conflict,' international peacebuilders, in abiding by their mandate, became blind to the continued fighting. Third, violence has been considered as endemic to the region and innate to the Congolese and has thus been largely overlooked. Finally, the fact that the focus of the international community has been on elections has served to overshadow the drivers of conflict on local, national, and regional levels, resulting in neglect of efforts that could have been made to counteract these.

Some of these arguments seem well founded, whereas others are rather weak. It is problematic to argue that defining DRC as a post-conflict country restricts peacebuilders' ability to assess and deal with continued violence, even on a gross scale. Even if there is no peace to keep, the 'post-conflict definition,' through a Security Council mandate, allows peacekeepers to deploy and activities to start. The alternative would be no presence of civilian peacebuilders, not from the UN or diplomatic circles, and no peace enforcers or peacekeepers either. Without security, humanitarian and development activities would have been at a minimum as well. In both *Rules for the World* as well as *The Trouble with the Congo*, I argue that the concept of 'culture' obscures more than it illuminates, as it does not adequately explain the fundamental tension between the basic norms of international relations and the role played by practices inside the organization and, even more importantly, by interaction between the UN and other classes of actors or ecologies in shaping and reshaping these norms and their interrelationship, in theory and in practice (Karlsrud 2011).[1]

While culture may be a useful concept for bringing out some defining features of the UN and more narrowly of peacekeeping and peacebuilding operations today, it also limits the understanding of how the UN interacts with others in informal policy alliances – internationally in the development of concepts, norms, and prescripts and nationally and locally in the daily implementation of peacekeeping operations. This book aims to explain instances of autonomous policy development processes in international organizations that cannot be described simply as pathologies or as organized hypocrisy, but where the organization engages in policy development processes that are more than what can be described by referring to 'organizational culture.' The book will examine who the main actors are, aside from member states and the organization itself, and how these actors from the UN, member states, and think tanks may form policy alliances to create norm change in international organizations.

24 *Theorizing linked ecologies*

In sum, it appears that much constructivist literature has lost the central part of Giddens's structuration theory when transferring it from an analysis of individual choice and action to analyze states and IOs (Giddens 1984). This has led to a Pavlovian understanding of socialization and individual action in IOs (see also Goddard 2009, Epstein 2012), with little explanatory power on individual and mid-level analyses of agency, norm transgression, and change in IOs. Put differently, the culture concept becomes a straitjacket on constructivist theorizing of international organizations, as it constrains the ability to explain other factors and actors that influence and shape actions and policy development processes and limits the ability to explain individual agency.

From bureaucracies to professions

Much of the constructivist theorizing of norms and change in international organizations is inspired by Max Weber's reflections on bureaucratic organization. According to Weber, the modern bureaucratic organization had "technical superiority over any other form of organization" (Weber et al. 1946, 214). Its key advantages were "precision, speed, unambiguity, knowledge of the files, continuity, discretion, unity, strict subordination, reduction of friction and of material and personal costs" (ibid.). Further, "bureaucratic authority" is established through three core elements: 1) regular activities are distributed in a stable way as official duties – clear roles and responsibilities follow the specific posts in the hierarchy; 2) authority to distribute tasks is also distributed in a stable way; and 3) those who fill established posts in the system need specialized competencies and qualifications. An official in the bureaucratic hierarchy is an "'objective' expert" (ibid., 216) with expert training and "jurisdictional competency" (197) and executes his or her tasks according to "*calculable rules* and without regard for persons" (215). Knowledge of the rules represents special technical learning and involves jurisprudence. This ensures the impersonal character of office work, but Weber also acknowledges that "in dubious cases, power interests tip the balance" (220).

Theorizing IOs as bureaucracies

Building on Weber and examining IOs as bureaucracies, Barnett and Finnemore give examples of IOs and their staff acting autonomously in ways originally unintended and unanticipated; they argue that IOs are capable of creating their own norms, rules, and practices independent of, and unintended by, their creators (2004). Dysfunctional behavior based on bureaucratic culture may occur when the IO and its officials must make difficult choices where several imperatives may apply at once. IOs may choose ways of solving problems not always in line with espoused goals. For instance, Barnett and Finnemore show how the UN Secretariat's handling of the genocide in Rwanda in 1994 resulted in dysfunctional and even pathological action and behavior, due to conflicting formal and informal rules within the organization (2004). The Secretariat's decision not to push for Security Council intervention in Rwanda in 1994 was based on the Secretariat's assessment that powerful states like the United States wanted to stay out of the conflict – particularly since this came shortly after the failure of Somalia – and that the likely failure of such an operation would be detrimental to the organization. While the contribution by Barnett and Finnemore demonstrates that IOs have agency and can act autonomously in line with their own interests in contradiction to the will of its member states, even powerful ones, their study suffers somewhat from a one-sided focus on the culture of the organization, not sufficiently considering what role other ecologies may have in IO change processes. While this shows that IOs have agency and can act in contradiction to the will of their member states, even powerful ones, it also points up the difficult balancing act IOs must undertake so as not to betray their ideals.

Critique of theorization of the UN as a bureaucratic international organization

There are thus several major flaws with Barnett and Finnemore's theory approach to the constructivist theorization of international organizations. First, by arguing that pathologies, dysfunctions, and organized hypocrisy take place, they presuppose that the UN can be understood as a single unitary actor, saying one thing but doing another. This may have been an error of omission on the part of Barnett and Finnemore, as the main focus of their project was to describe how IOs can have agency independent of member states. This book will take this as a starting point and seek to further open up the black box of IOs. First, the UN should not be seen as a single, unitary actor, but rather as an organization with several sources of agenda and agency. The UN consists of a range of different bodies, each with its particular dynamics, membership, and/or staff. The Security Council is the most important actor in the UN, and volumes have been written about the role of the Council with regard to peacekeeping (Malone 2004, Berdal and Economides 2007, Howard 2008). The General Assembly and various sub-committees play an important role and arrange meetings and plenary discussions, the discussions on Responsibility to Protect (R2P) being one relevant example (see e.g. United Nations General Assembly [UNGA] 2011). In chapter 3, the book expands the understanding of 'agency' to the special representatives of the secretary-general heading up peacekeeping missions in the field; in chapters 4 and 5 I argue that academic institutions and think tanks have agency through their participation in linked ecologies in norm change processes in the UN.

Second, by employing the concept of bureaucratic culture and stressing the uniformity of action that this imposes on UN staff, Barnett and Finnemore also underemphasize the potential impact that actors other than member states can have on the norm formation in the UN. Johnstone argues that the secretary-general can act as a norm entrepreneur, using high-level panels composed of statesmen, member state diplomats, and prominent researchers to advance thinking on topics of particular concern (2007, 134; Annan 2007, xii). Later in the chapter, I return to the theory of norm entrepreneurs and how it can be of significance for informal policy alliances. One case in point could be how the UN Secretariat sought to rebuild its

26 *Theorizing linked ecologies*

authority after Rwanda and Srebrenica through using reports, best practices, and lessons learned (Weinlich 2012, Benner et al. 2011). The significance of the combined involvement of statesmen, diplomats, bureaucrats, activists, and researchers in change processes has not yet been sufficiently explored. In the following, I begin to develop the theory framework of the book, examining how practice theory and the sociology of professions can help explain the actions and processes in focus in this book that elude the bureaucratic in-organization socialization and culture in constructivist theory. It is essential to recognize that international organizations and the individuals working within these also follow other incentives that lead them to link up with other ecologies in norm change processes.

Using practice theory and the sociology of professions to augment constructivist theorizing of norm change in international organizations

Existing theory does not sufficiently explain individual practices that break with existing norms and rules, and it is ill-suited for explaining new practices and norm change in IOs. This book sees norm change as change in established practices in the organization, change that transforms the relationship and relative balance between norms – for example, between the norms of sovereignty and the protection of civilians or between impartiality and supporting state authority.

Social practices accentuate the performative character of power (Guzzini 2005) and show the interplay between material and ideational factors in norm change.[2] Roxanne Lynn Doty was one of the first to emphasize the role of practices in the study of international relations (IR):

> Practices, because of their inextricable link with meaning, have an autonomy which cannot be reduced to either the intentions, will, motivations, or interpretations of choice-making subjects or to the constraining and enabling mechanisms of objective but socially constructed structures. Practices overflow that which can be accounted for in purely structural or agentic terms
>
> (Doty 1997, 377)

Doty thus indicates how practices can balance the understanding of the influence of material and ideational factors, a point this book also will emphasize.

In addition to the practices of peacekeeping, the book examines the practices of norm change by linked ecologies of the UN, member states, think tanks, and academic institutions. There are thus two main categories of practices to be examined:

1. Practices originating from the ground in peacekeeping operations, where senior leaders weigh norms against each other and decide on actions that form an inductive influence on norms in the UN system.
2. Social practices of alliance-building between different sets of actors or ecologies, seeking to advance particular sets of ideas or norms in the organization.

Practices and individual agency in peacekeeping

The first type of practices includes an element of background knowledge. This, according to Pouliot (2008), is an important element to consider. He holds that much practice theory relies too heavily on representational knowledge: "Conscious representations are emphasized to the detriment of background knowledge – the inarticulate know-how from which reflexive and intentional deliberation becomes possible" (ibid., 258). Quoting Bourdieu, Pouliot argues that "social scientists put themselves 'in a state of social weightlessness'" (2008, 260, translation by Pouliot). By virtue of their professions, social scientists are distanced from their object of study and focus instead on representational knowledge, which is readily available and can be theorized. However, social and individual action may not necessarily be premeditated, or informed, either consciously or unconsciously, by formal and informal norms and rules. According to Pouliot, practices rest on *background knowledge*, which is distinct from norms and ideas. Describing actions that are generated on the basis of background knowledge, he uses the words "self-evident" and "commonsense" (2008). To this list we could add terms like 'political acumen' and '*savoir-faire*' to describe qualities of actors who use background knowledge to perform practices. These descriptions and qualities all attempt to describe how an actor draws on prior experience, practical knowledge, and his or her reading of the political landscape and actors in making decisions on how to navigate the political landscape.

Background knowledge is practical and oriented toward action. Background knowledge also carries legitimacy – the UN special representative can diverge from his orders from headquarters due to his practical knowledge on the ground and the existence of conflicting norms guiding peacekeeping. When actors can choose between several sets of norms and rules, this may result in variation in action and practices. Chapter 3 on special representatives of the secretary-general (SRSGs) shows how peacekeeping is an area where conflicting norms and rules within the UN are particularly evident.

In his *Supplement to an Agenda for Peace*, UNSG Boutros-Ghali distinguished three levels of authority:

- Overall political direction, which belongs to the Security Council.
- Executive direction and command, for which the secretary-general is responsible.
- Command in the field, which is entrusted by the secretary-general to the chief of mission (special representative or force commander/chief military observer).

The distinctions between these three levels must be kept in mind in order to avoid any confusion of functions and responsibilities. It is as inappropriate for a chief of mission to take responsibility for formulating the mission's overall political objectives as it is for the Security Council or the secretary-general in New York to decide on matters that require a detailed understanding of operational conditions in the field (Boutros-Ghali 1995, 9–10).

28 *Theorizing linked ecologies*

The case study on SRSGs will show in greater detail how actors are situated in an uncertain environment where they must make difficult choices based on judgment, practical knowledge, and common sense. The chapter will give some practical examples of choices made where formal norms and rules were broken, shaping new norms and practices, and how an analysis of authority in peacekeeping, and particularly in the field, can offer a better understanding of these actions.

Background knowledge and practices have a geographical or locational aspect as well: they are formed and grounded in the local context of the actor. That different practices might occur between center and periphery applies not only to the UN and international relations. Several studies have shown how different norms and practices evolve between HQ and subsidiaries in multinational corporations, calling into question the traditional hierarchical understanding of how practices and action are based on following the rules and norms of a central authority (see e.g. Kristensen and Zeitlin 2005, Hotho et al. 2013, and Figure 1.1, chapter 1).

Pouliot focuses exclusively on non-representational or background knowledge, and to differentiate himself from Bourdieu he terms his approach "logic of practicality" (2008, 259). However, while acknowledging that background knowledge is important for understanding individual action, I will argue that excluding representational knowledge from the analysis would be throwing the baby out with the bathwater. The case studies in chapter 3 accentuate how a practice approach must focus on "the observable 'doings' of physical bodies and entities" (Andersen 2010, 16). We cannot accurately gauge what SRSG Kai Eide was thinking of, what common sense or experiences he was drawing on, and what norms he had considered in deciding to engage with the Taliban (see chapter 4). We can, however, see what his orders were, what norms guide peacekeeping today, the actions he took, and the consequences they had. Furthermore, we can analyze the sources of authority that a SRSG draws on when making decisions in the field.

Informal alliances for norm change as social practices

Agency will be explored at institutional as well as individual levels, including senior leadership at UN headquarters and in the field, but also other key actors in norm change processes. The book will examine the informal alliances or linked ecologies that are established to drive change in the processes of developing the norms guiding peacekeeping and the key actors in these alliances, whether they be individuals, institutions, or both.

Applying a practice approach in the social sciences amounts to

> a loose, but nevertheless definable movement of thought that is unified around the idea that the field of practices is the place to investigate such phenomena as agency, knowledge, language, ethics, power and science.
>
> (Schatzki et al. 2001, 13–14)

Schatzki argues that in social theory, "practice approaches promulgate a distinct social ontology" (ibid., 3). Social phenomena can be investigated as "a field of

Theorizing linked ecologies 29

embodied, materially interwoven practices centrally organized around shared practical understandings" (ibid., 3). Andersen distinguishes practice approaches from individualistic and structural theories, "as practice approaches locate their 'smallest theoretical unit' not in minds, discourses, interactions, structures or systems, but in practices that, however, can function as instantiations of all of the above" (Andersen 2010, 7).

A practice-oriented approach to studying norm change in UN peacekeeping can thus enable closer examination of the issues of agency and authority in norm change in international organizations and can help in identifying the important actors, whether institutions or individuals, or both. Most studies of practices are based on very concrete examples in established fields and are less focused on issues of emergence where the relative importance of competing norms are arbitrated or how new norms are championed by informal networks of heterogeneous actors. Here, the sociology of professions can be a useful tool to help understand how complex social practices occur and what impact they can have on norm change processes.

Sociology of professions

Professions have an organizational and a performative aspect, according to Anders Molander and Lars I. Terum (2010). Talcott Parsons describes the 'professional complex' as consisting of "occupational groups that perform certain rather specialized functions for others ('laymen') in the society on the basis of high-level and specialized competence, with the attendant fiduciary responsibility" (Parsons 1970, cited in Molander and Terum 2010, 14). Abbott defines 'professions' as "exclusive occupational groups applying somewhat abstract knowledge to particular cases" (Abbott 1988, 8). In this book I define 'professions' as exclusive occupational groups who try to achieve control over certain tasks due to their skills, specialist education and the organization they work for. Since professions have internal control over their tasks, this also implies that they have a certain degree of autonomy vis-à-vis the state or, in the case of the UN, the member states. Furthermore, a profession will seek to have jurisdictional control of the defined tasks, legitimized through expert authority and the delegation of these tasks by the member states (Molander and Terum 2010). The traditional professions include law, economics, and medicine, and it has been suggested that accounting, management, and nursing might also be considered as 'professions' (see e.g. Leicht and Fennell 2001). Peacekeeping consists of staff from a range of backgrounds but cannot be considered a separate profession if viewed through a strict definition of the term. However, if one takes an inductive approach, peacekeepers can be seen as 'issue professionals' who "combine knowledge and skills to enhance their attempts at control on a specific issue in transnational governance" (Seabrooke and Henriksen forthcoming 2016, 10).

The jurisdictional competencies of the UN bureaucracy are in part dictated by the development of a cadre of UN professionals working for various parts of the UN Secretariat, including the Office of the Secretary-General, the Department of

30 *Theorizing linked ecologies*

Peacekeeping Operations, the Department of Political Affairs, the Peacebuilding Commission and its Peacebuilding Support Office, and the Department of Field Support. Control of the area of peace and security relies on control of the abstractions that generate practical techniques and implementation – in other words, control of the profession-specific practices and concepts. Like Weber, Abbott identifies jurisdiction as the central connecting element between a profession and its work (Abbott 1988).

According to Talcott Parsons (cited in Molander and Terum 2010, 14), members of a profession also have a collective 'fiduciary responsibility' (see also Abbott 2005b, Fourcade 2006, Abbott 1988) – the relationship between the profession and the member states, as well as other stakeholders, is based on trust that the members will execute their tasks according to their mandate. To retain legitimacy, this implicitly requires the need for self-control, as well as ways of punishing those who break the professional code. The concept of fiduciary responsibility can also be useful in explaining anomalies where the organization acts *against* the will of its members, or at least some of them – including veto powers, as will be shown in the cases in chapter 3 on SRSGs. The chapter will recall the discussion around the attack on President Gbagbo in Côte d'Ivoire by UN helicopter gunships. On April 4 and 10, 2011, Choi Young-jin, UN special representative and head of UN operations in Côte d'Ivoire (ONUCI), authorized airstrikes against the troops of President Gbagbo, using MI-24 attack helicopters to defend civilian populations from heavy-weapon attacks by Gbagbo forces (BBC World News 2011). Russia reacted with strong condemnation and immediately questioned the legality of the attack (Anishchuk 2011). Here a tension was evident between Choi Young-jin's interpretation of the collective interest of member states as stated in UN Security Council Resolution 1975, in the UN Charter, and established by precedent, and the outcry of Russia after the attack. I will argue that individuals within the UN can influence the understanding of norms and what actions should be taken in a given situation (see also Karlsrud 2013). Finally, a profession is also a collective actor and will act as such in defending its tasks and legitimacy. From the aforementioned, we see that the sociology of professions has many affinities with constructivist theory and that they are both inspired in part by the work of Weber.

As highlighted earlier, practices constitute the performative aspect of professions. Professions execute services for clients. The services are solutions to particular specialized problems that require particular knowledge and that lead to change. The tasks or problems are often complex and require the use of common sense. The actions taken to solve the problem may prove wrong, and responsibility for the actions will lie with the professional. Over time, professions thus become communities of practice, gathering best practices and lessons learned that, together with established rules, norms, and values, form a repository of guidance and constitute jurisprudence for future problem-solving actions.

Finally, we need to distinguish between *professions* and *professionalism*. Eliot Freidson, investigating the increasing pressures under which professions have come from demands of "maximization of profit and the minimization of discretion" (2001, 220), sees a tension between these pressures and the ability of

Theorizing linked ecologies 31

professions to execute their work with professionalism. He argues that monopoly and "freedom of judgment or discretion in performance of work" (ibid., 3) are intrinsic to professionalism; in this he stands directly opposed to criticism from free-market supporters. Freidson defines professionalism as:

> the institutional circumstances in which the members of occupations rather than consumers or managers control work . . . Professionalism may be said to exist when an organized occupation gains the powers to determine who is qualified to perform a defined set of tasks, to prevent all others from performing that work, and to control the criteria by which to evaluate performance.
>
> (ibid., 12)

With increasing external pressures from consumers and managers (like host states of peacekeeping operations and member states in the case of UN peacekeeping), a profession must continuously develop its instruments of self-regulation, codes of conduct, guidelines, and accountability mechanisms in order to keep the consumers and managers at bay and avoid imposition of controls. Viewing the UN as a bureaucracy that has been allocated a certain number of tasks, and the development of these tasks in the area of peacekeeping, we note certain similarities. While the UN peacekeeping bureaucracy cannot be defined as a profession using a strict definition of professions, it has developed many of the features that define a profession, and it aims to professionalize the conduct of peacekeeping operations through the establishment of codes of conducts, policies, prescripts, and codification of best practices. It also seeks to contribute to the standards and goals according to which it will be measured by its constituencies – member states, host states, NGOs, civil society, and the general public. In international organizations it is quite common for individuals from heterogeneous occupational groups to work together on the same issue area, not as a profession in the original sense of the word, but grouped together due to the tasks they perform. Other examples outside of peacekeeping could be humanitarian workers and development workers who also can be considered 'issue professionals' (Seabrooke and Henriksen, forthcoming 2016). Individuals from traditional set professions are brought together – lawyers, economists, doctors, and others – and often work in teams, advising members of national ministries of host countries. I return to this in the final chapter as an area for further study.

Revolving doors and eminent personalities

Barnett and Finnemore, drawing on Weber, generally examine how IOs as bureaucracies establish 'jurisdictional competency' or rational-legal authority in their areas of expertise (2004) – excluding from their analysis how bureaucratic control of a policy area tends to be created in close cooperation with think tanks, donor governments, and other actors with similar interests in the area in question. Barnett and Finnemore do make reference to the importance of the external environment, but without further investigation of this. Understanding how actors move

32   Theorizing linked ecologies

between posts in the UN and in think tanks, member-state posts, and academia can offer additional insights into how policy alliances are formed to advance norm change in international organizations.

In the area of peacekeeping the UN has had to rely on funding and support from donor governments to develop doctrine and best practices since the end of the Cold War. Staff has been moving through 'revolving doors' as practitioners in IOs, policy-makers at think tanks, and officials in government institutions. Middle powers and donor governments in the club of "good states" (Lawler 2005) like the UK, Canada, the Netherlands, Norway, and Sweden have pushed the development of doctrine for peacekeeping, with dedicated government offices having peace-keeping on the agenda and funding the development of policy reports; discussions around new concepts and recommendations; and even best-practice positions on peacekeeping at UN headquarters (Jensen 2006, Benner et al. 2007, Benner and Rotmann 2008, Benner et al. 2011).[3]

A closer look at how this dynamic has evolved and the consequences for the development of doctrine and evolving practice within the UN is thus called for. Haas's concept of transnational epistemic communities naturally comes to mind here (1992). But that concept overemphasizes the role of technical expertise and does not sufficiently explain how policy alliances between technical experts in think tanks, NGOs, universities, and elsewhere, and bureaucrats in member states and international organizations, together can have an influence on processes of norm change. This book seeks to transcend the artificial divide between member-state decision-makers and transnational epistemic communities, showing that the likelihood of successfully influencing the global agenda increases with an alliance between these actors. Combined with the practice-oriented approach theorizing individual action in IOs sketched out earlier, the concept of basic norms in tension is better suited to explaining the existence of parallel sets of norms, rules, and practices than Barnett and Finnemore's concepts of dysfunctional behavior and pathologies.

Policy alliances and linked ecologies

Abbott has described how professional and political ecologies can form policy alliances (Abbott 2005b). Building on Abbott, Marion Fourcade, studying the transnationalization of economics, has identified how professions achieve juris-dictional competency and claims on a *global level*. She identifies transnational connectedness as one of the dimensions underlying the globalization of the economics profession (Fourcade 2006). According to Abbott, actors within different ecologies create "hinges" to form alliances – "strategies that work as well in one ecology as in the other" (Abbott 2005b, 255). The policy alliances can involve substantially different classes of actors, and a linkage can be made between a professional and a political ecology. In line with Abbott, in this book I define 'ecologies' as social structures that are composed of "actors, locations, and a rela-tion associating the one with the other" (Abbott 2005b, 248). By using the concept of ecology, we can see the similarities they display. Within ecologies there is

Theorizing linked ecologies 33

competition between coalitions who fight over control over how an issue should be defined and how it should be solved. In order to gain strength, a coalition can reach to other ecologies to form linked ecologies. By this they can gain strength and achieve change in "areas not formally within their remit" (Seabrooke and Tsingou 2009, 11).

I have already noted how the concept of epistemic communities takes the position of influence as already given, not explaining how epistemic communities become authoritative and policy relevant. The linked ecologies concept helps us understand how different ecologies connect and form formal and informal policy alliances and improves our understanding of not only who has authority, but the processes actors from different ecologies are involved in to come into those positions of authority. In the existing literature, such alliances have been described as, for example, networks, coalitions, and policy alliances. However, the literature on networks has mostly focused on how one actor *within* an ecology can play a central role in a network (Carpenter 2011) and how an actor can act as a broker (e.g. Goddard 2009), and not how multiple actors from *different* ecologies act together. What the linked ecologies can add to the literature is a process view of how heterogeneous actors can form linked ecologies and how individuals moving through revolving doors can ferry knowledge and ideas with them from one ecology to another.

By using the linked ecologies framework, I can better explain how it is the joint effort of actors from different ecologies that together make an impact on norm change processes, "where the actors do not conform to an ascribed public or private identity" (Seabrooke and Tsingou 2009, 8). Following Seabrooke and Tsingou, I understand ecologies as "social systems where the overall effect of interaction, rather than the capacities of any particular individual actor, is most important" (ibid., 11). In comparison to the use of the concept of bureaucratic culture by Barnett and Finnemore, the linked ecologies concept opens up for an understanding of how agency not only is formed by the organization that one is working for, but also the interaction with other organizations, and the how previous experience within other organizations can enable new linkages and facilitate change processes. This mix of public and private identity, and emphasis on how an individual carries knowledge and connections from one organization to another, is helpful when understanding how linked ecologies are formed and why they can have an impact on change processes. The linked ecologies concept then improves the understanding of individual agency within organizations, loosening the Pavlovian grip that the concept of 'bureaucratic culture' puts on individual agency in international relations.[4] Second, the linked ecologies concept opens up for a more process-oriented view of change and how knowledge, norms, and ideas can spread from one ecology to another through individuals who move through revolving doors. These individuals can bring with them new perspectives, ideas, and methods on how to solve old problems or can introduce their networks and open up for other resources that can be of use in the new ecology to which they have moved (ibid.; Seabrooke 2011; Seabrooke and Tsingou 2015; Stone 2013; Seabrooke and Nilsson 2015).

34 *Theorizing linked ecologies*

The main ecologies to be described and investigated in this book are as follows:

- Member states, in particular, officials dealing with UN peace and security issues.
- The UN as an international organization, with a special focus on the peacekeeping dimension.
- Think tank staff working on policy-oriented research on peacekeeping issues.
- Academic institutions focusing on peacekeeping.
- NGOs and activist groups focusing on peacekeeping.

In each of these ecologies, there are hierarchies and systems of tasks, particular entry requirements and systems of reward, and jurisdictional requirements concerning the tasks to be executed. The links between the ecologies occur on two levels. First, there is a substantively shared interest in peacekeeping, and informal and formal groups and partnerships are formed time and again to explore or advance this shared interest. Second, linkages are made through individuals moving between these ecologies through revolving doors, ferrying knowledge and networks with them (Strathern 2004).

One of the weaknesses of the theoretical approach of Barnett and Finnemore has been their focus on IOs, without enough attention to how norms, rules, and practices have been generated in cooperation with other ecologies such as

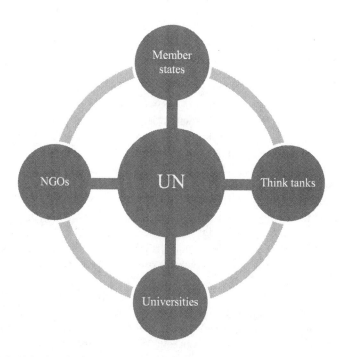

Figure 2.1 Linked ecologies in UN peacekeeping

Theorizing linked ecologies 35

government, think tanks, and academia. Seen through the lenses of Fourcade and Seabrooke and Tsingou (Seabrooke and Tsingou 2009), Abbott yields a more promising theoretical framework. According to Abbott, professions use abstract knowledge to attach subjective qualities and meaning of tasks through diagnosis, inference, and treatment (Abbott 1988). Through this process, the profession can take hold of a policy problem and canonize the treatment of the problem. On the global level, ecologies can link up in informal alliances and gain control over a policy 'location' on a global level (Fourcade 2006). The policy alliance will then be "able to influence how certain policy problems are understood and inform broader norms on how policy problems should be legitimately addressed" (Seabrooke and Tsingou 2009, 3). Based on the case studies in chapters 4 and 5, the book will argue that linked ecologies often are formed in order to further norm change.

Individuals act as brokers and forge links between different ecologies, moving from one ecology to another through 'revolving doors.' However, it would be unrealistic to assume that these individuals will completely change their identity to conform with their new institution and its culture, leaving behind their previous identity and networks. Thus, it seems odd that much of the literature on international organizations and public authority does not take account the frequent phenomenon of individuals moving through revolving doors when theorizing action and practices in international organizations.

The ability of an actor or linked ecology to affect change is dependent on the degree a linked ecology is able to incorporate members from various ecologies, drawing upon their ideas, skills, networks, and funding resources. This emphasis on heterogeneity as a potential asset distinguishes this theory from theories emphasizing that

> rather than finding complementary partners within an already-existing institutional framework or mindset, combination across linked ecologies opens up greater space for identifying how practices emerge across ecologies that would normally be treated as discrete categories. This should certainly assist us in identifying how transnational and international standard-setting processes are established.
>
> (Seabrooke and Tsingou 2009, 10)

The following section will further develop the theory framework to see how the agency of these linked ecologies can be framed in a reconceptualized understanding of the arena concept in international relations theory.

The United Nations as a competitive arena for informal policy alliances

According to Mearsheimer, neorealists view the international system as a "brutal arena where states look for opportunities to take advantage of each other . . . International relations is not a constant state of war, but is a state of relentless security

36   *Theorizing linked ecologies*

competition" (1994, 9). Principal-agent theory sees the UN as an arena where member states (principals) delegate authority to the UN (agent) or where the UN, acting as a second-level principal,[5] delegates some tasks to other actors such as NGOs, think tanks, and so forth. These are the most used understandings of arena in international relations today. Dijkstra argues that "to efficiently handle these increasing demands of peacekeeping, states have delegated planning and conduct functions to the Secretariat" and "weigh anticipated efficiency gains against sovereignty loss" (2012, 581–82).

This book would, however, like to expand the understanding of the arena concept in relation to norm change in the UN. In a narrow sense, the book agrees with the understandings of arena purported earlier, but in a wider sense, norm change processes seem to include actors other than only member states. As the case studies on R2P and integrated missions will show, linked ecologies are formed to advance norms. These processes occur partially inside and partially outside the UN, aiming to build support and momentum for a particular issue. In the wider understanding of arena, member states, think tanks, academia, and NGOs try to avoid internal UN spoiling, turf battles, and falling prey to political tug of wars by forming informal policy alliances to further norm goals. Such a wider view arguably also expands the understanding of which actors have authority and agency in the global arena, challenging realist and rationalist understandings of the arena concept.

This wider understanding of the arena concept is supported by the views of small activist member states like Norway regarding the UN and the functions it should fulfill. Norway sees the UN "as the world's central norm-setter, an arena for drawing up rules that many are bound by" (Johansen 2009). In fact, leading Norwegian diplomats have asserted that small powers together with other actors can influence norm change. Raymond Johansen, a former deputy minister, asserted:

> In our view, the supremacy of the great powers is an illusion. Reality is that there can be no permanent solution to common challenges unless the UN's norms and arena functions are used to bring states and *actors* together.
>
> (ibid., emphasis added)

Johansen expands the understanding of agency at the UN and includes actors other than member states. For many decades, Norway has been very active in advancing norms. Examples include the 1987 Brundtland report (Gro Harlem Brundtland, former Norwegian prime minister), support to the process leading up to the Mine Ban Convention in 1997, the integrated missions process (2004–7), and the still ongoing 'Delivering as One' process aimed at better UN coherence on the ground. In these processes Norway and other activist member states have teamed up with civil society, international non-governmental organizations (INGOs), the research community, and other classes of actors to advance a particular norm on the agenda of the UN that should be binding for all member states or should guide the UN's actions in a given area.

Theorizing linked ecologies 37

The wider understanding of the arena concept in norm change processes in the UN is also supported by recent studies on the role of the 'Third UN' (Weiss et al. 2009, Weiss and Thakur 2010, Kittikhoun and Weiss 2011). This literature shows how academics, civil society, and statesmen have had an impact on norm formation and change in the UN. Literature on global governance and who the important actors are has also greatly expanded agency. Deborah Avant and colleagues define global governors as "authorities who exercise power across borders for the purpose of affecting policy" (Avant et al. 2010, 2) and include NGOs, private companies, states, and international organizations among these authorities. Diane Stone has highlighted the role "transnational policy communities" can play in the "global agora" in global public policy processes (2008). This global agora concept shares the understanding of this book that there are other and less formal spaces where policy processes occur: "Networks, coalitions, and multilateral partnerships contribute to the shape, diversity and (in)equality in the global agora" (ibid., 31). Stone uses the agora concept as a common label for these spaces which "are multiple in character and variety" (ibid., 19). However, I will use the arena concept in relation to norm change in the UN, since the organization itself is very much involved (as an actor) in these processes, and it is an arena where member states still have a very important role. I return to the arena concept later in the book.

This book thus argues that the UN, in the area of peacekeeping, can be understood as a competitive arena, where linked ecologies compete to frame issues and build support for new norms, concepts, and rules. These processes often involve academic institutions, think tanks, and civil society, as well as diplomats on various levels. Taking a policy discussion out of the UN into the informal arena can be part of a strategy to avoid UN spoiling, turf battles, and substantive issues falling prey to political wrangling and horse-trading between member states in the General Assembly, seeking instead to build sufficient momentum and support for a norm before entering formal negotiations at the UN.

Conclusions

In this chapter I have looked at how norms and norm change have been theorized within various schools in international relations, ranging from realist to rationalist to constructivist approaches. Constructivist theories presented here support the view that, in the area of peacekeeping, the UN *qua* bureaucracy and *qua* a professional organization can act autonomously. Through its autonomous behavior, the organization is part of the processes of norm change that form and guide UN peacekeeping. However, theories differ considerably as to how and whether they can grasp and explain how autonomous acts come about. I have shown how the main strands of constructivist theory use pathologies and organized hypocrisy as terms to describe anomalous behavior in IOs and how this entails some significant shortcomings, such as not accounting for how agency is decentralized and including various actors within and outside of the UN.

This book argues that together, practices and linked ecologies are constitutive pillars for the change of norms. Norms become established as a result of practices

38 *Theorizing linked ecologies*

over time, slowly put into doctrine with those states driving UN reform and the peacebuilding agenda taking the lead. In the case studies, I investigate whether norms in the UN can enter into practice before they are codified, thereby establishing practices that may contradict established norms and rules – like engaging with terrorists in the case of Afghanistan or using force against a strategic actor in the case of Côte d'Ivoire.

We will see that there is a spatio-temporal lag in norm formation and codification between periphery and center in peacekeeping and peacebuilding. This can be explained by inadequate material resources or ideational factors. Material factors include the lack of institutional memory and resources for best-practices officers at HQ and the slow establishment of a lessons learned/best practices unit (Benner et al. 2011). Ideational factors include resistance to codification of practices on the ground that challenge the notion of sovereignty (Chesterman 2004, Krasner 2009). However, while the material and ideational factors are valid reasons for the spatio-temporal lag of norm formation, we have also seen that examining the development of peacekeeping as a developing *issue profession* through practices on the ground and the relationship with think tanks, government agencies, and academia can provide a fuller picture.

The book uses constructivist theory as its main theory framework, but couples this with the sociology of professions to account for how other actors affect the norm formation in organizations and uses a practice-oriented approach for grasping norm change at the 'coal face.' Together, practices and linked ecologies are constitutive pillars for new norms. Norms are established as a result of practices over time, and these are slowly being put into doctrine with the states, think tanks, and academic institutions driving UN reform. In chapter 1, Figure 1.1, I sketched out the relationship between practices, norms, and basic norms, and in the next chapters I will explore this relationship further through the case studies.

The case studies on R2P and integrated missions will show how informal alliances or linked ecologies are formed to drive change in the UN. This expands agency to actors other than member states. The book develops the concept of the UN as a competitive arena where linked ecologies advance new norms. This is further elaborated in chapter 6 in connection with the case studies, also adding further empirical evidence with a look at how some member states engage with academic institutions and think tanks on specific issues related to UN peacekeeping.

Notes

1   A previous version of this argument was published as a review of the book in: John Karlsrud (2011) 'The Trouble with the Congo: Local Violence and the Failure of International Peace-Building' [Review], *Forum for Development Studies*, 38 (2), pp. 227–30. The material is reprinted with permission from *Forum for Development Studies/* Taylor & Francis.
2   I am indebted to Katharina Glaab for this point.
3   In terms of Lawler's argument, the UK is somewhat of an outlier here, but it has devoted capacity to deal with UN peacekeeping. A point for further study could be to study whether the UK is pursuing change in UN peacekeeping that is more in line with liberal interventionist notions of internationalism compared to the more classical interventionalism displayed by the policies pursued by Nordic states.

4   In an unpublished section of the article on linked ecologies, *Ecologies and Fields*, Abbott acknowledges that there are many similarities between his concept of ecologies and Bourdieu's field concept:

> First, they are both concerned with locating actors relative to other actors. They refuse to consider social actors in unrelated, mass terms. Second, they agree that locations in social space are not given ex ante – by functions or by some rule system – but are rather enacted in the process of social life and in particular in the process of relating to other actors. Third, they both agree that there are units or collections of social locations that are usefully considered as macro structures – fields and ecologies. And we both see processes of conflict and competition as crucial to understanding the internal evolution of these collections of social locations.
>
> (Abbott 2005a, 1)

However, Abbott argues that Bourdieu is relying on economic metaphors in his descriptions, while the "ecology concept mixes the biological notions of the competition and coexistence of organisms in spaces with more strategic conceptions drawing on legal and political language" (ibid., 2). He also criticizes the concept of field for being static and based on a system of domination and subordination: "My concept of ecology arises not by the loosening up or putting into motion of structuralism, but by an attempt to find regularity in a social world first imagined as utterly fluid" (ibid., 6).

5   I would like to thank Catherine Weaver for this insight.

References

Abbott, Andrew D. (1988) *The System of Professions: An Essay on the Division of Expert Labor.* Chicago: University of Chicago Press.

Abbott, Andrew D. (2005a) *Ecologies and Fields*, http://home.uchicago.edu/~aabbott/Papers/BOURD.pdf. Accessed May 2, 2014.

Abbott, Andrew D. (2005b) 'Linked Ecologies: States and Universities as Environments for Professions', *Sociological Theory*, 23 (3), pp. 245–74.

Andersen, Morten S. (2010) *Putting Structure into Practice: The 'Practice' Turn in IR and Ontologies of Structural Inquiry.* MIMEO.

Anishchuk, Alexei (2011) 'Russia Criticises UN Force Role in Ivory Coast', Reuters, http://af.reuters.com/article/topNews/idAFJOE73D0C020110414?pageNumber=2&virtualBrandChannel=0. Accessed April 18, 2011.

Annan, Kofi A. (2007) 'Foreword,' in Chesterman, Simon ed. *Secretary or General? The UN Secretary-General in World Politics.* Cambridge: Cambridge University Press, pp. xi–xiii.

Autesserre, Severine (2010) *The Trouble with the Congo: Local Violence and the Failure of International Peacebuilding.* Cambridge: Cambridge University Press.

Avant, Deborah D., Martha Finnemore and Susan K. Sell (2010) *Who Governs the Globe?* Cambridge: Cambridge University Press.

Barnett, Michael N. and Martha Finnemore (1999) 'The Politics, Power, and Pathologies of International Organizations', *International Organization*, 53 (4), pp. 699–732.

Barnett, Michael N. and Martha Finnemore (2004) *Rules for the World: International Organizations in Global Politics.* Ithaca, NY: Cornell University Press.

BBC World News (2011) 'Ivory Coast: Besieged Gbagbo "in Basement" of Residence', BBC World News, www.bbc.co.uk/news/mobile/world-africa-12967610. Accessed April 18, 2011.

40   Theorizing linked ecologies

Benner, Thorsten, Andrea Binder and Philipp Rotmann (2007) 'Learning to Build Peace? United Nations Peacebuilding and Organizational Learning: Developing a Research Framework', *GPPi Research Paper Series No. 7*. Berlin: Global Public Policy Institute.

Benner, Thorsten, Stephan Mergenthaler and Philipp Rotmann (2011) *The New World of UN Peace Operations: Learning to Build Peace?* Oxford: Oxford University Press.

Benner, Thorsten and Philipp Rotmann (2008) 'Learning to Learn? UN Peacebuilding and the Challenges of Building a Learning Organization', *Journal of Intervention and State-building*, 2 (1), pp. 43–62.

Berdal, Mats R. and Spyros Economides (2007) *United Nations Interventionism, 1991–2004*. Cambridge: Cambridge University Press.

Bobbio, Norberto and Danilo Zolo (1998) 'Hans Kelsen, the Theory of Law and the International Legal System: A Talk', *European Journal of International Law*, 9 (2), pp. 355–67.

Boutros-Ghali, Boutros (1995) *A/RES/51/242: Supplement to An Agenda for Peace*. New York: United Nations.

Carpenter, R. Charli (2011) 'Vetting the Advocacy Agenda: Network Centrality and the Paradox of Weapons Norms', *International Organization*, 65 (1), pp. 69–102.

Checkel, Jeffrey T. (1998) 'Review: The Constructivist Turn in International Relations Theory', *World Politics*, 50 (2), pp. 324–48.

Chesterman, Simon (2004) *You, the People: The United Nations, Transitional Administration, and State-Building*. Oxford: Oxford University Press.

Dijkstra, Hylke (2012) 'Efficiency versus Sovereignty: Delegation to the UN Secretariat in Peacekeeping', *International Peacekeeping*, 19 (5), pp. 581–96.

Doty, Roxanne Lynn (1997) 'Aporia. A Critical Exploration of the Agent-Structure Problematique in International Relations Theory', *European Journal of International Relations*, 3 (3), pp. 365–92.

Epstein, Charlotte (2012) 'Stop Telling Us How to Behave: Socialization or Infantilization?' *International Studies Perspectives*, 13 (2), pp. 135–45.

Finnemore, Martha and Kathryn Sikkink (1998) 'International Norm Dynamics and Political Change', *International Organization*, 52 (4), pp. 887–917.

Fourcade, Marion (2006) 'The Construction of a Global Profession: The Transnationalization of Economics', *American Journal of Sociology*, 112 (1), pp. 145–94.

Freidson, Eliot (2001) *Professionalism: The Third Logic*. Cambridge: Polity Press.

Giddens, Anthony (1984) *The Constitution of Society: Outline of the Theory of Structuration*. Cambridge: Polity Press.

Goddard, Stacie E. (2009) 'Brokering Change: Networks and Entrepreneurs in International Politics', *International Theory*, 1 (2), 249–81.

Guzzini, Stefano (2005) 'The Concept of Power: A Constructivist Analysis', *Millennium – Journal of International Studies*, 33 (3), pp. 495–521.

Haas, Peter M. (1992) 'Epistemic Communities and International-Policy Coordination – Introduction', *International Organization*, 46 (1), pp. 1–35.

Hotho, Jasper J., Ayse Saka-Helmhout and Florian Becker-Ritterspach (2014) 'Bringing Context and Structure Back into Situated Learning', *Management Learning*, 45 (1), pp. 57–80.

Howard, Lise Morjé (2008) *UN Peacekeeping in Civil Wars*. Cambridge: Cambridge University Press.

Jensen, Elin G. (2006) 'Organisational Learning in UN Peacebuilding Operations: Efforts at Demilitarisation in Angola during the 1990s.' PhD dissertation, University of Oxford.

Johansen, Raymond (2009) 'Do We Need the United Nations? Address at ISFiT Conference, Trondheim, 27 February 2009', Norwegian Ministry of Foreign Affairs, www.regjeringen.no/nb/dep/ud/aktuelt/taler_artikler/taler_og_artikler_av_ovrig_politisk_lede/tidligere-statssekretaer-johansen/2009/isfit_un.html?id=547873. Accessed September 16, 2012.

Johnstone, Ian (2007) 'The Secretary-General as Norm Entrepreneur: Secretary or General?' in Chesterman, Simon ed. *Secretary or General? The UN Secretary-General in World Politics.* Cambridge: Cambridge University Press, pp. 123–38.

Karlsrud, John (2011) 'The Trouble with the Congo: Local Violence and the Failure of International Peace-Building' [Review], *Forum for Development Studies*, 38 (2), pp. 227–30.

Karlsrud, John (2013) 'SRSGs as Norm Arbitrators? Understanding Bottom-up Authority in UN Peacekeeping', *Global Governance*, 19 (4), pp. 525–44.

Kelsen, Hans (1961) *General Theory of Law and State.* New York: Russell & Russell.

Kittikhoun, Anoulak and Thomas G. Weiss (2011) 'The Myth of Scholarly Irrelevance for the United Nations', *International Studies Review*, 13 (1), pp. 18–23.

Koch, Martin (2009) 'Autonomization of IGOs', *International Political Sociology*, 3 (4), pp. 431–48.

Krasner, Stephen D. (2009) *Power, the State, and Sovereignty: Essays on International Relations.* London: Routledge.

Kristensen, Peer H. and Jonathan Zeitlin (2005) *Local Players in Global Games: The Strategic Constitution of a Multinational Corporation.* Oxford: Oxford University Press.

Lawler, Peter (2005) 'The Good State: In Praise of "Classical" Internationalism', *Review of International Studies*, 31 (3), pp. 427–49.

Leicht, Kevin T. and Mary L. Fennell (2001) *Professional Work: A Sociological Approach.* Oxford: Blackwell Publishers.

Lipson, Michael (2007) 'Peacekeeping: Organized Hypocrisy?' *European Journal of International Relations*, 13 (1), pp. 5–34.

Malone, David (2004) *The UN Security Council: From the Cold War to the 21st Century.* Boulder, CO: Lynne Rienner.

March, James G. and Johan P. Olsen (1995) *Democratic Governance.* New York: Free Press.

March, James G. and Johan P. Olsen (1998) 'The Institutional Dynamics of International Political Orders', *International Organization*, 52 (4), pp. 943–69.

Mearsheimer, John J. (1994) 'The False Promise of International Institutions', *International Security*, 19 (3), pp. 5–49.

Molander, Anders and Lars I. Terum (2010) 'Profesjonsstudier – en introduksjon,' in Molander, Anders and Lars I. Terum eds., *Profesjonsstudier.* Oslo: Universitetsforlaget, pp. 13–27.

Pouliot, Vincent (2008) 'The Logic of Practicality: A Theory of Practice of Security Communities', *International Organization*, 62 (2), pp. 257–88.

Reus-Smit, Christian (2001) 'Constructivism,' *Theories of International Relations.* 2nd ed. New York: Palgrave, pp. 209–30.

Reus-Smit, Christian (2004) 'The Politics of International Law', in Reus-Smit, Christian ed. *The Politics of International Law.* Cambridge: Cambridge University Press, pp. 14–44.

Risse, Thomas (2000) ' "Let's Argue!": Communicative Action in World Politics', *International Organization*, 54 (1), pp. 1–39.

42 *Theorizing linked ecologies*

Schatzki, Theodore R., K. Knorr-Cetina and Eike von Savigny (2001) *The Practice Turn in Contemporary Theory.* New York: Routledge.

Seabrooke, Leonard (2011) 'Economists and Diplomacy: Professions and the Practice of Economic Policy', *International Journal*, 66 (3), pp. 629–42.

Seabrooke, Leonard and Lasse F. Henriksen (forthcoming 2016) 'Issue Control in Transnational Professional Networks and Organizations,' in Seabrooke, Leonard and Lasse F. Henriksen eds., *Professional Networks in Transnational Governance.* Cambridge: Cambridge University Press.

Seabrooke, Leonard and Emelie Rebecca Nilsson (2015) 'Professional Skills in International Financial Surveillance: Assessing Change in IMF Policy Teams', *Governance*, 28 (2), pp. 267–54.

Seabrooke, Leonard and Eleni Tsingou (2009) *Revolving Doors and Linked Ecologies in the World Economy: Policy Locations and the Practice of International Financial Reform.* Warwick: University of Warwick, CSGR Working Papers.

Seabrooke, Leonard and Eleni Tsingou (2015) 'Professional Emergence on Transnational Issues: Linked Ecologies on Demographic Change', *Journal of Professions and Organization*, 2 (1), pp. 1–18.

Sending, Ole J. (2002) 'Constitution, Choice and Change: Problems with the "Logic of Appropriateness" and Its Use in Constructivist Theory', *European Journal of International Relations*, 8 (4), pp. 443–70.

Sending, Ole J. (2010) *Expertise and Field Dynamics in Global Governance.* MIMEO.

Stone, Diane (2008) 'Global Public Policy, Transnational Policy Communities, and Their Networks', *Policy Studies Journal*, 36 (1), pp. 19–38.

Stone, Diane (2013) '"Shades of Grey": The World Bank, Knowledge Networks and Linked Ecologies of Academic Engagement', *Global Networks*, 13 (2): pp. 241–60.

Strathern, Marilyn (2004) 'Working Paper One: Knowledge on Its Travels: Dispersal and Divergence in the Make-up of Communities,' in Strathern, Marilyn ed. *Commons and Borderlands:Working Papers on Interdisciplinarity, Accountability and the Flow of Knowledge.* Oxon, UK: Sean Kingston Publishing.

UN (1948) *A/RES/3/217. Universal Declaration of Human Rights.* New York: United Nations.

United Nations General Assembly (UNGA) (2011) 'United Nations General Assembly 65th Session. Informal Interactive Dialogue on the Role of Regional and Sub-regional Arrangements in Implementing the Responsibility to Protect, 12 July 2011', United Nations. www.un.org/en/ga/president/65/initiatives/RtoPdialogue.html. Accessed December 29, 2012.

Weaver, Catherine (2008) *Hypocrisy Trap: The World Bank and the Poverty of Reform.* . Princeton, NJ: Princeton University Press.

Weber, Max, Hans Heinrich Gerth and C. Wright Mills (1946) *From Max Weber: Essays in Sociology.* New York: Oxford University Press.

Weinlich, Silke (2012) '(Re)generating Peacekeeping Authority: The Brahimi Process', *Journal of Intervention and Statebuilding*, 6 (3), pp. 257–77.

Weiss, Thomas G., Tatiana Carayannis and Richard Jolly (2009) 'The "Third" United Nations', *Global Governance*, 15 (1), pp. 123–42.

Weiss, Thomas G. and Ramesh Thakur (2010) *Global Governance and the UN.* Bloomington; Indianapolis: Indiana University Press.

Wendt, Alexander E. (1987) 'The Agent-Structure Problem in International Relations Theory', *International Organization*, 41 (3): pp. 335–370.

Wendt, Alexander E. (1992) 'Anarchy Is What States Make of It – the Social Construction of Power-Politics', *International Organization*, 46 (2), pp. 3

3 SRSGs as norm arbitrators? Understanding bottom-up authority in UN peacekeeping

> Of course I met Taliban leaders during the time I was in Afghanistan. Anything else *for me* would have been *unthinkable*, given the emphasis I was placing on it *myself*, and the *mandate* that we have.
>
> Kai Eide, Special Representative of the UN Secretary-General in Afghanistan (Borger 2010a, emphases added)

Introduction[1]

On April 4 and 10, 2011, Choi Young-jin, SRSG[2] for the UN operation in Côte d'Ivoire (ONUCI), authorized airstrikes against the troops of President Gbagbo, using MI-24 attack helicopters to defend civilian populations from attacks with heavy weapons by Gbagbo forces (BBC World News 2011). Russia reacted with strong condemnation, immediately questioning the legality of the attack (Anishchuk 2011). One year earlier, Kai Eide had stepped down from his post as SRSG for the UN operation in Afghanistan, UNAMA, after admitting to having initiated contacts with the Taliban (Doucet 2010), challenging the US and UK policy of "sticks and carrots" (Lamb and Grey 2009).

Such controversial actions and the relationship between the basic norms they affect are pivotal to UN peacekeeping. In Afghanistan, what was at stake was the principle of impartiality and whether the UN should provide its good offices also to the Taliban, which the Security Council had designated as a terrorist organization. In Côte d'Ivoire, the tension was between the principles of impartiality and protection of civilians.

In both instances there was a clash between center and periphery, between UN headquarters and the field, with Security Council members showing diminishing support of the SRSGs involved. This chapter examines some potentially controversial actions of SRSGs, asking whether such actions or practices can reveal how authority is composed in the UN system and the roles of SRSGs in the norm change processes of that system. What can this indicate about norm change in UN peacekeeping operations and in international organizations more generally? How do new norms arise?

Rationalist theories stress the importance of interests of states, powerful ones in particular; constructivist theories have shown how the UN can act autonomously,

44 *SRSGs as norm arbitrators?*

even against the intent of its member states. The scholarly debate has focused on whether the UN can act autonomously against the intent of member states (Barnett and Finnemore 1999, 2004, Avant et al. 2010), the role of the Security Council in developing new norms (Johnstone 2008, 2010, Malone 2004), and whether the secretary-general can be considered a norm entrepreneur (Rivlin and Gordenker 1993, Chesterman 2007, Johnstone 2007). While these approaches have shed some light on norm change processes in the UN, they are marred by a top-down perspective that underestimates the role of the 'field' where actual operations unfold.

Some studies have examined bottom-up perspectives on norm change in international organizations (IOs) – for example, Finnemore and Sikkink's seminal work on non-governmental organizations (NGOs) as norm entrepreneurs (Finnemore and Sikkink 1998) – and organizational learning literature has focused on the role that assembling best practices and lessons learned has had for the development of guidelines for action and new norms in peacekeeping (Benner and Rotmann 2008). Here I seek to bring in a bottom-up perspective *from the field*. In peacekeeping, decisions have to be made on a daily basis in politically charged and fluctuating situations. The SRSG operates under authority delegated by the UN Security Council and the secretary-general through a Security Council mandate and general guidelines for action, but there remains considerable room for discretion.[3] Asking whether SRSGs can mediate between conflicting norms as *norm arbitrators*, I examine controversial decisions where there were no clear directions from UN HQ in New York or where several principles for peacekeeping clashed with each other or with instructions from headquarters.

Let us begin with two case studies from Afghanistan and Côte d'Ivoire, both involving situations where tensions between New York and the SRSG in the field were evident. In my view, SRSGs can operate as norm arbitrators in a field generally held to be dominated by member states, and their practices are an important source for norm change in the UN system, both historically and today. Arguing that SRSG practices cannot be deduced solely from their delegated authority from UN HQ and the UN Security Council, I will analyze the sources of SRSG authority, showing that SRSGs often move through 'revolving doors' with other ecologies and that this prior experience is being drawn upon in decision-making processes. SRSGs operate within a space where norms sometimes compete and where, also, other sources of authority have influence on their actions. Prior experience and personal prestige are important factors that should be taken into consideration. The experience from and interaction with other ecologies can have a decisive impact on SRSG actions. Finally, as normative closure and coherence between the various norms guiding peacekeeping is almost impossible, I argue that the *generative ambiguity* that SRSGs operate within can be of a positive nature.

Giving meaning to peacekeeping norms through actions: a bottom-up, practice-driven approach?

Peacekeeping operates according to three core traditional principles: impartiality, consent of the parties, and non-use of force. After the UN failures in Rwanda,

Somalia, and Bosnia, the Responsibility to Protect (R2P) and Protection of Civilians (PoC) have been advanced as important norms. While R2P is still in its infancy and has only recently been put into use in United Nations Security Council (UNSC) mandates,[4] PoC has become a staple ingredient in most UNSC mandates today (Holt et al. 2009). However, all these principles or norms are rarely found coexisting harmoniously in a peacekeeping context. As illustrated in Figure 1.1, norms exist in a competitive arena; according to the context of the peacekeeping operation, the norm composition is rebalanced each time. Bellamy et al. argue that there is an ongoing norm battle about what peacekeeping ought to be and do (Bellamy et al. 2010). This indicates that practices, and the normative reasoning backing up these practices, are significant when tracing how norms for peacekeeping operations wax and wane.

Social practices accentuate the "performative character of power" (Guzzini 2005). In pressed situations, SRSGs must make decisions that have an impact on people's lives as well as on the understanding of core norms guiding peacekeeping and must determine how these are weighed against each other. Individual action can form the foundation for norm change, as this chapter will show. It will show that there may be room for interpretation of norms between center and periphery and will expand our understanding of the role of practices in UN peacekeeping. The chapter studies the practices of SRSGs through "the observable 'doings' of physical bodies and entities" (Andersen 2010, 16), by the use of guidelines for peacekeeping, archive material, interviews with key actors, and other open sources. We then move on to an analysis of the sources of authority on which a SRSG draws, expanding on similar studies undertaken by Barnett and Finnemore (2004) and Avant et al. (2010).

Côte d'Ivoire – what does "robust peacekeeping" really mean?

In an unprecedented move on April 4 and 10, 2011, the UN peacekeeping operation in Côte d'Ivoire (ONUCI) carried out joint helicopter attacks on the residence of former president Gbagbo, together with French Licorne forces. SRSG Choi Young-jin was sharply criticized by Russian minister of foreign affairs Sergei Lavrov: "We are now looking into the legal side of the issue because peacekeepers had a mandate which requires them to be neutral and impartial" (BBC World News 2011). A few days later, Russian president Medvedev stated: "The United Nations cannot take sides, but that is de facto what happened" (Anishchuk 2011).

Only one month earlier, the UN had authorized the use of "all military means" to protect civilians in Libya, noting Libya's responsibility to protect its civilian population in UN Security Council Resolutions 1970 and 1973 (UNSC 2011a, UNSC 2011b). This was the first time the concept of R2P had been directly cited in a UN Security Council Resolution on a situation in a country. In previous resolutions on, for example, the situation in Darfur, the Security Council did not use the term "responsibility to protect," but reaffirmed "inter alia the provisions of paragraphs 138 and 139 of the 2005 United Nations World Summit outcome document" (UNSC 2006).[5] The use of R2P in the mandates on Libya, and the

46 *SRSGs as norm arbitrators?*

subsequent authorizations to use all necessary means to protect civilians in Libya as well as in Côte d'Ivoire,[6] seemed to set a new standard for mandates and the willingness of the Security Council to authorize robust action to protect civilians even against strategic-level actors.

In fact there have been historical precedents. In Haiti in 2005 the UN mission MINUSTAH engaged criminal gangs in Cité Soleil in direct confrontation, with civilian casualties, in Operation Iron Fist. In a matter of hours on August 15, Peruvian and Brazilian peacekeepers fired more than 20,000 rounds of ammunition, grenades, and mortar fire in a densely populated area, killing the gang leader Emmanuel "Dread" Wilme and many of his followers (Lynch 2005). Jean-Marie Guéhenno, UN under-secretary-general for peacekeeping operations at the time, said:

> it was necessary to stand up to armed groups that threaten to undermine peacekeeping missions. But he said U.N. commanders had to strike a balance between engaging in all-out warfare and resorting to the passive military posture that characterized U.N. operations in Srebrenica, where Dutch peacekeepers stood down as Bosnian Serb troops killed thousands of unarmed civilians.
>
> (ibid.)

Another precedent was the robust action taken by the UN mission, MONUC, against rebel groups in eastern Democratic Republic of the Congo (DRC) in 2006 (Terrie 2008). MONUC's support of the national Forces Armées de la République Démocratique du Congo (FARDC) resulted in MONUC being considered as a party to the conflict, even by some of its staff members (Holt et al. 2009, 168). Both these instances have since been cited as examples of robust action to protect civilians (New York University Center on International Cooperation [NYU CIC] 2009, 52; UN 2010, 2). Also, more recently, robust force has been used in DRC, with the use of helicopter gunships to stop the advancement of the M23 militia toward Goma in November 2012 and by the Force Intervention Brigade in 2013–14 (Kron 2012, Karlsrud 2015).

Back to Côte d'Ivoire: UN Security Council Resolution 1975, issued only a month after the historic resolutions for Libya, began by "reaffirming the primary responsibility of each State to protect civilians" (UNSC 2011c, 2) and then moved to consider the situation in Côte d'Ivoire, urging

> all Ivorian State institutions, including the Defence and Security Forces of Côte d'Ivoire (FDSCI), to yield to the authority vested by the Ivorian people in President Alassane Dramane Ouattara, condemns the attacks, threats, acts of obstructions and violence perpetrated by FDSCI, militias and mercenaries against United Nations personnel, obstructing them from protecting civilians, monitoring and helping investigate human rights violations and abuses, stresses that those responsible for such crimes under international law must be held accountable and calls upon all parties, in particular Mr. Laurent

SRSGs as norm arbitrators? 47

Gbagbo's supporters and forces, to fully cooperate with the United Nations Operation in Côte d'Ivoire (ONUCI) and cease interfering with ONUCI's activities in implementation of its mandate.

(ibid., 3)

In this very difficult situation, the SRSG was mandated to use all necessary means to protect civilians against the use of heavy weapons:

[The Security Council] [re]calls its authorization and stresses its full support given to the UNOCI [ONUCI], while *impartially* implementing its mandate, to *use all necessary means* to carry out its mandate to protect civilians under imminent threat of physical violence, *within its capabilities* and its areas of deployment, including to *prevent the use of heavy weapons against the civilian population* and requests the Secretary-General to keep it urgently informed of measures taken and efforts made in this regard.

(UNSC 2011c, 3, emphases added)

The SRSG was tasked with implementing the mandate impartially, while at the same time using all necessary means to prevent the use of heavy weapons against the civilian population. Also previously, UN SRSGs had been forced into similar situations, but only the UN mission in Somalia in the early 1990s had entered into confrontation with one of the principal parties to the conflict, and no mission had attacked the forces of an incumbent president. This seemed to run counter to how the UN had outlined the principle of "robust peacekeeping" only one year prior, in a concept note presented to the UN General Assembly Special Committee on Peacekeeping Operations (C34) for the February 2010 Substantive Session. Again, it is worth quoting an entire paragraph:

Robust peacekeeping is not peace enforcement. Robust peacekeeping is distinct from peace enforcement where use of force is at the strategic level and pursued often without the consent of the host nation/and or main parties to the conflict. The threat and use of force in robust peacekeeping is at the tactical level, limited in time and space, and aimed at countering or containing specific spoiler and residual or looming threat in a conflict or post-conflict environment. Large scale violence or one where the major parties are engaged in violent conflict is no longer a robust peacekeeping context. Robust, missions are not configured or intended to address any systemic breakdown in a political process.

(UN 2010, 3, emphasis in original)

This concept note was actually criticized for being too assertive when it was released (World Federalist Movement 2010). Morocco, representing the Non-Aligned Movement (NAM), said that peacekeeping was robust enough; and South Africa said that robust peacekeeping should not be used as a peace enforcement tool (Permanent Mission of South Africa to the United Nations 2010).[7]

48 *SRSGs as norm arbitrators?*

Certification as the key to understanding
the UN actions in Côte d'Ivoire

Already with the Pretoria Agreement of April 6, 2005, the parties to the conflict agreed that the UN would play a central role in the elections and should be part of the Independent Electoral Commission (South Africa 2005). The subsequent UN Security Council Resolution 1603 (2005) designated

> a High Representative for the elections in Côte d'Ivoire (the High Representative), autonomous from the United Nations Operation in Côte d'Ivoire (UNOCI/ONUCI), to assist in particular in the work of the Independent Electoral Commission and of the Constitutional Council, without prejudice to the responsibilities of the Special Representative of the Secretary-General and with the following mandate:
>
> To verify, on behalf of the international community, that all stages of the electoral process, including the establishment of a register of voters and the issuance of voters' cards, provide all the necessary guarantees for the holding of open, free, fair and transparent presidential and legislative elections within the ime limits laid down in the Constitution of the Republic of Côte d'Ivoire.
>
> (UNSC 2005, 3)

This responsibility was transferred to the head of UNOCI through Security Council Resolution 1765:

> *Decides* to terminate the mandate of the High Representative for the Elections, *decides* therefore that the Special Representative of the Secretary-General in Côte d'Ivoire shall certify that all stages of the electoral process provide all the necessary guarantees for the holding of open, free, fair and transparent presidential and legislative elections in accordance with international standards, and *requests* the Secretary-General to take all the necessary steps so that the Special Representative has at his disposal a support cell providing him all the appropriate assistance to fulfil this task.
>
> (UNSC 2007, 2, emphasis in original)

Lori-Anne Théroux-Bénoni argues that "the UN should avoid being perceived as both a judge and a party to the dispute" (Théroux-Bénoni 2012, 7). By both certifying the elections, as well as providing technical assistance, ONUCI had put itself in "a rather awkward position" (ibid., 7). This argument is also supported by other seasoned UN staff: "Too much focus on elections is too narrow and opens the doors for additional conflict" (interview with senior UN official, June 20, 2011). In a frequently asked questions (FAQ) memo that the Certification Cell of ONUCI had posted on its website and circulated prior to the elections (ONUCI 2010), the mission had underscored that the UN had a mandate to *guarantee and uphold* the outcome of the elections:

SRSGs as norm arbitrators? 49

The Certifier has received a mandate from the Security Council to *certify that all stages of the electoral process provide all the necessary guarantees for the holding of open, free, fair and transparent presidential and legislative elections in accordance with international standards.* The Certifier therefore has to ensure that all the necessary guarantees are met for the holding of successful elections in Côte d'Ivoire. This means safeguarding both the process and the results of the elections.

(ibid., 1, emphasis in original)

SRSG Choi also made it clear that he was willing to go very far in order to guarantee and uphold the outcome of the elections:

In the improbable event that the legitimate results are contested through non-democratic means, the Certifier, who as Head of UNOCI has also the mandate of maintaining peace and stability in Côte d'Ivoire, *will safeguard the results by all means at his disposal* to serve the Ivorian people.

(ibid., my emphasis)

Elections and the ensuing violence

The first round of elections took place on October 31, 2010, and the second round, in which President Gbagbo lost to opposition leader Ouattara, was held on November 28, 2010. The elections had already been postponed several times, as they were originally scheduled to be held in 2005, so the international community was playing close attention to the event. After the second round, both candidates claimed to have won, but the UN supported Ouattara's claim, and President Gbagbo asked the UN mission to leave the country (BBC 2010). With both candidates claiming to have won the elections, clashes continued between supporters of the two, leaving hundreds of people dead. Both sides were accused of atrocities, and the International Criminal Court decided to investigate the post-election violence (BBC 2011a).

On March 3, a group of women, pro-Ouattara supporters, demonstrated against the government. "FDSCI [Côte d'Ivoire] fired with a 20 mm cannon from an armored personnel carrier into the crowd" (interview with senior UN official, November 14, 2012). This incident was one of the key reasons for the UN Security Council giving the mandate to ONUCI to protect civilians against the use of heavy weapons. Moreover,

most of the time, the FDSCI strategy was to withdraw to Abidjan, and offered very little resistance along the way. Within three days they were at the outskirts of Abidjan, and at this time Ouattara halted his troops and wanted to give Gbagbo the chance to withdraw. This did not happen and on 31 March they entered Abidjan.

(ibid.)

50 *SRSGs as norm arbitrators?*

During the post-election violence, ONUCI and the SRSG were criticized for not taking action, but after the Duékoué massacre on March 28/29 (BBC 2011b) and increasing fighting over the capital Abidjan, international attention built up, and UN Security Council Resolution 1975 was adopted. By March 31, the pro-Ouattara Forces républicaines de Côte d'Ivoire (FRCI) were standing outside the city, and "urban guerrilla warfare was fought in Abidjan" (interview with senior UN official, November 14, 2012). Pro-Gbagbo forces had built up strongholds at a few key places in the city – the radio station, the presidential palace, and the presidential residence – and these were fortified with heavy weapons, and "the situation had become very difficult for the UN operation, very difficult for us to have the freedom of movement, and we had to use convoys with armored vehicles" (ibid.). Fighting had broken out in various parts of Abidjan, several police officers had been killed, and some supporters of Ouattara abducted and disappeared (ibid.). Further, according to this interviewee, the Forces de Défense et de Sécurité de Côte d'Ivoire "declared the area a war zone and used mortars and fired mortars into the Abobo area," an area with many Ouattara supporters. "A lot of heavy weapons were used against civilians" (ibid.). The same heavy weapons would be central in the later use of force by the UN, as it was argued that the "same heavy weapons were also used to target certain civilian areas" (ibid.). With a full-scale civil war imminent, the Security Council took action and gave the mission a robust mandate, bordering on peace enforcement.

On April 10, having already vowed to guarantee the outcome of the elections, facing the possible escalation of the post-election violence to full-scale civil war, and equipped with a mandate that spelled out the responsibility to protect civilian populations against heavy weapons, SRSG Choi, the French Licorne forces, and the Forces Nouvelles supporting Ouattara, who had been reconstituted as the FRCI, went after President Gbagbo. With the linkage established that the heavy weapons guarding President Gbagbo also were used to attack civilian populations, the ground was prepared for the UN using force:

> At this time, the UN gave SCR 1975, which mandated Licorne and UN forces to take out the heavy weapons of Gbagbo. On April 4, the force took action against several positions with heavy weapons. On April 5, the Foreign Minister asked for a cease-fire and wanted to surrender. But Gbagbo refused to accept and the fighting continued for another week. Fighting resumed and heavy weapons were again used against civilians.
>
> The order came after a SMG [Senior Management Group] meeting where the military had made its assessment of the situation. The political side had to leave it to the military, because it was now a military operation. The military coordinated with Licorne. The MI-24 did not have night-fighting capability, so it was decided that the UN would start just before dusk and the French would then continue.
>
> (interview with senior UN official, November 14, 2012)

According to the member of the senior management team of SRSG Choi,

> the SRSG did not give a formal order in writing, but we had regular meetings – like a council of war – and during these a green light to link up with Licorne. Behind the scenes there were political maneuvers. The UNSG [UN secretary-general] had to link up with President Sarkozy. Then the SG [secretary-general] gave the green light through the SRSG.
>
> (ibid.)

The same person also argues that UNSC Resolution 1975 enabled the mission to "level the playing field":

> We had rules of engagement and we followed them to the letter. But the rules of engagement were also a limiting factor in some areas. The initial mandate was protection of civilians, the responsibility of protection also lies with the government, and how do you assess whether the government is failing to protect and step in? Resolution 1975 made it easier as it showed that the government was failing to protect its citizens and we could step in and take out the heavy weapons and level the playing field.
>
> (ibid.)

Finally, "on April 10, French Licorne forces and the UN attacked with heavy weapons and ground forces moved in on the presidential residence and captured Gbagbo."

> (ibid.)

Navigating uncharted waters

ONUCI was equipped with MI-24 gunship helicopters, which could and indeed did make a big difference in joint attacks with French Licorne forces on April 4 and 10. After the two attacks, President Gbagbo's troops were finally overpowered, and President Gbagbo was taken into custody. The SRSG could have avoided entering the conflict, citing the need for impartiality and the limited capabilities of the mission. He could have argued, as many SRSGs had done before him, that he would need more troops to be able to protect civilians and that the use of helicopters would risk involving the UN in a protracted direct confrontation with Gbagbo's forces. Instead, the SRSG took responsibility for changing the mission from a peacekeeping to a peace enforcement mission, operating in tandem with the French Licorne forces and the FRCI. The UN gunship helicopters took part in a joint attack with French Licorne forces that could bring substantial firepower to bear. As the UN did not have night-flight capability, they attacked the positions of President Gbagbo's forces until nightfall (ibid.). After this, the French Licorne force continued to bomb the positions during the night. According to the same respondent, the action of the UN gunship helicopters had an impact and

52   SRSGs as norm arbitrators?

also helped FRCI achieve their objective of conquering the forces of President Gbagbo: "Indirectly, our actions also helped the FRCI to carry out their operations" (ibid.).

Navigating these uncharted waters, the SRSG could well anticipate that his actions would be controversial no matter what – had he chosen to ignore the continued fighting, he would have joined the list of SRSGs who had been condemned for doing nothing when faced with the killing of civilians. Instead he was attacked for taking sides and forcibly changing the regime of an African country, installing a pro-Western president. Clearly, the actions of this SRSG violated the principle of robust peacekeeping as outlined in the 2010 concept note. Two major parties were engaged in violent conflict at the strategic level, and the use of force was pursued without the consent of the main parties. As the UN is wary of member-state skepticism, the concept outline on robust peacekeeping had taken into consideration how practices had evolved over the last decade, with the actions taken to protect civilians against gangs in Haiti and rebels in eastern DRC (UN 2010). No one foresaw that the UN would become engaged in peace *enforcement* in Côte d'Ivoire only one year later. This indicates a time gap between practice and policy, with practice preceding the development of policy and doctrine at UN headquarters.

The concept note had also stressed that "the Security Council should be clearly informed of the risks before the decision is taken" (UN 2010, 3). In Côte d'Ivoire, the SRSG warned that he was in the process of using force and that action was imminent, only hours before launching the first attack (CNN 2011). According to one interviewee, the SRSG informally consulted with the SG (interview with senior UN official, November 14, 2012), but there was no time for the Security Council to convene to discuss the potential risks of the action, and the SRSG proceeded to authorize the attack without Council intervention.

What emerges from Côte d'Ivoire is a case where the norms of protection of civilians and of robust peacekeeping were redefined through actions on the ground. This has a significant impact on the balance between protection of civilians and the other norms of peacekeeping – impartiality, consent of the parties, and minimal use of force. To protect civilians and prevent or stop mass atrocities and crimes against humanity, the UN may at times be willing to use force at the strategic level against one of the main parties to the conflict, turning the operation into a peace enforcement mission and enforcing the responsibility to protect that the government has failed to respect and uphold. While the Security Council provides the mandate for action, it is within the prerogative of the SRSG to determine whether the mission has sufficient capabilities to undertake such action. This indicates the level of independence that the SRSG has vis-à-vis headquarters to decide the appropriate action to protect civilians.

Afghanistan – upholding the principle of impartiality or undermining the operation?

After the terrorist events of 9/11, the United States launched Operation Enduring Freedom on October 7, 2001, to fight the Taliban and Al-Qaida. With UNSC

SRSGs as norm arbitrators? 53

Resolution 1378 of November 14, 2001 (UNSC 2001), the Security Council affirmed that the UN would have an important role to play. Following the Bonn Agreement in December 2001, the Security Council established the UN Assistance Mission in Afghanistan (UNAMA) on March 28, 2002. UNAMA was tasked with:

> providing political and strategic advice for the peace process, promoting international engagement in the country, assisting the Government towards implementing the Afghanistan Compact of 2006 – a five-year strategy for rebuilding the country – and contributing to the protection and promotion of human rights. In addition, UNAMA continued to manage UN humanitarian relief, recovery, reconstruction and development activities in Afghanistan in coordination with the Government.
>
> (UNAMA 2010)

Overnight, the War on Terror changed the environment in which UN staff operated. In many Middle Eastern countries, interlocutors were now termed "terrorists" by the United States and the UN Security Council. The Taliban did not participate in the negotiations for the Bonn Agreement in December 2001: at that point, the US-led coalition had control of most of Afghanistan and saw no need to include the Taliban. The Security Council established a special counterterrorism unit to track members of Al-Qaida and the Taliban, effectively designating these groups and their members as 'beyond the pale' (de Soto 2007). Lakhdar Brahimi, the first SRSG to be sent to Afghanistan after 9/11, has since admitted that it was a mistake not to reach out to moderate factions of the Taliban already in early 2002 (Brahimi 2007, Ackerman 2008). Engagement has proven complicated because of the reluctance of the Afghan government as well as of the United States.

In late 2007, Mervyn Patterson, a high-ranking UN official, and Michael Semple, acting head of the EU mission, were expelled from Afghanistan after talking with and allegedly trying to "turn" a senior Taliban commander (Nelson 2008). A spokesperson for Afghan president Karzai said that the men had been involved in activities that "were not their jobs" (Meo et al. 2007). Aleem Siddique, a UN spokesperson, explained in the same interview that the UN was barred from meeting with Taliban leaders due to a Security Council Resolution but that the two men had met with tribal elders as part of a fact-finding mission (ibid.).

In March 2010, just before leaving his post as SRSG, Kai Eide admitted to regular contacts with Taliban members, including the leadership (Borger 2010a, Eide 2010). In fact, engagement had begun much earlier than this: "We started careful contact with the rebel movement [Taliban] during the autumn of 2008, with a humanitarian focus to provide food and vaccines" (interview with Kai Eide, former SRSG, UNAMA, September 4, 2012, Oslo). Mindful of the Patterson/Semple incident, Eide made sure that he had the support of President Karzai before engaging in talks. To Eide, it was important to be able to sit down with the president and discuss possible engagement to make sure that "the president supported the initiative" (ibid.). This was also something he was required to do by the UNAMA mandate as stipulated by UN SCR 1806, issued March 20, 2008: "Provide good

54 *SRSGs as norm arbitrators?*

offices to support, if requested by the Afghan Government, the implementation of Afghan-led reconciliation programmes, within the framework of the Afghan Constitution" (UNSC 2008a, 3). In the autumn of 2008, concurrently with when the engagement with the Taliban started, according to Eide, the clause of a pre-request from the Afghan government was dropped from the mandate. In the new mandate adopted in UN SC Resolution 1833 on September 22, 2008, the Security Council encouraged "the implementation of Afghan-led reconciliation programs within the framework of the Afghan Constitution" (UNSC 2008b, 3).

Eide underscored that before initiating contact, he had "warmed up" member states to the idea, particularly the Permanent Five on the Security Council, by talking about the need to engage in public. In the Security Council, SRSG Eide brought up the need to talk with the rebel movement, but "both the Russians and Teheran were opposed to such contacts" (interview with Kai Eide). While the EU special representative for Afghanistan, Francesc Vendrell, and the UK ambassador, Cowper-Coles, on a personal basis supported the engagement with the Taliban, the governments they represented were much more reluctant. Ambassador Cowper-Coles was forced to take 'extended leave' in 2010 and eventually quit the UK Foreign Service after insisting "that the military-driven counter-insurgency effort was headed for failure, and that talks with the Taliban should be prioritised" (Walsh and Boone 2010). The engagement was also "supported by Barney [Barnett] Rubin, but he was not yet inside [the US] State [Department]" (interview with Kai Eide).[8]

A deal was struck for the UN Peace Day on September 21, 2008: indeed, according to the UN Department of Safety and Security (UNDSS), there was a 70 percent decrease in security incidents on that day. SRSG Eide stated that "hostilities were almost brought to a halt, including by the Taliban, following an appeal by the United Nations. Further successful initiatives towards the Taliban resulted in a successful polio vaccination program in 2009 were 1.6 million vaccinated" (UNAMA 2009). While the UN Peace Day had been a success according to Eide, his positive assessment was not shared by the International Security Assistance Force, ISAF (interview with Kai Eide).

The presidential elections in Afghanistan in 2009 made engagement more difficult and put the talks with the rebel movement on hold. This coincided with Barack Obama taking over at the helm in the United States, which also had an impact on relations with Karzai – "the new administration wanted that Karzai should be held at an arm's length during the election" (ibid.). However, Eide argues that he was able to establish a good relationship with Karzai and gain his respect, both because he met more often with Karzai than many of his peers and predecessors, but also because he dared to criticize the United States, the UK, and the Afghans – "this protected me . . . and made Karzai think it was useful to talk with me . . . Karzai has to talk with the American Ambassador and the chief of the US Forces, but he doesn't have to talk with the UN SRSG if he's a carbon copy of USA" (ibid.). Civilian deaths – 'collateral damage' in military parlance – was one issue on which Eide criticized ISAF and the United States.

Contacts picked up in 2009, but on January 28, 2010, in connection with the meeting on Afghanistan held in London, "it was incorrectly leaked to a British newspaper that I had had meetings with the Taliban in Dubai early that month. This, together with the arrest of Taliban's number two, Mullah Baradar, ruined any possibility for further dialogue" (ibid.; see also Borger 2010b). Looking at the talks in retrospect, Eide argues that "we established connections that were important and interesting, and later we also had confirmation that these went all the way to the top" (interview with Kai Eide).

Operating between conflicting imperatives

What can the UN engagement with the Taliban and Hamas reveal about how norms develop in the UN and the influence of powerful states like the United States as regards the autonomy and influence of the world organization itself?

In most UN missions, there is a built-in dilemma for SRSGs: they are given conflicting mandates, like extending state authority, while at the same time mediating between the parties when the state is one of the main parties to the conflict. In Afghanistan, this dilemma was brought to a head, as the mandate tasked the UN to cooperate more closely with one of the parties to the conflict (ISAF), while also tasking the SRSG to work toward reconciliation. For Eide, the inclusion of closer civil–military cooperation in the mandate "had a negative effect by complicating efforts to engage as an impartial partner for dialogue" (interview with Kai Eide).

In addition, the UN Security Council had established the UNSC 'Al-Qaida and Taliban Sanctions Committee,' which contained a list of persons labeled as terrorists. The list "made it operationally more complicated and sensitive to initiate contacts with Taliban members" (ibid.). The list included several persons whom UNAMA wanted removed from the list, in order to engage with them, including Mullah Muttawakil, "who we wanted to be able to travel" (ibid.). Another person who was eventually removed was Mullah Zaeef, which was "symbolically important for our relationship with the Taliban" (ibid.). Interestingly, the list has been renamed the 'Al-Qaida Sanctions Committee' (UNSC 2012). The removal of 'Taliban' from the title also shows how the UN Security Council has been changing its stance on engagement, and the list has been divided into two lists, one for Al-Qaida and one for the Taliban.

On the surface, SRSG Eide's engagement with the Taliban seems to contradict the views of several key members of the Security Council. Eide himself holds that he had been given a *political* mandate to work for the long-term peace and stability of Afghanistan. For him, *not* talking with the Taliban was not an option since they had to be an integral part of a sustainable and long-term solution. Here it was not a new norm that was being generated, but rather the interpretation of the norm of impartiality that was used as the main argument for engagement. Like de Soto, Eide stressed the importance of being able to meet with everyone so that he could execute the political mandate of the mission:

> We met senior people in the Taliban leadership and we also met people who have the authority of the Quetta Shura to engage in that kind of discussion.

I have always believed in an engagement policy. I have always believed that it is better to try to talk than to refrain from talking. But I have no illusions with regard to the complexity of such a process and the time that such a process may require.

(Borger 2010a)

Eide was here drawing upon the moral authority of the established norm of impartiality – like de Soto, he underscored the importance of being able to engage and talk with all involved parties. This came in conflict with the newer post-9/11 norm of 'not talking to terrorists.' Through his practices, Eide thus reaffirmed the traditional norm of impartiality, and knowingly risked conflict with UN headquarters and key member states, in ways similar to de Soto in the Middle East. Eide is today convinced that "the way we handled this had an effect on the way the international community viewed the issue of negotiating . . . When asked whether I was prepared to talk with Mullah Omar, my answer always was 'You have to talk with relevant people to get relevant results!'" (interview with Kai Eide).

SRSG autonomy – the composition of authority in peacekeeping

The case studies presented here show instances where SRSGs have navigated in difficult norm environments. The norms guiding peacekeeping have not been in concordance,[9] and the SRSGs have been forced to make choices. The ensuing actions have been controversial, stirring the waters in the UN Secretariat, in the UN Security Council, and among member states.

Despite strong imperatives from UN HQ, senior leaders in the field have had considerable autonomy and have at times acted contradictory to guidance from HQ. In Afghanistan, there was considerable pressure from UN headquarters and the Security Council against engagement with the Taliban, but, as shown from the quote in the introduction to this chapter, operational imperatives and the long-term goals of the UN, as interpreted by SRSG Eide, dictated another approach. Secret talks and low-profile engagement continued, the argument being that all parties had to be involved if sustainable peace and security were to be established – particularly as the Taliban represented a significant part of the population in Afghanistan.

Over the past two decades, the UN has carved out a role for itself in some of the world's most intractable conflicts. It has established a tradition of talking with everyone, including those deemed 'beyond the pale.' This practice has been central to peacemaking and mediation in conflicts in Latin America, Central Africa, and the Middle East, and UN representatives have had frequent meetings with such groups as the Lord's Resistance Army (LRA) in Uganda, the Revolutionary United Front (RUF) in Sierra Leone, Hezbollah and Hamas in the Middle East, and the Revolutionary Armed Forces of Columbia (FARC) – all frequently labeled as terrorist organizations.[10]

SRSGs as norm arbitrators? 57

After 9/11, engaging with these groups has proven difficult. In the Middle East, Alvaro de Soto resigned from his post because of the restrictions on engaging with Hamas and Syria. In his *End of Mission Report*, he warned against establishing a new precedent for UN officials – of talking only with those actors seen to be in the clear: "Since the late 1980s the UN has become rather adept dealing with groups that most governments can't or won't touch. If this ability is removed we would seriously weaken our hand as a peacemaking tool" (de Soto 2007, 34).

The literature on the role of SRSGs and their relative authority vis-à-vis UN headquarters has been evolving – in particular, with a special issue of *Global Governance*: 'Special Focus: Postwar Mediation in UN Peace Operations: The Role of the Special Representatives of the Secretary-General,' but also Puchala (1993), Vance and Hamburg (1997), Fafo (1999), and Peck (2004, 2006).[11] Some claims have already been made regarding the responsibility of SRSGs for making difficult choices in tight situations when civilians are at risk. Victoria Holt, examining implementation of the PoC concept in MONUC, asserts:

> the authorization for civilian protection is clear, but the Council's resolution leaves the decision to protect civilians up to the Special Representative of the Secretary General (SRSG), the force commander or another actor further down the chain to "deem" it to be within the scope of "its capabilities."
>
> (Holt et al. 2009, 14, see also de Carvalho and Lie 2011)

Similarly, Lise Morjé Howard has argued that UN peace operations that attract high interest from the Security Council tend to be less successful and that the success of UN peace operations hinges on the relative autonomy of the operation vis-à-vis headquarters, as well as the degree to which SRSGs interpret their mandate independently (Howard 2008, 13). However, there is no doubt that the SRSG needs the support of the Security Council and the secretary-general to maintain credibility with the main actors on the ground (Fafo 1999, de Coning 2010).

De Carvalho and Lie argue that the PoC concept has been made deliberately vague so as to decentralize intent and responsibility for interpreting the mandate to the SRSG in the field:

> The ambiguous protection language recognises the case-by-case applicability, as it lacks clearly demarcated thresholds and criteria for what constitutes a protection situation, and its decentralised intent, that the mission head is responsible to deem the when and what of protection activities. The "what" of protection activities, in Côte d'Ivoire as well as in DRC and Haiti, included using force against one of the parties to the conflict.
>
> (De Carvalho and Lie 2011, 350)

It may be argued that SRSGs have some relative autonomy to implement UN Security Council mandates and UN Department of Peacekeeping Operations (DPKO) policies with a certain amount of discretion. But what if this brings them

58 *SRSGs as norm arbitrators?*

into conflict with the Security Council and/or the secretary-general? What other sources of authority can SRSGs invoke to explain this form of anomalous behavior? I argue that SRSGs have access to several different forms of authority in decision-making processes. Drawing on some of the literature on authority and the UN system, I distinguish five such sources of authority: delegated authority from the Security Council and the secretary-general, expert authority, moral authority, charismatic authority, and prestige.[12]

Delegated authority

Member states create IOs, delegating authority to them for dealing with various tasks, including the maintenance of peace and security. The Security Council can deem a situation in a country to be a threat to international peace and security and delegate to the secretary-general appropriate tasks for tackling the threat; in turn, the UNSG may delegate these tasks to an SRSG. The delegated authority of the SRSG can be subdivided into two components – operational guidance from the secretary-general and the Secretariat and strategic guidance from the Security Council.

The secretary-general has delegated executive responsibilities to the SRSGs, who carry out their assignments under authority given to the secretary-general to appoint his staff – in Article 101 of the Charter; in Article 99, which gives the UNSG the opportunity to open good offices and have an independent political role; and in Article 33, which invites the parties to select mediators of their own choice (UN 1945).

Donald Puchala argues that, because of staffing constraints at the SG's office, the *ad hoc* nature of special representation, and their history of relative autonomy, SRSGs have been granted wide latitude that opens for personal initiatives, critical thinking, and inventiveness (1993). While this has permitted swift action on the ground, it has also

> tempted special representatives to ignore or go beyond their mandates and instructions, thus creating tensions in center–mission relations or otherwise raising questions about the structure of authority. *Sometimes it becomes unclear who is the tail and who is the dog.*
>
> (ibid., 94, emphasis added)

To adapt to the changing circumstances on the ground, the SRSG needs to keep the Security Council abreast of developments through regular reporting. This practice, instituted by Secretary-General Kofi Annan, has been greatly appreciated by the Council (Peck 2004, 331). Moreover, the Council often makes field visits to get their own impressions of the situation. Besides briefing the Security Council, many SRSGs also choose to brief a selection of ambassadors at regular intervals. This can reinforce messages that the SRSG wants to send, to garner support for a particular strategy.[13] The SRSG depends on Security Council support to maintain a strong standing and the respect of the parties in the field. However, members of the Security Council may well act in contradicting manners, supporting the SRSG in the Council but effectively undermining the position of the SRSG in the field. Eide argues:

> the Security Council gives you legitimacy, but not enough. The members of the Security Council may well run you over in the field – there are many examples of this. [UNAMA] had for example a mandate to coordinate [international aid] that the Americans did not care much about.
>
> (interview with Kai Eide)

Expert authority

Delegated authority can be further divided into the expert authority conferred to the SRSG on behalf of the UN system and the collective experience and guidelines established for the role to be executed and the moral authority conferred on the SRSG by executing the will of the member states according to the established principles and values of the UN. SRSGs have expert or rational-legal authority, drawing on personal experience, knowledge of previous cases, and established precedence. Further, SRSGs have the assistance of their offices, technical sections and units, and the senior management team, forming a mini-bureaucracy with expertise at their disposal (see also Haas 1992). Similarly, the expanding body of lessons learned and formal guidance is also part of the repository of expert authority (Benner et al. 2011). After a long career as a diplomat representing a member state, as a UN career staff, or both, the SRSG will also be able to draw upon his or her experience. Eide underscored this aspect – as "the SRSG in Bosnia from 1997–8 [I] could draw on my experience from that context, as well as from my period as NATO Ambassador in Brussels [for Norway from 2002–6] and as UN Special Envoy to Kosovo [in 2005]" (interview with Kai Eide).

Moral authority

SRSGs are to execute their mandates according to the established principles and norms for peacekeeping. As noted, the traditional norms here are consent of the parties, minimal use of force, and impartiality; after the failures in Bosnia, Somalia, and Rwanda, protection of civilians has been established as an important new norm. However, these principles do not always form a coherent framework for action: they may conflict with each other. Which norm is paramount, and who is to decide?

The SRSG, through years of experience as a UN official or a career diplomat, will be inculcated with these norms and will have personal views on how they should be interpreted, weighed against each other, and implemented. SRSGs are vested with moral authority as representatives of the UN. They are to embody the values of the UN and act "as agents of the international community and purveyors of UN norms" (Puchala 1993, 89). In the course of years as a UN official or career diplomat, an SRSG will have developed personal views on how the values of the UN should be interpreted and implemented. Not violating these personal views on UN values may be more important than actually keeping the position as

60 *SRSGs as norm arbitrators?*

a special envoy for the UN. A particularly clear example of this was the *End of Mission Report* of the former special envoy for the Middle East process, Alvaro de Soto, who chose to resign because he felt he could not perform his functions. In the report, leaked to the *Guardian*, de Soto slammed the secretary-general for not standing up for the core value of impartiality of the UN; he said he had been dissuaded from meeting with Syria, a member state of the UN, and Hamas, the winning political party after the elections in 2006 (BBC 2006, de Soto 2007, McCarthy and Williams 2007).

Charismatic authority

Weber differentiates between bureaucratic and charismatic authority, arguing that the modern bureaucracy has advanced beyond charismatic authority as expressed through the patriarchal structure. While this is an important distinction, I argue that SRSGs draw on both forms of authority in executing their roles. Weber defines "charismatic authority" as "a rule over men, whether predominantly external or predominantly internal, to which the governed submit because of their belief in the extraordinary quality of the specific *person*" (Weber et al. 1946, 295). SRSGs are often charismatic personalities – frequently top diplomats of their country or high in the ranks of the UN.

Moreover, the UN can be vested with extraordinary powers in a post-conflict country, and it is the job of the SRSG to execute these. Many missions have been given executive mandates, effectively instituting the SRSG as a "viceroy," as in Kosovo and Timor Leste (Boot 2000, Chesterman 2004). But also where the UN mission has only a mandate to support what may be a fledgling state, the SRSGs have very influential roles vis-à-vis national politics and dynamics. The influence they are able to wield is affected not only by the relative degree of executive power included in the mandate, but also by the support of important states. SRSGs form the focal point for sources of power of potentially formidable size. Their position at the intersection between the international and the national confers charismatic authority, akin to the authority that Weber held the monarch wielded over his subjects (Weber et al. 1946). Compared to the leader of the country to which the UN mission is deployed, an SRSG often controls and coordinates vast financial, material, and human resources and can have significant influence on how the situation in the country is portrayed internationally, for example, through his or her regular briefings to ambassadors of interested countries present on the ground and to the Security Council in New York and through contact with international media, NGOs, and the research community. The decisions of the SRSG can at times seem opaque and hard to understand from a national point of view, and there has been continuing criticism that there is too little national ownership in peace operations (Pouligny 2006, Autesserre 2010).

Prestige or 'revolving doors' authority

We have seen that SRSGs are sometimes willing to go out on a limb, taking controversial decisions that the member states may not support or indeed may oppose.

What source of authority do SRSGs draw on in instances where they risk losing significant political capital and support from the Security Council and the secretary-general? They can draw on the moral authority vested in the position, balancing the various guiding norms of peacekeeping against each other. Perhaps more importantly, SRSG are enabled to make controversial decisions because of their prior career backgrounds through a combination of articulate and background knowledge (Pouliot 2008).

SRSGs have normally developed long and distinguished careers in the service of their country or as UN staff members. Some SRSGs also have come from national parliaments or NGOs. While they are required to be managers of a peace operation, they are first and foremost diplomats with a keen sense of politics. Over the years they may have built up considerable political capital and prestige – which they may be willing to risk, at least in part, in defending a controversial decision. Breaking norms creates stigma (Finnemore and Sikkink 1998, 892), but in these cases one norm is broken to uphold another. The prestige of an SRSG is composed of the reputation for integrity and accountability built up through a lengthy career. Prestige grows on investment – by making a controversial decision, involving exposure to risk, an SRSG may actually gain more prestige and credibility if the decision proves correct. In arbitrating between the different norms, SRSGs thus risk their credibility – but they may also increase their prestige. The relationship between credibility and prestige is flexible: SRSGs may be willing to lose their credibility and their post in order to uphold their values and, ultimately, their prestige.

Moreover, most SRSGs will have some sort of exit option. On finishing their assignment or if relieved of their duty, they may be able to return to the diplomatic service at home, move to a distinguished fellowship position at a prestigious university, or serve as senior fellow at a highly reputed think tank. In these postings they continue to engage with the issues they have worked with as SRSGs and may act as advisors to the secretary-general, for instance by chairing a senior advisory panel. Throughout their careers they may have moved back and forth between these various roles – a 'revolving doors' phenomenon in the field of peace operations. This leads to exit options – if disagreement arises because of difference of opinion as to how to interpret the UN Charter and the norms guiding peace operations, the SRSG may choose to go elsewhere, without losing his or her pride, understanding of UN values, and prestige.

Autonomous behavior of IOs – the role of SRSG norm arbitration

The UN has several sources of agenda and agency. It consists of a range of bodies, each with its particular dynamics, membership, and staff. The Security Council is the most important actor, and volumes have been written about the role of the Council as regards peacekeeping (see e.g. Malone 2004, Berdal and Economides 2007, Howard 2008). The General Assembly and the C34 Committee on Peacekeeping meet each year to discuss matters pertaining to peacekeeping. Further, the General Assembly has plenary discussions on peacekeeping matters from time

62 SRSGs as norm arbitrators?

to time. The UN Secretariat is an important actor in its own right, led by the UN secretary-general. In addition to these various centers of agency at the UN HQ, the SRSG adds another bottom-up layer of agency in the organization.

I introduced the concept of norm entrepreneurs developed by Finnemore and Sikkink in chapter 2. Using the analytical framework developed by Finnemore and Sikkink, Ian Johnstone argues that the secretary-general can act as a norm entrepreneur, helping push the norm of Responsibility to Protect to a "tipping point" at the 2005 World Summit (Johnstone 2007, 134, Bellamy 2009, 27–8).

The SRSGs in the case studies presented here were navigating in difficult norm waters, seeking to balance and arbitrate between different peacekeeping norms – always with a view to the context, their interpretation of UN values and norms, their experience, and the risks to their own credibility and position vis-à-vis local stakeholders, the secretary-general, and the Security Council. SRSGs Choi and Eide took actions for which they were criticized, but they also received support. Talking with the Taliban, which in 2008 was highly controversial, was two years later supported by most international actors, and Côte d'Ivoire has now reached a calm period where the economy can restart and normal life return.

SRSGs have to take risks, and sometimes it is better to ask for forgiveness than permission. The need to trust the discretion of the SRSG to take the right action in pressed circumstances has major implications for the selection process. An SRSG must be well versed in the intricacies of UN politics and bureaucratic procedures, intimately familiar with international diplomacy, able to build and nurture relationships with the main powers with vested interests in a particular conflict, as well as perceived by the host-state stakeholders – from top to bottom – as a legitimate, credible, and accountable partner.

SRSGs are either long-term UN employees or diplomats with extensive experience from working with their national service and in or with international organizations. Puchala distinguishes between "insiders" and "outsiders" and argues that the division depends on the level of interest from the permanent member states of the Security Council, as well as the personal taste of various UN secretary-generals (Puchala 1993). As SRSGs, they must juggle a series of roles. In UN integrated missions, the SRSG is the top political representative of the secretary-general and the Security Council. The SRSG provides the good offices of the secretary-general, acts as the eyes and ears of the secretary-general in the field, the overall coordinator of the UN system, and the general manager of the peace operation. Puchala, quoting Cyrus Vance and David A. Hamburg, argues that the SRSG must be "a bona fide surrogate" of the secretary-general (ibid., 83). The SRSG will often be expected to play a coordinating role outside of the UN, interacting with national counterparts, bilateral development donors, and the humanitarian community and chairing coordination efforts in these widely varying domains.

Making strategic decisions, also with a mandate from the Security Council, involves considerable discretion. SRSGs will interpret the mandate (delegated authority) in light of their own interpretation of the UN Charter (expert and moral authority) and in terms of personal gain or loss of prestige (revolving doors authority). The sources of authority guiding SRSG action are inherently complex, offering a range of different arguments and solutions. This in turn opens up for contextualized responses, depending on the personal analysis of the political economy on the ground, the personalities involved, the guidance given from UN headquarters, and the personal experience and fallback options of the SRSG. SRSGs receive guidance from their department in New York, either the DPKO or the Department of Political Affairs (DPA), and advice from their senior management team on the ground. In the end, however, they alone are responsible for their actions.

One of the first special representatives of the secretary-general, Count Folke Bernadotte, deployed to mediate in Palestine in 1948, had a relatively free hand to devise and propose possible solutions to the parties – indeed, the parties expected him to do so even though he had too little time to consult with the secretary-general:

> the two parties had made it quite clear that they expected to receive from me, during the period of the truce, an indication of my ideas as to a possible basis of settlement . . . Notwithstanding, therefore, the complete divergence of aims and the very short time left at my disposal, I decided to submit to the two parties a set of tentative suggestions.
>
> (Bernadotte cited in Puchala 1993, 88)

From the history of individual actions of SRSGs, ranging from Folke Bernadotte to Kai Eide and Choi Young-jin, can we deduce anything in terms of norm change in IOs? Or is this too small a unit of analysis for theorizing as to norm change?

There is a growing literature on organizational learning in IOs in general and peacekeeping in particular (Benner and Rotmann 2008, Benner et al. 2011). In 2008, UN DPKO finally issued a set of guidelines for peacekeeping operations – the 'Capstone Doctrine' (UN 2008); moreover, various reviews have been conducted, gradually developing the aforementioned cornerstones of peacekeeping operations and developing new norms like the Responsibility to Protect and its conceptual sibling, Protection of Civilians.

They point to how practices have been instrumental in the development of doctrine for UN peacekeeping. In the cases shown in this chapter, practices emanating from the ground up have become potential turning points in how the UN deals with a particular problem and perhaps also have influenced more long-term change and the arbitration between norms in the UN system. These practices have supported the argument that SRSGs can be seen as a focal point for bottom-up influence on norm change in UN peacekeeping, as illustrated in Figure 1.1 in chapter 1 in this book.

Conclusions

Overnight, the War on Terror changed the norm framework for senior UN staff in Afghanistan. Established practices of talking with everyone had to yield to a more restrained mode of operation where some groups were now considered 'beyond the pale.' However, when senior staff realized their loss of freedom, they set about

64 *SRSGs as norm arbitrators?*

regaining lost territory through assertive practices in the field. Alvaro de Soto argued for this principled approach in his *End of Mission Report*:

> The UN is not in business of recognizing governments; we deal pragmatically with whoever are the authorities. In good offices, we deal with the players who need to be part of peace agreements. We should practice *realpolitik* in the purest sense, by removing *politik* and dealing with reality.
>
> (de Soto 2007, 32, emphases in original)

The role of the good offices of the UN secretary-general was developed during the Cold War, when the Security Council was deadlocked between East and West. The secretary-general, through his special representatives, mediated in various conflicts, gradually establishing a mechanism for peaceable settlement that also enhanced the authority and autonomy of the secretary-general as regards the General Assembly and the Security Council. The SRSGs are an extension of this authority; by being deployed in the field, they enjoy considerable discretion in strategic questions as well as in their day-to-day activities. In peace operations today, they have the main responsibility for navigating the tension between the norms of non-use of force, impartiality, and consent of all parties, on the one hand, and the Responsibility to Protect and its conceptual sibling Protection of Civilians on the other.

The cases of Côte d'Ivoire and Afghanistan show how SRSGs have engaged in controversial practices that could give impetus to important doctrinal developments and change. These have been clear examples of tensions between center and periphery, where the SRSGs have chosen to take initiative to controversial actions, stepping out of the 'comfort zone' and actively interpreting their mandates. In fact, this is a necessary feature of their role if SRSGs are to be relevant and useful to the countries where they are deployed. In every peacekeeping operation, the relationship between the core principles is contested again and again, particularly with the addition of protection of civilians as a staple ingredient in most mandates today.

The actions of the SRSGs in these two cases examined here showed a certain level of decentralized authority and relative autonomy of the SRSGs in the UN system. The concept of prestige can help explain why SRSGs engage in potentially controversial practices. Further research should examine the various sources of authority on which SRSGs draw.

The literature has studied how the UN occasionally acts counter to its rules and mandates, but only in a negative way, focusing on "dysfunctions" and "pathologies" and "organized hypocrisy" (Barnett and Finnemore 2004, Lipson 2007). By contrast, I argue that the gap between theory, doctrine, and practice is often of a positive nature and can create a *generative ambiguity* within which senior field staff can operate.[14] The literature has dealt with these ambiguities in a simplistic manner: the real world is highly complex and differentiated. The rules and norms of an organization are more than bounded rationality, distinct from the environment: they shape the rationality of the organization's actors and guide individual action. The relationship between rules and bureaucrats is mutually constitutive and dynamic, and at any given time several rules may be applicable. I thus argue the need for senior leaders to have considerable leeway in the field and caution against an overly fine-grained and detailed norm framework that limits the freedom of action of special representatives and envoys. The drive to conceptualize and codify peacekeeping experience may at times be counterproductive. Using their local knowledge and previous experience, UN special representatives and envoys can utilize the generative ambiguity of mandates and guidelines that do not spell out rules for all possible forms of behavior.

Competence does not arise solely from the bureaucracy that the SRSG is part of (and the inculcated norms that follow from this bureaucracy), but also from other sources on the individual level and from the complex interplay of linked ecologies where the SRSG is at the center. I have previously introduced the theory of Adler and Pouliot on how background knowledge is important to understand competent performances and practices (2011). However, they do not provide the tools for analyzing and understanding competent practices. I have sought to address this gap in this chapter by analyzing the sources of authority SRSGs draw upon and by introducing the concept of linked ecologies to better understand the interplay of various classes of actors in the day-to-day operations of UN peace operations and in the personal career trajectories of SRSGs themselves. I have showed that SRSGs operate in conflictual normative spaces, where their practices may violate one norm, but strengthen another. For practice theory, this implies bringing context back into the analysis of practices, loosening the Pavlovian grip that has dominated constructivist theorizing of IOs, and focusing on the culture of a given organization.

The insight that professionals in bureaucracies may be able to influence the balance between norms and act as norm arbitrators should, according to principle-agent (PA) theory, lead to the imposition of more controls by principals (i.e. member states) on bureaucracies, and senior leaders in particular. Is this the case? That would be a pertinent question for further study by PA theorists.

Examining the practices of peacekeeping practitioners alone cannot fully capture how new norms evolve in the area of peacekeeping. The actors involved rely on their experience, frequently from other institutional settings like diplomacy, think tanks, and academia, and these environments also play a crucial role in the development of new norms. In part, this is due to the low capacity of the UN Secretariat to generate lessons learned and best practices that can guide the formation of new norms, but also because of the general lack of guidelines in the area of peacekeeping, which creates a temporal lag between the formation of norms for peacekeeping in the field and their codification at headquarters. The role of experience and prestige in the decision-making processes of SRSGs also points to the role of external actors or ecologies emphasized by this book.

Examining the practices of senior leaders of the UN, not only the secretary-general, may offer a promising new avenue for theorizing on norm change in IOs. Norm change is constant and non-linear, and norms wax and wane through decision-making at the Security Council as well as through practices in the field.

66 *SRSGs as norm arbitrators?*

However, the latter often precede the former, with a temporal-spatial lag between periphery and center, where practices in the field and codified norms at HQ may differ. Practices precede and lead to codification of norms – and that has important consequences for how we understand norm change processes in the UN.

I have argued that decisions on the ground are often taken by individuals using their various sources of authority and cannot be seen solely as the collective output of the organization. Within the UN, various parallel sets of norms, rules, and practices coexist, at times at odds with and even in contradiction to each other. This underscores the dynamic situation in which norms are generated and solidified, but also change significantly over time.

The literature has dealt with these contradictions simplistically: in the real world, things are more complex and differentiated. Senior managers in the field rely on their prestige and experience when they perform actions apparently in contradiction to established norms and rules, and they enjoy relative safety in challenging the central authority through their own networks and exit options. SRSGs are norm arbitrators – arbitrating the relationship between conflicting norms in each case. In Côte d'Ivoire, R2P and protection of civilians trumped impartiality; in Afghanistan, impartiality made a comeback and trumped the new norm of War on Terror after being sidelined because of US pressure. In arbitrating between the various norms, SRSGs risk their credibility, but may also increase their own prestige and the relevance of the UN to host populations.

The findings of this chapter confirm the first argument of the book – that authority will center on those who can arbitrate when there is conflict between the norms guiding peacekeeping. SRSG practices in the field form a prism where central issues concerning IOs converge. By examining the practices of SRSGs, we can learn more about how new practices are formed and how norms and rules are arbitrated and maintained, but also broken. Ultimately, we can learn more about bottom-up influences on norm change in IOs. The relationships and evolving practices involve important, perhaps crucial, insights and implications for the evolving and changing basic norm of sovereignty.

Notes

1 I wish to thank Connie Peck and Giulia Piccolino for incisive and very helpful comments, as well as participants at the European Consortium for Political Research (ECPR) General Conference in Reykjavik, August 25–7, 2011; the Millennium conference in London, October 22–3, 2011; the NUPI annual theory seminar in December 2011; and the ISA Annual Convention in San Diego, California, April 1–4, 2012. A previous version of this chapter was published as 'SRSGs as Norm Arbitrators? Understanding Bottom-Up Authority in UN Peacekeeping', *Global Governance*, 19 (4), pp. 525–44. Copyright © 2013 by Lynne Rienner Publishers, Inc. Used with permission of the publisher.
2 The term 'SRSG' is used here to refer to the various types of representatives of the secretary-general, who may be titled special representative, personal representative, executive representative, special envoy, or special adviser.
3 Examining the relationship between HQ and the field, Lise Morjé Howard (2008, 13) finds that a peacekeeping mission is most likely to be successful when it receives moderate attention from the Security Council.

4 Used in UN SCR 1970 and 1973 on Libya, 2011.
5 These are the relevant paragraphs outlining the R2P concept in the World Summit Outcome Document.
6 In Côte d'Ivoire this came with the caveat that force could be used only to protect civilians against the use of heavy weapons.
7 However, one year later, South Africa, after a short visit by President Zuma to Paris, supported UN SC Resolution 1975 on Côte d'Ivoire authorizing the use of force to protect civilians against heavy weapons (UNSC 2011c), thus completely changing their position on this issue.
8 Dr. Barnett Rubin was later appointed senior adviser to the special representative of the president for Afghanistan and Pakistan in the US Department of State.
9 This touches on an interesting argument by Legro, who holds that norms should be in concordance. This book argues the opposite: that several norms exist in parallel – they are not necessarily in harmony with each other, and the relationship between them must be adjudicated according to the specific context (Legro 1997).
10 Except for the LRA, but their leader, Joseph Kony, has been indicted by the International Criminal Court for crimes against humanity, so I have included this organization. It is generally considered 'beyond the pale,' but senior UN officials have met with Kony and other leaders (interview with Jan Egeland, at the time director, NUPI, and former head of UN Office for the Coordination of Humanitarian Affairs [OCHA], May 29, 2011). For a list that compares organizations listed as terrorist by Australia, Canada, the EU, the UK, the United States, India, and Russia, see Wikipedia (2010).
11 Peck (2006) is an instruction handbook intended for internal use in the training of new SRSGs. It contains interview material on a range of issues gathered by its author from interviews with SRSGs before 2006.
12 Barnett and Finnemore list only three sources of authority in *Rules for the World*: delegated, moral, and expert authority. I include also charismatic authority and prestige due to the particular nature of the role of the SRSG as both an official within the UN system but also drawing upon his or her personal experience.
13 See SRSG Aldo Ajello in Peck 2004, 333. The present author, having worked as a special assistant to the SRSG in MINURCAT, also arranged and attended similar monthly meetings that the SRSG had with the diplomatic community.
14 I am indebted to Chris Wilson for this concept, helping me to put my thoughts into words.

References

Ackerman, Spencer (2008) 'Diplomat Lends Credence to Talks with Taliban', *Washington Independent*, http://washingtonindependent.com/22577/lakhdar-brahimi. Accessed August 28, 2012.

Adler, Emanuel and Vincent Pouliot (2011) 'International Practices: Introduction and Framework,' in Adler, Emanuel and Vincent Pouliot eds., *International Practices*. Cambridge: Cambridge University Press, pp. 3–35.

Andersen, Morten S. (2010) *Putting Structure into Practice: The 'Practice' Turn in IR and Ontologies of Structural Inquiry*. MIMEO.

Anishchuk, Alexei (2011) 'Russia Criticises UN Force Role in Ivory Coast', Reuters, http://af.reuters.com/article/topNews/idAFJOE73D0C020110414?pageNumber=2&virtualBrandChannel=0. Accessed April 18, 2011.

Autesserre, Severine (2010) *The Trouble with the Congo: Local Violence and the Failure of International Peacebuilding*. Cambridge: Cambridge University Press.

Avant, Deborah D., Martha Finnemore and Susan K. Sell (2010) *Who Governs the Globe?* Cambridge: Cambridge University Press.

68 *SRSGs as norm arbitrators?*

Barnett, Michael N. and Martha Finnemore (1999) 'The Politics, Power, and Pathologies of International Organizations', *International Organization*, 53 (4), pp. 699–732.

Barnett, Michael N. and Martha Finnemore (2004) *Rules for the World: International Organizations in Global Politics.* Ithaca, NY: Cornell University Press.

BBC (2006) 'Hamas Sweeps to Election Victory', BBC News, http://news.bbc.co.uk/2/hi/4650788.stm. Accessed January 18, 2013.

BBC (2010) 'Gbagbo Orders Peacekeepers to Leave Ivory Coast', BBC News Africa, www.bbc.co.uk/news/world-africa-12028263. Accessed September 17, 2012.

BBC (2011a) 'ICC to Investigate Ivory Coast Post-Election Violence', BBC News Africa, www.bbc.co.uk/news/world-africa-15148801. Accessed September 17, 2012.

BBC (2011b) 'Ivory Coast: UN Presses Ouattara over Duekoue Massacre', BBC News Africa, www.bbc.co.uk/news/world-africa-12951990. Accessed September 17, 2012.

BBC World News (2011) 'Ivory Coast: Besieged Gbagbo "in Basement" of Residence', BBC World News, www.bbc.co.uk/news/mobile/world-africa-12967610. Accessed April 18, 2011.

Bellamy, Alex J. (2009) *Responsibility to Protect: The Global Effort to End Mass Atrocities.* Cambridge: Polity.

Bellamy, Alex J., Paul Williams and Stuart Griffin (2010) *Understanding Peacekeeping.* Cambridge: Polity.

Benner, Thorsten, Stephan Mergenthaler and Philipp Rotmann (2011) *The New World of UN Peace Operations: Learning to Build Peace?* Oxford: Oxford University Press.

Benner, Thorsten and Philipp Rotmann (2008) 'Learning to Learn? UN Peacebuilding and the Challenges of Building a Learning Organization', *Journal of Intervention and Statebuilding*, 2 (1), pp. 43–62.

Berdal, Mats R. and Spyros Economides (2007) *United Nations Interventionism, 1991–2004.* Cambridge: Cambridge University Press.

Boot, Max (2000) 'Paving the Road to Hell: The Failure of U.N. Peacekeeping', *Foreign Affairs*, March/April, pp. 143–48.

Borger, Julian (2010a) 'Kai Eide Lashes Out', *Guardian*, www.guardian.co.uk/world/julian-borger-global-security-blog/2010/mar/18/afghanistan-taliban. Accessed September 9, 2011.

Borger, Julian (2010b) 'UN in Secret Peace Talks with Taliban', *Guardian*, www.guardian.co.uk/world/2010/jan/28/taliban-united-nations-afghanistan. Accessed January 18, 2013.

Brahimi, Lakhdar (2007) 'Afghanistan and Iraq: Failed States or Failed Wars?' Lakhdar Brahimi Lecture on Public Policy, Princeton University, March 28, 2007 [Video], http://video.ias.edu/node/65. Accessed September 4, 2013.Chesterman, Simon (2004) *You, the People: The United Nations, Transitional Administration, and State-Building.* Oxford: Oxford University Press.

Chesterman, Simon (2007) *Secretary or General? The UN Secretary-General in World Politics.* Cambridge: Cambridge University Press.

CNN (2011) 'World Report', CNN, March 18, 2011 [Television].

de Carvalho, Benjamin and Jon Harald Sande Lie (2011) 'Chronicle of a Frustration Foretold? The Implementation of a Broad Protection Agenda in the United Nations', *Journal of International Peacekeeping*, 15 (3–4), pp. 341–62.

de Coning, Cedric (2010) 'Mediation and Peacebuilding: SRSGs and DSRSGs in Integrated Missions', *Global Governance*, 16 (2), pp. 281–99.

de Soto, Alvaro (2007) *End of Mission Report.* New York: United Nations.

Doucet, Lyse (2010) 'Afghanistan: A Job Half Done', BBC News, http://news.bbc.co.uk/2/hi/south_asia/6205220.stm. Accessed September 6, 2010.

Eide, Kai (2010) *Høyt spill om Afghanistan.* Oslo: Cappelen Damm.

Fafo (1999) *Command from the Saddle: Managing United Nations Peace-Building Missions.* Oslo: Fafo Institute for Applied Social Science.

Finnemore, Martha and Kathryn Sikkink (1998) 'International Norm Dynamics and Political Change', *International Organization*, 52 (4), pp. 887–917.

Guzzini, Stefano (2005) 'The Concept of Power: A Constructivist Analysis', *Millennium – Journal of International Studies*, 33 (3), pp. 495–521.

Haas, Peter M. (1992) 'Epistemic Communities and International-Policy Coordination – Introduction', *International Organization*, 46 (1), pp. 1–35.

Holt, Victoria, Glyn Taylor and Max Kelly (2009) *Protecting Civilians in the Context of UN Peacekeeping Operations: Successes, Setbacks and Remaining Challenges.* New York: UN DPKO and UN OCHA.

Howard, Lise Morjé (2008) *UN Peacekeeping in Civil Wars.* Cambridge: Cambridge University Press.

Johnstone, Ian (2007) 'The Secretary-General as Norm Entrepreneur: Secretary or General?' in Chesterman, Simon ed. *Secretary or General? The UN Secretary-General in World Politics.* Cambridge: Cambridge University Press, pp. 123–38.

Johnstone, Ian (2008) 'Legislation and Adjudication in the UN Security Council: Bringing Down the Deliberative Deficit', *American Journal of International Law*, 102 (2), pp. 275–83.

Johnstone, Ian (2010) 'Normative Evolution at the UN: Impact on Operational Imperatives,' in Jones, Bruce D., Shepard Forman and Richard Gowan eds., *Cooperating for Peace and Security: Evolving Institutions and Arrangements in a Context of Changing U.S. Security Policy.* Cambridge: Cambridge University Press, pp. 187–214.

Karlsrud, John (2013) 'SRSGs as Norm Arbitrators? Understanding Bottom-up Authority in UN Peacekeeping', *Global Governance*, 19 (4), pp. 525–44.

Karlsrud, John (2015) 'The UN at War: Examining the Consequences of Peace Enforcement Mandates for the UN Peacekeeping Operations in the CAR, the DRC and Mali', *Third World Quarterly*, 36 (1), pp. 40–54.

Kron, Josh (2012) 'Congo Rebels Advancing on Major City', *New York Times*, www.nytimes.com/2012/11/19/world/africa/congo-rebels-advancing-on-city-of-goma.html?smid=tw-share. Accessed November 19, 2012.

Lamb, Christina and Stephen Grey (2009) 'UN Chief Scorns Miliband Plan for Taliban talks', *Times*, www.timesonline.co.uk/tol/news/world/asia/article6736047.ece. Accessed April 20, 2011.

Legro, Jeffrey W. (1997) 'Which Norms Matter? Revisiting the "Failure" of Internationalism', *International Organization*, 51 (1), pp. 31–63.

Lipson, Michael (2007) 'Peacekeeping: Organized Hypocrisy?' *European Journal of International Relations*, 13 (1), pp. 5–34.

Lynch, Colum (2005) 'U.N. Peacekeeping More Assertive, Creating Risk for Civilians', *Washington Post*, www.washingtonpost.com/wp-dyn/content/article/2005/08/14/AR2005081400946.html. Accessed September 4, 2013.

Malone, David (2004) *The UN Security Council: From the Cold War to the 21st Century.* Boulder, CO: Lynne Rienner.

McCarthy, Rory and Ian Williams (2007) 'Secret UN Report Condemns US for Middle East Failures', *Guardian*, www.guardian.co.uk/world/2007/jun/13/usa.israel. Accessed May 19, 2011.

70 *SRSGs as norm arbitrators?*

Meo, Nick, Michael Evans and Sam Coates (2007) 'Diplomats Expelled over Talks with Taleban', *Times*, www.thetimes.co.uk/tto/news/world/asia/article2608083.ece. Accessed September 4, 2013.

Nelson, Dean (2008) 'Expelled British Envoys Tried to Turn Taliban Chief', *Sunday Times*, www.thesundaytimes.co.uk/sto/news/uk_news/article78157.ece. Accessed September 4, 2013.

New York University Center on International Cooperation [NYU CIC] (2009) *Robust Peacekeeping: The Politics of Force*. New York: Center on International Cooperation, New York University.

ONUCI (2010) 'FAQ: The Certification of Elections in Côte d'Ivoire', ONUCI, www.onuci.org/spip.php?rubrique117. Accessed October 1, 2012.

Permanent Mission of South Africa to the United Nations (2010) 'Statement by Ambassadro Baso Sangqu, Permanent Representative of the Republic of South Africa to the United Nations at the Meeting of the Special Committee on Peacekeeping Operations 2010 Substantive Session. United Nations, New York, 22 February 2010', Permanent Mission of South Africa to the United Nations, www.betterpeace.org/files/c34_south_africa_22feb10.pdf. Accessed May 12, 2011.

Peck, Connie (2004) 'Special Representatives of the Secretary General,' in Malone, David ed. *The UN Security Council: From the Cold War to the 21st Century*. Boulder, CO: Lynne Rienner, pp. 325–39.

Peck, Connie (2006) *On Being a Special Representative to the Secretary-General*. Geneva: UNITAR.

Pouligny, Béatrice (2006) *Peace Operations Seen from Below: UN Missions and Local People*. London: Hurst & Co.

Pouliot, Vincent (2008) 'The Logic of Practicality: A Theory of Practice of Security Communities', *International Organization*, 62 (2), pp. 257–88.

Puchala, Donald J. (1993) 'The Secretary-General and His Special Representatives,' in Rivlin, Benjamin and Leon Gordenker eds., *The Challenging Role of the UN Secretary-General: Making "the Most Impossible Job in the World" Possible*. Westport, CN: Praeger, pp. 81–97.

Rivlin, Benjamin and Leon Gordenker (1993) *The Challenging Role of the UN Secretary-General: Making "the Most Impossible Job in the World" Possible*. Westport, CN: Praeger.

South Africa (2005) *Pretoria Agreement on the Peace Process in Côte d'Ivoire, 6 April 2005*. Pretoria: Government of South Africa.

Terrie, Jim (2008) 'The Use of Force in UN Peacekeeping: The Experience of MONUC', *African Security Review*, 18 (1), pp. 21–34.

Théroux-Bénoni, Lori-Anne (2012) *Lessons for UN Electoral Certification from the 2010 Disputed Presidential Poll in Côte d'Ivoire*. Waterloo, Ontario, Canada: Centre for International Governance Innovation; Africa Initiative.

UN (1945) *Charter of the United Nations*. New York: United Nations.

UN (2008) *United Nations Peacekeeping Operations: Principles and Guidelines*. New York: United Nations Department of Peacekeeping Operations and Department of Field Support.

UN (2010) *Draft DPKO/DFS Concept Note on Robust Peacekeeping*. New York: United Nations Department of Peacekeeping Operations and Department of Field Support.

UNAMA (2009) 'UN 100 Day Countdown Begins – What Are You Doing for Peace?' UNAMA, http://unama.unmissions.org/Default.aspx?tabid=12254&ctl=Details&mid=15756&ItemID=31640&language=en-US. Accessed September 18, 2012.

UNAMA (2010) 'United Nations Assistance Mission in Afghanistan', UNAMA, http://unama.unmissions.org/Default.aspx?tabid=1741. Accessed August 20, 2010.

United Nations Security Council (UNSC) (2001) *'Resolution 1378'*, *Security Council Resolution, UN doc. S/RES/1378, 1 November 2001.* New York: United Nations.

United Nations Security Council (UNSC) (2005) *'Resolution 1603'*, *Security Council Resolution, UN doc. S/RES/1603, 3 June 2005.* New York: United Nations.

United Nations Security Council (UNSC) (2006) *'Resolution 1706'*, *Security Council Resolution, UN doc. S/RES/1706, 31 August 2006.* New York: United Nations.

United Nations Security Council (UNSC) (2007) *'Resolution 1765'*, *Security Council Resolution, UN doc. S/RES/1765, 16 July 2007.* New York: United Nations.

United Nations Security Council (UNSC) (2008a) *'Resolution 1806'*, *Security Council Resolution, UN doc. S/RES/1833, 22 September 2008.* New York: United Nations.

United Nations Security Council (UNSC) (2008b) *'Resolution 1833'*, *Security Council Resolution, UN doc. S/RES/1806, 20 March 2008.* New York: United Nations.

United Nations Security Council (UNSC) (2011a) *'Resolution 1970'*, *Security Council Resolution, UN doc. S/RES/1970, 26 February 2011.* New York: United Nations.

United Nations Security Council (UNSC) (2011b) *'Resolution 1973'*, *Security Council Resolution, UN doc. S/RES/1973, 17 March 2011.* New York: United Nations.

United Nations Security Council (UNSC) (2011c) *'Resolution 1975'*, *Security Council Resolution, UN doc. S/RES/1975, 30 March 2011.* New York: United Nations.

United Nations Security Council (UNSC) (2012) 'Al-Qaida Sanctions Committee', United Nations Security Council, www.un.org/sc/committees/1267/. Accessed September 18, 2012.

Vance, Cyrus R. and David A. Hamburg (1997) *Pathfinders for Peace. A Report to the UN Secretary-General on the Role of Special Representatives and Personal Envoys.* New York: Carnegie Commission on Preventing Deadly Conflict.

Walsh, Declan and Jon Boone (2010) 'UK Special Envoy to Afghanistan Who Called for Talks with Taliban Quits', *Guardian.*

Weber, Max, Hans Heinrich Gerth and C. Wright Mills (1946) *From Max Weber: Essays in Sociology.* New York: Oxford University Press.

Wikipedia (2010) 'List of Designated Terrorist Organizations', Wikipedia, http://en.wikipedia.org/wiki/List_of_designated_terrorist_organizations. Accessed September 7, 2010.

World Federalist Movement (2010) 'IGP Matrix of Issues: General Debate of the Special Committee on Peacekeeping Operations (C34) 2010 Substantive Session', World Federalist Movement – Institute for Global Policy (WFM-IGP), www.betterpeace.org/files/C34_Matrix_General_Debate_22_23Feb10Final_0.pdf. Accessed May 12, 2011.

4 Linked ecologies and Responsibility to Protect

The role of academic institutions and think tanks in norm change

> There are certain issues that are better done outside and there are certain issues that can only be done inside . . . But take a look at the intervention issue. I couldn't have done it inside. It would have been very divisive.
>
> UN Secretary-General Kofi A. Annan (Weiss 2007, 17–18)

> Today, the responsibility to protect is a concept, not yet a policy; an aspiration, not yet a reality.
>
> UN Secretary-General Ban Ki-moon
> (United Nations Secretary-General [UNSG] 2008)

Introduction[1]

The opening quote by Kofi Annan is indicative of what this book aims to investigate. Certain issues, such as the humanitarian intervention issue, can be highly divisive, and discussions between member states can end up in deadlock. In this chapter I examine the Responsibility to Protect (R2P) process and how Kofi Annan and the UN engaged with the 'outside' to deal with the 'intervention issue' and come up with a solution to it.

The second quote tellingly describes the status of the R2P norm prior to the two UN Security Council Resolutions (UN SCR) 1970 and 1973 on Libya (United Nations Security Council [UNSC] 2011a, UNSC 2011b) and UN SCR 1975 on Côte d'Ivoire (UNSC 2011c). Even after more than ten years of debate, and after the adoption of the principle through the World Summit outcome document in 2005 (United Nations General Assembly [UNGA] 2005), the understanding remained hotly contested (UN 2009a, Global Centre for the Responsibility to Protect 2009).

References to R2P to authorize the robust use of force in the two Security Council Resolutions on Libya were the first in a UN context. However, the preventive pillar of R2P had been invoked several times earlier. According to the secretary-general,

> the Special Advisers on the Prevention of Genocide and on the Responsibility to Protect have made public statements over the past year regarding

developments in Kyrgyzstan, Guinea, Côte d'Ivoire, Libya, the Sudan, and Syria, as well as providing me with internal assessments of a number of other situations.

(UNSG 2011, 8)

Simon Adams, Director of the Global Centre for the R2P, asserts that "discussions now are not whether R2P is a good norm, but what Pillar 3 on 'coercive means' means" (interview with Simon Adams, Director of the Global Centre for the R2P, September 26, 2011, New York). Contestation over the meaning of R2P has thus been an ongoing feature of the norm, long after its adoption.

This chapter examines the norm change process concerning R2P, from when the term was first coined until today (see also Karlsrud 2013). It does so by asking who the main actors have been in the drive to establish the norm and what consequences this can have for understanding and theorizing norm change in international organizations. I employ the conceptual framework describing R2P developed by Bellamy (2009), who distinguishes between describing R2P as a concept, a principle, or a norm. He argues that for the period prior to the adoption of R2P by UN member states in 2005, R2P should be considered as a concept, whereas since its adoption it should be recognized as a principle, since the member states have "agreed on its content and have pledged to act in accordance with it" (ibid., 7). Discussing R2P as a norm is a separate question, he holds; it involves inquiring into how the norm is translated from concept to principle and how the norm has evolved, using theories of norm change. This chapter seeks to elucidate the norm change process concerning R2P using a blend of constructivist theories, the sociology of professions, and practice theory.

I begin with a short narrative of the development of R2P, tracing its historical antecedents until the inclusion of R2P in UN Security Council Resolution 1970 on Libya in 2011 (UNSC 2011a) and the subsequent discussion on R2P. In the second section, applying the theory framework, I show how the sociology of professions can enrich constructivist theories of norm change in international organizations. In this section I analyze the process in greater detail, highlighting what actors were involved and the roles they played. The next section takes one step back and examines the process of R2P and the roles of the various actors and their interaction during the process. That section draws on the sociology of professions to augment our understanding of how R2P has been advanced as a norm through informal alliances. At the end of the section I emphasize how the interaction with other ecologies has been instrumental in advancing the R2P norm and the role of policy alliances. In concluding, I note the need for further exploration of the potentially fruitful application of the theory framework and the need for a fundamental rethink concerning agency in norm change processes of international organizations.

The evolution of R2P – from concept to principle?

External intervention by the UN where it took on executive tasks can be traced back to its interventions during the Suez crisis in 1956 and in Congo in 1960

74 *Linked ecologies and R2P*

(Organisation des Nations Unies au Congo – ONUC). These missions included fact-finding, technical support, civilian administration, and peacekeeping. None of these practices were included in the UN Charter, so the missions expanded the tools available to the UN for dealing with threats to international peace and stability (Orford 2011). The UN mission in Congo has since been considered as an exception in UN peacekeeping history, as it was not only a matter of monitoring a peace agreement, but included technical support and civilian administration, similar to present-day peacekeeping. The tension between UN peacekeeping and the basic norm of sovereignty was evident already at this stage and would resurface again in the operations mounted after the end of the Cold War. This tension could be described as a conflict between *de jure* and *de facto* sources of sovereignty, according to Anne Orford (ibid., 16, 41) or between statutory sovereignty and empirical sovereignty (Evans and Thakur 2013). Arthur Mühlen-Schulte traces the antecedents to the protection of civilians concept to the just war and *jus in bello* tradition, with thinking about how to ensure civilian protection and compassion to civilian bystanders stretching back to St. Augustine, Thomas Aquinas, Hugo Grotius, and others, and carried into contemporary warfare through international humanitarian law (IHL), particularly with the Geneva Conventions; international human rights law (HRL) (in particular the 1948 Declaration of Human Rights); and refugee law (in particular the 1951 Refugee Protocols) (Mühlen-Schulte 2012).

R2P has been advanced as a norm for more than a decade now. The process has not been a unilinear one: there have been advances and setbacks. In the academic literature, the norm change process around R2P has generally been described by focusing on specific outputs, such as significant reports and articles that have advanced the debate. Against the backdrop of the failures of Bosnia and Rwanda, the genealogy of R2P starts with Francis Deng and Roberta Cohen's conceptual redefinition of "sovereignty as responsibility" (Deng 1996, Cohen and Deng 1998), emerging from work on locating responsibility for internally displaced persons (IDPs), who lacked the rights enjoyed by refugees under international law.

The failures of the UN to act in Bosnia and in Rwanda brought the conflict between the basic norm of sovereignty and core humanitarian principles and human rights to the fore. The world should not sit idly by if atrocities are committed and the host state is either unable or unwilling to prevent them or takes an active part in committing them. After two years in office as secretary-general, Kofi Annan in 1999 commissioned two reports on the UN's inaction in Rwanda and in Srebrenica (UN 1999a, UN 1999b) that were unusually harsh for being from within the UN system. In a speech to the General Assembly, he challenged the Security Council and the United Nations to "forge unity behind the principle that massive and systematic violations of human rights . . . cannot be allowed to stand" (Annan 1999a), and he supported the view of sovereignty as responsibility in a watershed article in the *Economist* (Annan 1999b). Subsequently, Canada set up the International Commission on Intervention and State Sovereignty (ICISS) in September 2000. The ICISS first coined the term 'responsibility to protect' when releasing its report (ICISS 2001). It was then picked up in the report of the High-Level Panel on Threats, Challenges and Change commissioned by Secretary-General Kofi Annan (UN 2004) and in his subsequent report *In Larger Freedom* (UN 2005). After much debate in the run-up to the 2005 World Summit (Stedman 2007, 51–4, Johnstone 2010), a watered-down version of R2P as set out in the ICISS report was adopted in the outcome document (UNGA 2005). This outcome document narrowed the scope of R2P from "population is suffering serious harm" in the ICISS document (ICISS 2001, xi) to four serious crimes: "Each individual State has the responsibility to protect its populations from genocide, war crimes, ethnic cleansing and crimes against humanity" (UNGA 2005, 31). In 2006, R2P was reaffirmed by the Security Council in its resolution on the protection of civilians (UNSC 2006, 6).

In 2009, the secretary-general sought to further clarify the principle with the release of the report *Implementing the Responsibility to Protect* (UN 2009b), and the General Assembly had a broad discussion about R2P, involving 94 speakers representing 180 nations and two observer missions (Global Centre for the Responsibility to Protect 2009). An informal interactive dialogue on R2P has been underway at the General Assembly on an annual basis. In September 2011, Secretary-General Ban Ki-moon asserted that the debate was no longer about the principle, but about how to implement it in practice: "Our debates are now about how, not whether, to implement the Responsibility to Protect. No government questions the principle" (Ki-moon 2011). This turn of events is closely linked with the situation in Libya from 2010 to 2012.

Responsibility to Protect – from words to deeds?

With UN Security Council Resolution (UN SCR) 1970 on Libya in February 2011, the coercive part of pillar three of R2P was for the first time translated into practice.[2] In accordance with the principles for R2P established in paragraph 139 of the World Summit outcome document and the principles for implementing R2P set out by the secretary-general in 2009, UN SCR 1970 on Libya established the necessary justification "to take collective action, in a timely and decisive manner, through the Security Council, in accordance with the Charter, including Chapter VII" (UN 2009b, 27):

> *Deploring* the gross and systematic violation of human rights, including the repression of peaceful demonstrators, expressing deep concern at the deaths of civilians, and rejecting unequivocally the incitement to hostility and violence against the civilian population made from the highest level of the Libyan government . . . *Considering* that the widespread and systematic attacks currently taking place . . . against the civilian population may amount to crimes against humanity . . . *Recalling* the Libyan authorities' **responsibility to protect** its population . . . *Acting* under Chapter VII of the Charter of the United Nations, and taking measures under its Article 41.
>
> (UNSC 2011a, 1–2, bold emphasis added)

76 Linked ecologies and R2P

The resolution also decided to refer the situation in Libya to the Prosecutor of the International Criminal Court, to impose sanctions including the freezing of assets as well as an arms embargo (UNSC 2011a, 2–7). Some commentators wished for a stronger reaction, arguing for a no-fly zone and even a humanitarian intervention (Thakur 2011, Global Centre for the Responsibility to Protect 2011). Nicholas Wheeler argues that, while there has been an expansive interpretation of the occasions when the Security Council gives authorization for the use of force ('Chapter VII mandates'), the Security Council did not take action where it was most needed, as in Rwanda, Bosnia, and Darfur, and that most likely the Security Council would not authorize a humanitarian intervention even if R2P were adopted (Wheeler 2008, 16–18, Lie 2008). Others argued for a more cautious approach so as not to undermine the popular support for the Libyan revolution (Libya 2011, Ash 2011, Milne 2011). Eli Stamnes has advocated for limiting use of direct reference to R2P to situations where there is a threat of mass atrocities (Stamnes 2008).

Since March 2011, discussions have been fierce and many, also involving members of the Security Council who voted in favor of the resolutions but later argued that the coalition took the mandate too far. For example South Africa was "condemning the continuing aerial bombardments of Libya by western forces" (*Sydney Morning Herald* 2011). David Rieff has argued that "instead of strengthening R2P as a new global norm, the NATO intervention in Libya may well serve as its "high water mark" (Rieff 2011). We will return to this later, in connection with the introduction of the concept of Responsibility while Protecting (RwP) by Brazil, which can be seen as an attempt to save R2P from controversy after the Libya intervention.

Viewing the R2P process in terms of a constructivist/sociology of professions framework

Writing on the phenomenon of shell shock during World War I, Andrew Abbott argues that defining shell shock as a task that psychiatrists could and should take care of also redefined the psychiatric profession as such: "Creating a psychiatric approach to shell shock in World War I, for example, redefined who psychiatrists were and what shell shock was more than it defined a relation between a preexisting group and a given task" (Abbott 2005, 248–49). In other words, there is reciprocal relationship between the profession and the tasks the profession is making jurisdictional claims over. In the area of peacekeeping, we have seen how the UN has, with the support of member states, taken jurisdictional control over a range of tasks, starting with fact-finding and monitoring of cease-fires and peace agreements and expanding to technical support with its mission to Congo (ONUC) to various civilian tasks connected to peace- and statebuilding since the mid-1990s until today.

Anne Orford argues that "the responsibility to protect concept offers a coherent framework for understanding practices of international executive rule" by the UN ever since the leadership of Secretary-General Dag Hammarskjöld (Orford 2011, 42). In order to pre-empt intervention by powerful states that had vested interests, Hammarskjöld successfully asserted the role of the UN as a guarantor of order and protection of life in Egypt (United Nations Emergency Force – UNEF) and in Congo (ONUC) with the support of the Security Council. Since then, according to Orford, practices have preceded and informed the development of norms – the concept of responsibility to protect can thus be seen as a *post facto* explanation and framework legitimizing protective intervention by the UN in cases where there has been a need to intervene – in the words of UN Secretary-General Dag Hammarskjöld arguing for the UN involvement in Congo "to achieve 'the maintenance of order in the country and the protection of life'" (cited in Orford, 2011, 30). Simon Chesterman holds that, in one way, the most important contribution of the adoption of R2P was not in a legal sense, as it has only formalized actions that the Security Council has "been authorizing for more than a decade," but political and rhetorical (Chesterman 2011, 2). Johnstone offers a similar argument about how practices can precede norm- and law-making activities in international organizations (Johnstone 2008). The previous chapter has also shown how practices in the field impact and can precede codification of norms at UN headquarters, rebalancing the relationship between the various, and at times conflicting, norms guiding UN peacekeeping.

The secretary-general as a norm entrepreneur

Using the analytical framework developed by Finnemore and Sikkink, Johnstone argues that the secretary-general can act as a norm entrepreneur and helped "to push the R2P norm to a 'tipping point' which it may have reached at the 2005 World Summit" (Johnstone 2007, 134, see also, Bellamy 2009, 27–8, Johnstone 2010). While stressing that states like Canada, the UK, "and other like-minded governments" were probably the most important actors in advancing the R2P principle (Johnstone 2007, 134), he argues that the secretary-general played a significant role in institutionalizing the norm – by commissioning the report on the failure of the UN in Srebrenica, which found that the failure was due not only to a mismatch between means and mandate, but also to a gap in the ideology of peacekeeping (UN 1999a, 108), and the Brahimi Report, which stressed that impartiality does not mean indifference (UN 2000). This brought further momentum, with the aforementioned reports from the ICISS and the High-Level Panel on Threats, Challenges and Change leading up to the World Summit in 2005 (ICISS et al. 2001, UN 2004).

It is a fine balancing act that the UN secretary-general has to perform when advancing new norms – being ambitious, but at the same time taking care to resonate with the prevailing sentiment among member states. As Kofi Annan expressed it: "[The secretary-general] has to challenge member states to aim high, yet also convince them what he is suggesting is within their reach" (Annan 2007, xii, see also Johnstone 2007, 138, Rivlin and Gordenker 1993, 5). In an article defending the outcome document published in the *Wall Street Journal*, Kofi Annan was even more clear: "When I proposed an agenda for the Summit, I deliberately set the bar high, since in international negotiations you never get everything you ask" (Annan 2005).

However, focusing solely on the secretary-general will reveal only part of the picture of how R2P came into being. Other actors were instrumental as well, and

78 *Linked ecologies and R2P*

the process that guided the development was also key to the success. Kofi Annan deliberately reached out to member states and the academic community, as he recognized that the UN was not able to extract itself from the quagmire in which the concept of 'humanitarian intervention' had landed it:

> *KA* [Kofi Annan]: There are certain issues that are better done outside and there are certain issues that can only be done inside . . . But take a look at the intervention issue. I couldn't have done it inside. It would have been very divisive. And the member-states were very uncomfortable because, as an organization, *sovereignty is our bedrock and bible – here is someone coming with ideas which are almost challenging it.* So I had to sow the seed and let them digest it, but take the study outside and then bring in the results for them to look at it. And what I intend to do, for example, after the Security Council has reviewed it and discussed it, I may find a way of getting the document distributed to the membership at large, for them to continue their own dialogue and discussions on it . . .
>
> I find that when you are dealing with issues where the member-states are divided and have very strong views, and very strong regional reviews, if you do the work inside, the discussions become so acrimonious that, however good a document is, sometimes you have problems. And in fact, they begin to look at who did the report, where do they come from, who influenced them. But if you bring it from outside – that Professor Weiss investigated it, this is a really, very good document that could help our discussions – they accept it.
>
> And I must say there are also times when I go outside because quite frankly I don't think we have the expertise in the house. If I go and ask my people, they will say, "We can do it." Bureaucrats never admit that they cannot do it. So there are, at times, areas where I think there is stronger expertise outside, and I should reach out to them. And in fact, the infusion of outside views would also help our processes.
>
> *TGW* [Thomas G. Weiss]: So sometimes it's tactical, and sometimes it's –
> *KA*: Substantive, yes. Content.
>
> (Weiss 2007, 17–18, emphasis added)

This lengthy quotation is an excerpt from a transcript of an interview with Kofi Annan done by Thomas G. Weiss, who himself played an important role in the R2P process. In the following I explore in depth the various arguments Annan is making, but let me briefly summarize them here:

1. The UN may have limited capacity to deal with substantive issues.
2. Academia matters – divisive issues among member states can be solved by establishing commissions and receiving expert opinions that are broadly representative.
3. Reaching out to academia may be for tactical reasons, substantive reasons, or both.

Setting up the commission

On September 16, 1999, Kofi Annan published an article in the *Economist* just prior to the meeting of the UN General Assembly. Here he laid out two understandings of sovereignty, counterpoising the sovereignty of the state with the sovereignty of the individual, and the responsibility of the former to protect the latter (Annan 1999b). A few days later, on September 20 at the opening of the General Assembly, he asked, "How should we respond to a Rwanda, to a Srebrenica – to gross and systematic violations of human rights that affect every precept of our common humanity?" He repeated that question in his report *We the Peoples: The Role of the United Nations in the 21st Century* (Annan 2000, 48), released in March 2000. Indirectly, he also gave the answer: "States bent on criminal behavior [should] know that frontiers are not the absolute defence . . . that massive and systematic violations of human rights – wherever they may take place – should not be allowed to stand" (Annan 1999a, cited in Weiss 2000, 11).

Canada, and Lloyd Axworthy, its foreign minister at the time, picked up the challenge that Kofi Annan had given the international community and created a commission of high-level statesmen and diplomats, researchers, and former UN officials – the International Commission on Intervention and State Sovereignty. Canada had been a champion of humanitarian interventions since the failures in Bosnia and Rwanda. However, humanitarian interventions had become a highly divisive issue after the NATO bombing in Kosovo, conducted from March until June of the same year Annan issued his challenge. There was a need to find common ground between the atrocities in Bosnia and Rwanda that had shocked the conscience of world, while avoiding the divisive debate around humanitarian interventions stirred up by the NATO bombing in Kosovo.

The Commission – composed of a high-level panel and a research directorate – was part of a pattern of how Kofi Annan advanced thinking and new norms in the UN, as shown also in previous quotes. The UN secretary-general can use high-level panels and Senior Advisory Groups as independent constituencies that can explore a particular issue and inform member states. Government officials, prominent statesmen and international diplomats, think tanks, and academic institutions outside the UN have been crucial to the process of advancing R2P.

Academics and statesmen as norm entrepreneurs

Some of the members of the Commission could be seen as norm entrepreneurs in their own right during the R2P process, and the 'revolving doors' phenomenon was clearly discernible. Commission members included Gareth Evans, former minister of foreign affairs of Australia; Ramesh Thakur, Edward C. Luck; Francis Deng, Stephen J. Stedman; and Bruce Jones.

Ramesh Thakur was vice rector and senior vice rector of the United Nations University from 1998–2007 and one of the principal authors of the ICISS report,

80   *Linked ecologies and R2P*

and he has continued to support the principle vigorously through regular inputs in the debate (Thakur 2006, Thakur 2011). Thakur has also argued for the influence of his and other academic members of the ICISS commission in his book *International Commissions and the Power of Ideas* (Thakur et al. 2005) and *Global Governance and the UN* (Weiss and Thakur 2010).

The work of Gareth Evans has over the last decade been closely intertwined with the fate of R2P – he was co-chair of the ICISS and a member of the secretary-general's High-Level Panel on Threats, Challenges and Change, where he played a vital role in the drafting of the report (Norwegian Institute of International Affairs [NUPI] 2006, 65, Bellamy 2009); he has published extensively on R2P and also took part in the General Assembly debate on R2P in 2009. Gareth Evans's most recent book is *The Responsibility to Protect: Ending Mass Atrocity Crimes Once and for All*. He served as president and CEO of the International Crisis Group from 2000 to 2009 and is also the co-chair of the International Advisory Board of the Global Centre for the Responsibility to Protect (Evans 2008).

Francis Deng had, together with Roberta Cohen, proposed the concept of 'sovereignty as responsibility', which initiated the paradigmatic turn in understanding the relationship between sovereignty and the protection of civilians. He served as special adviser on the prevention of genocide, sharing a joint office with Edward C. Luck, who was the special adviser on the Responsibility to Protect and mandated to work for "conceptual development and consensus-building, in recognition of the fledgling nature of the international agreement on the responsibility to protect" (UN 2007). Luck was also senior vice president for research and programs at the International Peace Institute and was on leave from his post as director of the Center on International Organization of the School of International and Public Affairs, Columbia University, while serving as special adviser. Having served as a special adviser, he has been characterized as "particularly influential" by fellow proponents Evans and Thakur (Evans and Thakur 2013, 201).

Stephen J. Stedman was the research director of the High-Level Panel on Threats, Challenges and Change and special advisor to the UN secretary-general in the crucial period leading up to the UN World Summit in 2005 "to help gain worldwide support in implementing the panel's recommendations" (Stedman 2012).

The director of the Center on International Cooperation (CIC), Bruce Jones, held several key positions in the process leading up to the adoption of the principle of R2P in 2005, first as a deputy research director of the High-Level Panel on Threats, Challenges and Change, and in the crucial period ahead of the General Assembly in 2005, where the principle was agreed upon and adopted at the eleventh hour (Stedman 2007), he was a senior advisor to the secretary-general.[3]

The careers of all these individuals can be characterized as a 'revolving doors' phenomenon: they have created close-knit networks between the various institutions they have worked for and moved between.

Role of think tanks and academic institutions

Think tanks and academic institutions often have an explicit goal of norm change in the international system and have also been central actors in the R2P process. As Weiss and Thakur argue:

> The normative advances of the concept of the responsibility to protect can in no small measure be traced to early efforts by the Brookings Project on Internal Displacement to give concrete meaning to the mandate of the representative of the secretary-general for internally displaced persons, a position held at the time by Francis Deng.
>
> (Weiss and Thakur 2010, 313–14)

They report that it was Deng who introduced the notion to Lloyd Axworthy, then Canadian foreign minister, who launched the ICISS commission: "The first time I heard the notion of 'responsibility to protect' was when Deng visited me in Ottawa and argued for a clear commitment by the international community to deal with the IDP issue" (Axworthy 2003, cited in Weiss and Thakur 2010, 314).

The high-level panel was supported by a research directorate housed at the Ralph Bunche Institute for International Studies at the Graduate Center of the City University of New York (CUNY). This research directorate was led by "Thomas G. Weiss, Director of the Ralph Bunche Institute and Presidential Professor, Stanlake J.T.M. Samkange, a lawyer from Zimbabwe and former UN staff member, and Don Hubert, of the Peacebuilding and Human Security Division at Foreign Affairs Canada (FAC)" (CUNY 2000). Weiss and Hubert were the leading authors of a supplementary volume to the report issued by ICISS, with participation by another fifty-one contributing authors from around the globe (Weiss and Hubert 2001). When working with ICISS, Don Hubert had experience from another successful norm change process – on establishing the Mine Ban Treaty. Besides being a government official, he was well acquainted with the academic field, with a Ph.D. under his belt, and had made some reflections on how to best advance norms in the international arena in his *The Landmine Ban: A Case Study in Humanitarian Advocacy* (2000). In the book, Hubert listed three core criteria for successful humanitarian advocacy that, with few modifications, also would apply to other substantive areas:

- Favorable negotiating conditions (a strong chairperson, NGO [non-governmental organization] access, and provision for voting).
- Effective coalition building (among and between NGOs, governments and international organizations).
- Clear campaign messaging (advocating stringent provisions within an explicitly humanitarian discourse). (Hubert 2000, 57)

Indeed, the ICISS report stands as a prime example of coalition building and extensive use of think-tank, academic and civil society expertise and input. In

82 *Linked ecologies and R2P*

addition to the supplementary volume, the ICISS also added an extensive bibliography including more than 2,000 listings, "to reflect the best writing of the range of material published on all aspects of humanitarian intervention through the middle of 2001" (CUNY 2008). This bibliography was continuously updated with new entries and contained 3,600 references when the updates stopped in 2008 (CUNY 2008).

The CIC has been another key institution here, in the development of the R2P concept as well as others. It publishes the *Annual Review of Global Peace Operations* and conducts applied research on a range of concepts related to peacekeeping. According to its web page, the Center "works to enhance international responses to humanitarian crises and global security threats through applied research and direct engagement with multilateral institutions and the wider policy community. It has an international reputation for agenda-setting work on post-conflict peace-building, global peace operations, and UN reform" (NYU CIC 2011a). CIC relies on funding from traditional donor governments such as the UK, Norway, Sweden, and the Netherlands, as well as charitable trusts and foundations.

Also on the website of the Asia-Pacific Centre for the Responsibility to Protect, the goal of contributing to norm change is clearly stated:

> Despite the progress achieved to date in terms of the development, initial codification and state acceptance in principle of the R2P norm, much remains to be done to effectively implement the concept of the responsibility to protect if civilians are not to continue to be the victims of mass-atrocity crimes.
> (Asia-Pacific Centre for the Responsibility to Protect [APCR2P] 2011)

The Asia-Pacific Centre for the Responsibility to Protect is housed at the University of Queensland, Australia. It also publishes *Global Responsibility to Protect*, a peer-reviewed academic journal that

> seeks to publish the best and latest research on the R2P principle, its development as a new norm in global politics, its operationalization through the work of governments, international and regional organizations and NGOs, and finally, its relationship and applicability to past and present cases of genocide and mass atrocities including the global response to those cases.
> (APCR2P 2012).

This is but a narrow selection of the many think tanks and academic institutions active in this area, but it suffices to show that these appear to measure their standing by the degree they are able to participate in and influence international agenda-setting, in this case with regard to R2P.

Diane Stone has looked at how linked ecologies are formed to advance policy processes in the World Bank (Stone 2013). Formal research networks have been formed involving scholars from think tanks and academia, and Stone emphasizes that enduring concerns for the "policy engaged scholar" are questions of "co-option, epistemic capture and becoming 'templated by the field'" (ibid., 242).

However, she also notes that scholars, aware of the danger of being coopted and " 'socially bound' to the organizations they study" (ibid., 242), still choose to engage, as this give them "access to data, people and funding opportunities as well as incorporation into policy fora" (ibid., 245) and, perhaps most importantly, the opportunity to influence policy-makers with their own ideas and research.

Civil society

Civil society has also been very active in advancing R2P. The International Coalition for Responsibility to Protect (ICRtoP), housed at the World Federalist Movement Institute for Global Policy and sponsored by Canada, has been a central actor, with thirty NGOs worldwide as members (ICRtoP 2012a). Together with Oxfam they ran the Responsibility to Protect – Engaging Civil Society (R2P-CS) project and organized global consultations, one of them at the 2003 World Social Forum in Brazil. The coalition has played an important role "by marshalling the support of NGOs globally, fostering efforts to inform the public better, and by actively lobbying permanent delegations in New York" (Bellamy 2009, 71). The Global Centre for R2P is another important New York–based NGO. According to its director, "it is not a classic NGO, it is inside and outside the policy circle, gets to speak with policy makers, and is a privileged mechanism to push forward R2P" (interview with Simon Adams). This NGO conducts policy-oriented research and helps UN member states build capacity by supporting focal points for R2P in the delegations to the UN in New York – "doing some of the intellectual heavy-lifting for member states" (ibid.).

The role of civil society and NGOs in norm change processes is perhaps the facet that has been most investigated in international relations theory. Margaret E. Keck and Kathryn Sikkink have explored and highlighted the role of transnational advocacy networks (1998), Charli R. Carpenter has shown how certain NGOs can steer the agenda of a wider network (2011), and Evans and Thakur have underscored the important role civil society has played in the R2P process, noting the establishment and efforts of the Global Centre for R2P, the International Coalition for the Responsibility to Protect, and the Asia-Pacific Centre for the Responsibility to Protect (Evans and Thakur 2013, 202).

Member states

A few UN member states were at the helm during the R2P process. Canada sponsored the work of the ICISS, and the UK, Australia, Norway, and Sweden were among those that supported think tanks and academic circles to undertake research, in parallel with vigorous activism at the UN. Support from non-permanent members of the Security Council like Canada and Norway for expanded mandates for peacekeeping also helped persuade the United States, according to CIC director Bruce Jones (Jones and Forman 2010, 15). Major funders of the report were Canada, as well as Switzerland, the UK, and various philanthropic foundations.

84 *Linked ecologies and R2P*

Regional consultations

The process was a highly inclusive and participatory process. The Commission itself met five times in Ottawa, Canada; New Delhi, India; Maputo, Mozambique; Wakefield, Canada; and Brussels, Belgium. Another eleven regional roundtables and national consultations took place in Ottawa; Geneva; London; Maputo; Washington, DC; Santiago de Chile; Cairo; Paris; New Delhi; Beijing; and St Petersburg and aimed at engaging "members of the academic community and civil society" (Thakur et al. 2005, 199). According to Thakur, "The consultations were intended to take the issue beyond the confines of the Western liberal internationalism and ensure a broader consensus on the Commission's findings" (ibid., 199). Fifty pages of the report were devoted to summaries from these consultations (Weiss and Hubert 2001, 349–98). According to the ICISS report, the result was quite successful – "the text on which we have found consensus does reflect the shared views of all Commissioners as to what is politically achievable in the world as we know it today" (ICISS 2001, viii).

The high-level panel was composed of a multi-cultural blend of eminent personalities – statesmen, international diplomats, and academic heavyweights who had significant standing in the international community and could provide legitimacy to the R2P principle. This is a common element for all the high-level panels the UN has established to advance new ideas and norms: "Their names lend credibility to an idea which might otherwise have appeared utopian or fanciful" (Annan 2007, xii). Also Kittikhoun and Weiss (2011) argue that these panels influence UN ideas and policies. This was particularly important with R2P: the concept had been accused of being a Western norm, and it became important to defend what was argued to be its universality: "Although western governments were central in forming the concept, and it was based on the failures of Bosnia and Rwanda, the term was coined by Francis Deng, an African scholar and senior UN official" (Gowan and Jones 2010, 315). Proponents of R2P also never fail to mention that the Constitutive Act of the African Union also supported the concept (African Union [AU] 2000). Thakur, one of the members of the ICISS and a champion of the norm, argues that the norm also has roots in ancient Indian culture: "In India, Emperor Ashoka (3rd Century BC) inscribed the following message on a rock edict: 'this is my rule: government by the law, administration according to the law, gratification of my subjects under the law, and protection [sic] through the law'" (Wolpert, 1977, 66–7, cited in Thakur 2012, 3).

The Joint Office

In its work, the Joint Office intersects with all the aforementioned actors. It was led by Deng and Luck, two of the key individuals who had formed extensive networks with the other actors.[4] The Joint Office issued statements on country situations, provided training to UN and member-state officials, and collaborated with partners – defined broadly, including UN funds, programs and agencies, regional and sub-regional organizations, and civil society organizations (UN 2012). It could gauge member-state interest in the norm, noting where resistance might originate; it worked to build capacity and knowledge among member states to galvanize support and create consensus; and it sought to refine conceptual thinking around the norm and its three pillars. Interestingly, in addition to serving as special advisor on R2P, Ed Luck was also the vice president of the International Peace Institute, IPI. His UN post did not include a salary or funding for an office, so the IPI was instrumental in providing support to the special advisor to perform his tasks.[5]

With donor funding from a range of states, the IPI established several task forces to implement the reform agenda of the 2005 outcome document and arranged a series of consultations in 2008. "The Task Forces were funded by Sweden, Norway, etc., as part of the Coping with Crisis Program. It was designed as a vehicle to push forward a lot of the recommendations of the outcome document" (interview with think tank official, New York, March 12, 2012). This process engaged more than sixty member states, ranging from Switzerland to South Africa. The UN was seen as unable to reform itself, so consultations in an informal setting were deemed necessary for advancing the reform agenda: "Funding IPA was seen as a way to fuel the machinery a little bit, if you took ambassadors to Greentree and had discussions you could move the position forward" (ibid.).[6] The final report from the consultations, presented to the UN secretary-general in 2009, "mirrored a lot of the first SG Report, but also went a bit further" (ibid.; IPI 2009). The IPI has a useful insider/outsider position, according to its former executive director, Thomas G. Weiss (interview with Thomas G. Weiss, April 2, 2012, San Diego.).[7] Examining how ideas and policies are formed in the UN, he supports the view that the 'revolving door' phenomenon is a key factor in norm change processes in the organization and that this phenomenon has increased "enormously over the last twenty years," significantly impacting the way the UN operates (Kittikhoun and Weiss 2011).

Advancing the principle inside and outside the UN

The chapter has detailed the participation and influence of several scholars on the process of establishing and adopting the R2P principle. This is in itself not a new finding: Thakur, Weiss, and others have pointed to the role of scholars in academia and think tanks in recent years (Thakur et al. 2005, Weiss and Thakur 2010, Evans and Thakur 2013). However, their analyses have used the existing conceptual frameworks to explain this interaction in theoretical terms. Weiss and Thakur talk of norm entrepreneurs, champions, and brokers in their analysis of the R2P process, seeing Annan as the norm entrepreneur, Canada as the norm champion, and the Commission as the norm broker (Weiss and Thakur 2010, 317–19). Although generally agreeing with this analysis, I would argue that there is a need to dig deeper and better understand the process and who the important actors were in analytical terms as well, aside from Annan, Canada, and the Commission.

86 *Linked ecologies and R2P*

Revolving doors, policy alliances, and R2P

First of all, as noted, Annan did indeed play an important role, but insufficient attention has been paid to how he included academia, think tanks, and other non-state actors in the process. He and the UN reached out to academia and other expert communities either because they lacked the capacity to deal with an issue substantively or as a tactical move to avoid divisive debates within the organization between member states.

Looking further, beyond the institutions, we can note a few key actors who were walking through revolving doors, as part of the high-level panel at one point and then moving to become part of the UN, advising the secretary-general. This was clear during the R2P process and has been evident also in other reform processes in the UN, most notably the process leading up to the 2005 World Summit, where the adoption of the R2P concept as a norm was on the agenda.

Evans and Thakur have admitted that although the ICISS report was purportedly a document that was the result of a series of inclusive consultations, it was still "an advocacy document, not the final word, and it succeeded admirably in its objective of producing an authoritative political response" (Evans and Thakur 2013, 203–4). Evans and Thakur hailed from the same region, and although Thakur is from India, he had lived in the Australian capital, Canberra, as the head of the Peace Research Centre at Australia National University from 1995 to 1998, prior to taking up his post as vice rector (peace and governance) at the United Nations University (UNU) in Tokyo in 1998 (Thakur 2007). Evans was Australian foreign minister from 1988 to 1996 (Evans 2012). Other members of the Commission also knew each other from previous interactions and across various environments and ecologies.

Such interaction between ecologies can stimulate debate and open up for different perspectives. Geographical and gender diversity can help strengthen the legitimacy of the outcome document. Moreover, the Commission had a research directorate that strengthened the knowledge base and supported the arguments of the commission. This knowledge base was not impartial, however: while it helped explore the concept, it did so in a general direction that supported adopting R2P.

Academic scholars can have a special 'straddling role,' having autonomy through their research, while at the same time attending to clients, including students in their own ecology (Larson 1977, 196) and customers of knowledge products in other ecologies. This also applies to staff at think tanks who perform varying degrees of independent research, while aiming to inform national and global policy processes as well (Stone 2013). Statesmen can also play this straddling, or go-between, role, mediating interests, ideas, and knowledge between different ecologies.

Conclusions

This chapter has examined the development of R2P and the interplay between various classes of actors, or linked ecologies, in this process. The process reveals important insights about how norms develop, and that a blend of constructivist and sociological theories can provide a conceptual framework to improve our understanding of how norms develop and change and which actors it may be relevant to follow. While constructivist theories have shown that international organizations (IOs) may act autonomously, these theories are less suited for explaining how processes of norm change occur, which actors are important, and what roles they play.

The sociology of professions, as presented here, can augment constructivist theorizing in this area, in part because the norms are advanced by linked ecologies rather than singular norm entrepreneurs – and this is a specific feature of norm change processes detailed in this book. Practice theory provides a tool for grasping the practices of informal alliances for policy change.

Weber's views on the organization of bureaucracy and the role of its officials have informed the theories of norm change developed by Finnemore, Sikkink, and Barnett, as well as thinking on how professions develop and change. The constructivist theories outlined in this book share several features, including the autonomy that IOs can display toward member states, the role of knowledge in developing authority for the organization and its officials on a topic, and how the UN secretary-general and others can act as norm entrepreneurs in promoting an agenda.

However, while rationalist and constructivist theories have emphasized how the organization is able to act autonomously from its member states, they have not sufficiently explored how staff members at various levels in the UN engage with other ecologies to advance change. This has led to a Pavlovian understanding of socialization and individual action in IOs with little explanatory power on individual and mid-level practices of norm transgression and change in IOs.

The sociology of professions theory shows that the UN secretary-general must perform a balancing act within his fiduciary responsibility and that the bureaucratic nature of the UN is important for understanding how norms change. In the area of peacekeeping, there is a continuous process of change underway through best practices and lessons learned, where the staff of the organization wields their expert authority in working for jurisdictional control of the field of peacekeeping. Using the theory of professions highlights the complementary nature of organizational and performative aspects; supplemented by the concepts of linked ecologies and revolving doors, this chapter has also accounted for how policy alliances are formed to promote principles like R2P. The chapter has supported the second hypothesis of the book, emphasizing the role of external actors in situations when basic norms clash, as evidenced in the tension between the norm of sovereignty and the norm of protecting civilians coming to the fore in the R2P process.

Member states, think tanks, and academic institutions are free to argue for whatever norm they want, but the secretary-general was repeatedly criticized during the UN reform process for overstepping his mandate. Reverting to Parsons, we could say that in the view of some member states, the secretary-general overstepped his fiduciary responsibility and mandate by advancing R2P. However, as shown in various quotes presented here, he was well aware of this danger and

88 *Linked ecologies and R2P*

deemed it within his mandate to pick up on emerging trends by using means like high-level panels, at times pushing the boundary of what the member states were ready to accept.

But while the secretary-general may have an important role advancing norms mature enough to be considered by UN member states, he is far from the only actor. The UN relies on donors, think tanks, and academic institutions to develop policy and analysis capacity. Fiduciary responsibility for the values of the UN Charter in general, and the R2P norm in this case, is not solely the responsibility of the secretary-general and the staff of the UN – it is shared in equal measure by academic institutions, advocacy NGOs, think tanks, and member states that have been championing a norm. This gives these actors a more central role than previously argued in norm evolution or codification processes in the UN. We should not underestimate the effect of the work of a few special individuals, think tanks, and dedicated foreign ministry staff in advancing R2P. Within a close-knit circle, the same persons may shift roles, from advancing a norm and issuing reports from prominent think tanks and academic institutions with the support of a few member states, to serving on UN high-level panels or acting as secretariat to these panels. The 'revolving doors' phenomenon is clearly evident here. Using the linked ecologies framework of the sociology of professions makes it possible to grasp this phenomenon also in terms of theory.

In this chapter, I have showed how think tanks and the academic community have been important in broadening the knowledge base for the R2P norm, staffing the research directorate of the Commission, supporting the secretary-general during the crucial period before the World Summit, and staffing the Joint Office. Regional consultations were also important in fostering consensus for R2P. Recently we have seen the Global South developing and advancing their understanding of how the norm should be understood and implemented. The initiative of Brazil to focus on how the norm is implemented – Responsibility while Protecting (RwP) – may in fact be the only way of saving the norm from an early demise after the Libya debacle. I return to Brazil and this question in chapter 5.

Notes

1 A previous and shorter version of this chapter was published as Karlsrud, John (2013) 'Responsibility to Protect and Theorising Normative Change in International Organisations: From Weber to the Sociology of Professions', *Global Responsibility to Protect*, 5 (1), pp. 3–27. The material is reprinted with permission from *Global Responsibility to Protect*/Brill. © Koninklijke Brill NV, Leiden, 2013.
2 In previous resolutions, for example, on the situation in Darfur, the Security Council did not use the phrase "responsibility to protect," but reaffirmed "*inter alia* the provisions of paragraphs 138 and 139 of the 2005 United Nations World Summit outcome document" (UNSC 2006, 1) and reaffirmed "responsibility of the Government of the Sudan, to protect civilians under threat of physical violence" (UNSC 2006, 6). Gareth Evans has argued that Darfur has continued to be a R2P situation (2008, 61).
3 From the CIC website: Dr Jones 'was Senior Advisor in the Office of the Secretary-General during the UN reform effort leading up to the World Summit 2005, and in the

same period was Acting Secretary of the Secretary-General's Policy Committee. In 2004/5, he was Deputy Research Director of the High-Level Panel on Threats, Challenges and Change. From 2000 until 2002 he was special assistant to the UN Special Coordinator for the Middle East peace process; and held assignments in the UN Interim Mission in Kosovo, and in the Office for the Coordination of Humanitarian Affairs' (NYU CIC 2011b).

4   In 2013, Adama Dieng of Senegal took over as special adviser on the prevention of genocide (UN 2013).
5   Luck has since returned to the academic world as a dean of the Kroc School at the University of California, San Diego.
6   Greentree is an estate in Manhasset, Long Island, New York, owned by the Greentree Foundation.
7   Weiss is now professor at the City University of New York.

References

Abbott, Andrew D. (2005) 'Linked Ecologies: States and Universities as Environments for Professions', *Sociological Theory*, 23 (3), pp. 245–74.

African Union (AU) (2000) *Constitutive Act of the African Union*, African Union, www. au2002.gov.za/docs/key_oau/au_act.htm. Accessed March 3, 2011.

Annan, Kofi A. (1999a) *Address to the General Assembly, UN Press Release SG/SM/7136 (20 September 1999)*. New York: United Nations.

Annan, Kofi A. (1999b) 'Two Concepts of Sovereignty', *Economist*, www.economist.com/ node/324795. Accessed September 4, 2013.

Annan, Kofi A. (2000) *We the Peoples: The Role of the United Nations in the 21st Century*. New York: United Nations.

Annan, Kofi A. (2005) 'A Glass At Least Half Full. 19 September 2005', *Wall Street Journal*, http://archive1.globalsolutions.org/programs/intl_instit/annan_oped.pdf. Accessed March 7, 2011.

Annan, Kofi A. (2007) 'Foreword', in Chesterman, Simon ed. *Secretary or General? The UN Secretary-General in World Politics*. Cambridge University Press, pp. xi–xiii.

Asia-Pacific Centre for the Responsibility to Protect (APCR2P) (2011) 'Asia-Pacific Centre for the Responsibility to Protect', Asia-Pacific Centre for the Responsibility to Protect, University of Queensland, http://r2pasiapacific.org/index.php?option=com_ content&task=view&id=8&Itemid=12. Accessed March 5, 2011.

Asia-Pacific Centre for the Responsibility to Protect (APCR2P) (2012) 'Global Responsibility to Protect Journal', University of Queensland, www.r2pasiapacific.org/ global-responsibility-to-protect-journal. Accessed December 28, 2012.

Ash, Timothy Garton (2011) 'Libya's Escalating Drama Reopens the Case for Liberal Intervention', *Guardian*, www.theguardian.com/commentisfree/2011/mar/03/ libya-escalating-drama-case-liberal-intervention. Accessed March 4, 2011.

Axworthy, Lloyd (2003) *Navigating a New World: Canada's Global Future*. Toronto: Alfred A. Knopf.

Bellamy, Alex J. (2009) *Responsibility to Protect: The Global Effort to End Mass Atrocities*. Cambridge: Polity.

Carpenter, R. Charli (2011) 'Vetting the Advocacy Agenda: Network Centrality and the Paradox of Weapons Norms', *International Organization*, 65 (1), pp. 69–102.

Chesterman, Simon (2011) ' "Leading from Behind": The Responsibility to Protect, the Obama Doctrine, and Humanitarian Intervention after Libya', *Ethics & International Affairs*, 25 (3), pp. 279–85.

90 Linked ecologies and R2P

City University of New York (CUNY) (2000) 'International Commission on Intervention and State Sovereignty; The Responsibility to Protect; Research Directorate', City University of New York, http://web.gc.cuny.edu/dept/rbins/ICISS/index.htm. Accessed September 27, 2012.

Cohen, Roberta and Francis M. Deng (1998) *Masses in Flight: The Global Crisis of Internal Displacement.* Washington, DC: Brookings Institution Press.

Deng, Francis M. (1996) *Sovereignty as Responsibility: Conflict Management in Africa.* Washington, DC: Brookings Institution.

Evans, Gareth J. (2008) *The Responsibility to Protect: Ending Mass Atrocity Crimes Once and for All.* Washington, DC: Brookings Institution Press.

Evans, Gareth (2012) 'Biography' [Personal blog], www.gevans.org/biography.html. Accessed December 29, 2012.

Evans, Gareth and Ramesh Thakur (2013) 'Correspondence: Humanitarian Intervention and the Responsibility to Protect (R2P)', *International Security*, 37, pp. 199–214.

Global Centre for the Responsibility to Protect (2009) *Implementing the Responsibility to Protect. The 2009 General Assembly Debate: An Assessment. GCR2P Report, August 2009.* New York: Global Centre for the Responsibility to Protect.

Global Centre for the Responsibility to Protect (2011) 'Open Statement on the Situation in Libya', Global Centre for the Responsibility to Protect, www.globalr2p.org/publications/48. Accessed September 4, 2013.

Gowan, Richard and Bruce D. Jones (2010) 'Conclusion: International Institutions and the Problems of Adaptation,' in Jones, Bruce D., Shepard Forman and Richard Gowan eds., *Cooperating for Peace and Security: Evolving Institutions and Arrangements in a Context of Changing U.S. Security Policy.* Cambridge: Cambridge University Press, pp. 311–19.

Hubert, Don (2000) *The Landmine Ban: A Case Study in Humanitarian Advocacy.* Providence, RI: Thomas J. Watson Jr. Institute for International Studies.

International Coaltion for the Responsibility to Protect (ICRtoP) (2012a) 'International Coaltion for the Responsibility to Protect', International Coaltion for the Responsibility to Protect, www.responsibilitytoprotect.org/. Accessed August 29, 2012.

International Coaltion for the Responsibility to Protect (ICRtoP) (2012b) 'United Nations Informal Discussion on "Responsibility While Protecting". 21 February 2012', International Coalition for the Responsibility to Protect, www.responsibilitytoprotect.org/index.php/component/content/article/35-r2pcs-topics/4002-informal-discussion-on-brazils-concept-of-responsibility-while-protecting. Accessed January 1, 2013.

International Commission on Intervention and State Sovereignty (ICISS) (2001) *The Responsibility to Protect: Report of the International Commission on Intervention and State Sovereignty.* Ottawa: International Development Research Centre.

International Peace Institute (IPI) (2009) *Conflict Prevention and the Responsibility to Protect. Task Forces on Strengthening Multilateral Security Capacity, No. 7.* New York: International Peace Institute.

Johnstone, Ian (2007) 'The Secretary-General as Norm Entrepreneur: Secretary or General?' in Chesterman, Simon ed. *Secretary or General? The UN Secretary-General in World Politics.* Cambridge: Cambridge University Press, pp. 123–38.

Johnstone, Ian (2008) 'Law-Making through the Operational Activities of International Organizations', *George Washington International Law Review*, 40, pp. 87–122.

Johnstone, Ian (2010) 'Normative Evolution at the UN: Impact on Operational Imperatives', in Jones, Bruce D., Shepard Forman and Richard Gowan eds., *Cooperating for Peace and Security: Evolving Institutions and Arrangements in a Context of Changing U.S. Security Policy.* Cambridge: Cambridge University Press, pp. 187–214.

Jones, Bruce D. and Shepard Forman (2010) Introduction', in Jones, Bruce D., Shepard Forman and Richard Gowan eds., *Cooperating for Peace and Security: Evolving Institutions and Arrangements in a Context of Changing U.S. Security Policy.* Cambridge: Cambridge University Press.

Karlsrud, John (2013) 'Responsibility to Protect and Theorising Normative Change in International Organisations: From Weber to the Sociology of Professions', *Global Responsibility to Protect,* 5 (1), pp. 3–27.

Keck, Margaret E. and Kathryn Sikkink (1998) *Activists Beyond Borders: Advocacy Networks in International Politics.* Ithaca, NY: Cornell University Press.

Ki-moon, Ban (2011) 'Remarks at Breakfast Roundtable with Foreign Ministers on "The Responsibility to Protect: Responding to Imminent Threats of Mass Atrocities" [as prepared for delivery]', United Nations, www.un.org/apps/news/infocus/sgspeeches/search_full.asp?statID=1325. Accessed December 28, 2012.

Kittikhoun, Anoulak and Thomas G. Weiss (2011) 'The Myth of Scholarly Irrelevance for the United Nations', *International Studies Review,* 13 (1), pp. 18–23.

Larson, Magali S. (1977) *The Rise of Professionalism: A Sociological Analysis.* Berkeley: University of California Press.

Libya, Muhammad min (2011) 'Libya Is United in Popular Revolution – Please Don't Intervene', *Guardian,* www.theguardian.com/commentisfree/cifamerica/2011/mar/01/libya-revolution-no-fly-zone. Accessed March 4, 2011.

Lie, Jon Harald Sande (2008) 'Protection of Civilians, the Responsibility to Protect and Peace Operations', *NUPI Report: Responsibility to Protect. No. 4–2008.* Oslo: Norwegian Institute of International Affairs (NUPI).

Milne, Seumas (2011) 'Intervention in Libya Would Poison the Arab Revolution', *Guardian,* www.theguardian.com/commentisfree/2011/mar/02/intervention-libya-poison-arab-revolution. Accessed March 4, 2011.

Mühlen-Schulte, Arthur (2012) 'Evolving Discourses of Protection', in Sending, Ole J. and Benjamin de Caravalho eds., *The Protection of Civilians in UN Peacekeeping.* Baden-Baden, Germany: Nomos Verlagsgesellschaft, pp. 25–46.

New York University Center on International Cooperation (NYU CIC) (2011a) 'About', New York University Center on International Cooperation, www.cic.nyu.edu/about.html. Accessed August 12, 2011.

New York University Center on International Cooperation (NYU CIC) (2011b) 'Bruce Jones', New York University Center on International Cooperation, www.cic.nyu.edu/staff/brucejones.html. Accessed March 5, 2011.

Norwegian Institute of International Affairs (NUPI) (2006) *A Fork in the Road or a Roundabout? A Narrative of the UN Reform Process 2003–2005.* Oslo: Norwegian Institute of International Affairs.

Orford, Anne (2011) *International Authority and the Responsibility to Protect.* Cambridge: Cambridge University Press.

Rieff, David (2011) 'R2P, R.I.P.', *New York Times,* www.nytimes.com/2011/11/08/opinion/r2p-rip.html?_r=1&pagewanted=all. Accessed December 29, 2012.

Rivlin, Benjamin and Leon Gordenker (1993) *The Challenging Role of the UN Secretary-General: Making "the Most Impossible Job in the World" Possible.* Westport, CT: Praeger.

Stamnes, Eli (2008) *Operationalising the Preventive Aspects of the Responsibility to Protect.* Oslo: Norwegian Institute of International Affairs (NUPI).

Stedman, Stephen J. (2007) 'UN Transformation in an Era of Soft Balancing', *International Affairs,* 83 (5), pp. 933–44.

92 Linked ecologies and R2P

Stedman, Stephen J. (2012) 'Profile: Stephen J. Stedman', Stanford University, http://cisac.stanford.edu/people/stephenjstedman/. Accessed February 29, 2012.

Stone, Diane (2013) '"Shades of Grey": The World Bank, Knowledge Networks and Linked Ecologies of Academic Engagement', *Global Networks*, 13, pp. 241–60.

Sydney Morning Herald (2011) 'South Africa Slams Libya Strikes before Gaddafi Talks', *Sydney Morning Herald*, www.smh.com.au/world/south-africa-slams-libya-strikes-before-gaddafi-talks-20110530–1fbe5.html. Accessed August 30, 2011.

Thakur, Ramesh C. (2006) *The United Nations, Peace and Security: From Collective Security to the Responsibility to Protect.* Cambridge: Cambridge University Press.

Thakur, Ramesh C. (2007) 'Vita: Ramesh Chandra Thakur', Centre for International Governance Innovation, www.cigionline.org/sites/default/files/RThakurCV.pdf. Accessed Deember 29, 2012.

Thakur, Ramesh C. (2011) 'We Have a Duty to Stop Libyan Slaughter', *Star*, www.thestar.com/opinion/editorialopinion/article/946306—we-have-a-duty-to-stop-libyan-slaughter. Accessed March 3, 2011.

Thakur, Ramesh C. (2012) *Emerging Powers and the Responsibility to Protect after Libya.* Oslo: Norwegian Institute of International Affairs.

Thakur, Ramesh, Andrew F. Cooper and John English (eds.) (2005) *International Commissions and the Power of Ideas.* Tokyo: United Nations University Press.

UN (1999a) *A/54/549. Report of the Secretary-General Pursuant to General Assembly Resolution 53/35: The Fall of Srebrenica, 15 November 1999.* New York: United Nations.

UN (1999b) *S/1999/1257. Report of the Independent Inquiry into the Actions of the United Nations during the 1994 Genocide in Rwanda, 16 December 1999.* New York: United Nations.

UN (2000) *Report of the Panel on United Nations Peace Operations.* New York: United Nations.

UN (2004) *A More Secure World: Our Shared Responsibility: Report of the High-Level Panel on Threats, Challenges and Change.* New York: United Nations.

UN (2005) *A/59/2005. In Larger Freedom: Towards Development, Security and Human Rights for All. Report of the Secretary-General, 25 March 2005.* New York: United Nations.

UN (2007) 'Appointment Confirmed of UN Special Adviser on Responsibility to Protect', United Nations, www.un.org/apps/news/story.asp?NewsID=25010&Cr=appoint&Cr1=. Accessed February 29, 2012.

UN (2009a) *Concept Note on Responsibility to Protect Populations from Genocide, War Crimes, Ethnic Cleansing and Crimes against Humanity.* New York: Office of the President of the General Assembly, United Nations.

UN (2009b) *GA/63/677. Implementing the Responsibility to Protect. Report of the Secretary-General, 12 January 2009.* New York: United Nations.

UN (2012) 'Office of the Special Adviser on the Prevention of Genocide', United Nations, www.un.org/en/preventgenocide/adviser/index.shtml. Accessed February 29, 2012.

UN (2013) 'Office of the Special Adviser on the Prevention of Genocide', UN, www.un.org/en/preventgenocide/adviser/adviser.shtml. Accessed September 11, 2013.

United Nations General Assembly (UNGA) (2005) *A/RES/60/1. 2005 World Summit Outcome.* New York: United Nations General Assembly.

United Nations Security Council (UNSC) (2006) *'Resolution 1706', Security Council Resolution, UN doc. S/RES/1706, 31 August 2006.* New York: United Nations.

United Nations Security Council (UNSC) (2011a) *'Resolution 1970', Security Council Resolution, UN doc. S/RES/1970, 26 February 2011.* New York: United Nations.

United Nations Security Council (UNSC) (2011b) *'Resolution 1973', Security Council Resolution, UN doc. S/RES/1973, 17 March 2011.* New York: United Nations.

United Nations Security Council (UNSC) (2011c) *'Resolution 1975', Security Council Resolution, UN doc. S/RES/1975, 30 March 2011.* New York: United Nations.

United Nations Secretary-General (UNSG) (2011) *A/65/877–S/2011/393. The Role of Regional and Sub-Regional Arrangements in Implementing the Responsibility to Protect, 27 June 2011.* New York: United Nations.

Weiss, Thomas G. (2000) 'The Politics of Humanitarian Ideas', *Security Dialogue*, 31 (1), pp. 11–23.

Weiss, Thomas G. (2007) 'The Oral History Interview of Kofi A. Annan, 29 April 2002', *The Complete Oral History Transcripts from UN Voices* [CD-ROM]. New York: United Nations Intellectual History Project.

Weiss, Thomas G. and Don Hubert (2001) *The Responsibility to Protect: Research, Bibliography, Background. Supplementary Volume to the Report of the International Commission on Intervention and State Sovereignty.* Ottawa: International Research Development Centre.

Weiss, Thomas G. and Ramesh Thakur (2010) *Global Governance and the UN.* Bloomington; Indianapolis: Indiana University Press.

Wheeler, Nicholas J. (2008) 'Operationalising the Responsibility to Protect. The Continuing Debate over Where Authority Should Be Located for the Use of Force', *NUPI Report: Responsibility to Protect. No. 3–2008.* Oslo: Norwegian Institute of International Affairs.

Wolpert, Stanley (1977) *A New History of India.* New York: Oxford University Press.

5 Linked ecologies and revolving doors for norm change in peacekeeping operations

The development of the Integrated Missions concept

Action 4: In the field, the Special Representative of the Secretary-General will have authority over all UN entities.

Kofi Annan (UN 1997, 39)

There is a gaping hole in the United Nations institutional machinery: no part of the United Nations system effectively addresses the challenge of helping countries with the transition from war to lasting peace.

Kofi Annan (UN 2005, 2)

Introduction[1]

When Kofi Annan presented his program for reform in 1997, he started on an endeavor that would last for his entire tenure. Central to his exertions were the efforts to make the UN work in a more integrated way on the ground in conflict-ravaged countries. As the first quote in this chapter shows, he strengthened the powers of the special representatives of the secretary-general on the ground to have authority over UN force commanders, civilian police commissioners, resident coordinators, and humanitarian coordinators. By this action "the Special Representative will ensure that the efforts of the different components of the system are mutually reinforcing" (UN 1997, 39). But the decision was controversial; in the ensuing years, the debate on how and to what extent the UN should be integrated continued with unabated strength. By 2005, some progress had been made, but as the second quote shows, there was still a strong wish to integrate the UN further.

This chapter examines the process of the integrated missions concept in the UN, focusing particularly on the period from 2003 to 2007. It analyzes the debate around the concept of integrated missions as an example of how norms, principles, and concepts are advanced in international organizations (IOs) and seeks to identify the principal actors of these processes. The second part of the chapter, honing in on the role of linked ecologies and the 'revolving doors' phenomenon, provides a more detailed analysis, establishing key features evident also in other norm change processes in the international system.

In the area of peacekeeping, the UN has had to rely on funding and support from donor governments to develop doctrine and best practices since the end of the Cold War. Staff members has moved through 'revolving doors' – as practitioners in IOs, activists in non-governmental organizations (NGOs), researchers at think tanks, and policy-makers in government institutions. Middle powers and donor governments like the UK, Canada, the Netherlands, Norway, and Sweden have pushed the development of doctrine for peacekeeping, with dedicated government offices having peacekeeping on the agenda and funding the development of policy reports, enabling discussions around new concepts and recommendations, and even developing best-practices positions on peacekeeping at UN headquarters (Benner et al. 2007, Benner and Rotmann 2008, Benner et al. 2011).

This chapter takes a closer look at this phenomenon, focusing on the integrated missions process. I begin with a brief introduction to what the integrated missions concept is and why it can be studied as an important norm change process and then proceed with a historical narrative of how the concept was established and put into practice, focusing on the period from 2003–7. We will follow the development and the follow-up process of the *Report on Integrated Missions* (Eide et al. 2005) closely. The chapter examines the role of Norway, asking whether Norway can be seen as a norm entrepreneur employing a linked ecology strategy, working with the UN Department of Peacekeeping Operations (DPKO) and other parts of the UN, as well as with scholars in think tanks and academic institutions. Next, eight features of international norm change processes are identified and presented. Finally, I conclude that, although the integrated missions process cannot be considered a success, it is a useful case study for better understanding processes of norm change in the international system in general and in UN peacekeeping in particular. Here I highlight the contribution of this chapter in terms of identifying the key features of these norm change processes. The chapter also points to the theoretical implications of these features – that more actors have agency in norm change processes, including research institutes, think tanks, and academia, and that change processes are often driven from the working level up.

Evolution of the integrated missions concept

An 'integrated mission' is a peacekeeping mission in which the UN seeks to help countries in the transition from war to lasting peace or to deal with a similarly complex situation that requires a system-wide UN response, through subsuming actors and approaches within an overall political-strategic crisis management framework (Eide et al. 2005). This means that the UN actors normally present on the ground and part of the UN Country Team – such as the UN Development Programme (UNDP), United Nations Children's Fund (UNICEF), World Food Programme (WFP), United Nations High Commissioner for Refugees (UNHCR), and other programs, funds, and agencies – are integrated with a peacekeeping mission that is deployed once a mandate has been given by the UN Security Council. This is done under the leadership of a special representative of the secretary-general (SRSG), who will also serve as head of the peacekeeping mission with two deputy SRSGs (DSRSG) under his or her command. In an integrated mission, one of these will normally be a triple-hatted DSRSG who will also be the UN

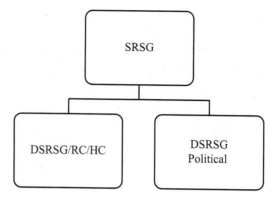

Figure 5.1 Organization of leadership tasks in integrated missions

resident coordinator (RC) for the UN system. The same person will also normally be the UN humanitarian coordinator (HC). I return to this in more detail later in the chapter.

The period from 2003–7 was selected for study because it coincided with the latter part of the reform agenda of former UN secretary-general Kofi Annan, who ended his second term in 2006. It was Annan who initiated the integrated missions process to improve the provision of UN support in post-conflict countries, across organizational silos. This chapter focuses on the process around the *Report on Integrated Missions* (Eide et al. 2005), from which the opening quote is taken. We will examine the composition of the team who wrote the report and the follow-up process initiated and funded by Norway.

The report was prepared for the expanded UN Executive Committee on Humanitarian Affairs. It identified three dilemmas: 1) The "contraposition of the *partiality* involved in supporting a political transition process as opposed to the continued need for *impartiality* (or neutrality in providing certain forms of humanitarian assistance" (ibid., 7); 2) The recurring tension between the UN's mandate to further human rights and seek an end to impunity and the need for a stable peace agreement; and 3) The dilemma of local ownership, where there is a tension between the universalist aspirations of the statebuilding agenda of the UN and other international actors and the frequent reluctance to relinquish power and resources among transitional government leaders, warlords, and other central actors (ibid., 7–8).

The integrated missions concept can be seen as an organizational reform process, but its norm implications were also significant. Those opposed to the concept wanted humanitarian assistance to continue to be impartial and feared that humanitarian aid could be securitized and politicized through integration. Supporters of the concept wanted the various pillars of the UN to work more closely together, for better efficiency and delivery to host populations, and to avoid having the different pillars working at cross-purposes.

The dilemmas mentioned here are very real and have been discussed at length in the academic literature and in policy circles, so my chief aim here is not to try to add more to these discussions. Instead, I ask whether and how change was achieved and by whom. But first a short historical narrative.

Establishing the integrated missions concept

With the expansion of UN involvement in internal conflicts after the end of the Cold War, the question of how the different parts of the UN should work together on the ground quickly surfaced. In the years prior to becoming secretary-general in 1997, Kofi Annan had a series of postings that gave him clear insight into the challenges confronting the UN within this area. Kofi Annan served as assistant secretary-general (ASG) for human resources management and security coordinator for the UN system (1987–90), ASG for programme planning, budget and finance, and controller (1990–2), and ASG for peacekeeping operations (PKOs) (March 1992–February 1993), later promoted to under-secretary-general (USG) (March 1993–December 1996) for the same PKOs. His tenure coincided with the unprecedented growth of UN peacekeeping operations, with a total deployment at its peak in 1995 of almost 70,000 military and civilian personnel. After the Dayton Agreement establishing a peace agreement for Bosnia and Herzegovina was signed, he also served as special representative of the secretary-general to the former Yugoslavia (November 1995–March 1996). On taking up the post as secretary-general, he launched a reform program that sought, *inter alia*, to improve the effectiveness and efficiency of the UN on the ground in countries where peacekeeping operations were deployed, to better serve host populations (UN 1997). The peacekeeping and special political missions are headed by special or personal representatives of the secretary-general, and these were to "have authority over all UN entities" (UN 1997, 39). It was the combination of the peacekeeping mission and the other UN entities that would constitute an 'integrated mission.'

Following the decision on better integration of peacekeeping missions with the other UN entities on the ground, the secretary-general issued a *Note of Guidance* in 2000 (United Nations Secretary-General [UNSG] 2000), where the initial statement – the "SRSG will have authority over all UN entities" (UN 1997, 39) – was significantly watered down. Instead, the guidance merely gave the SRSG/RSG the authority to establish the political framework and the responsibility for providing overall leadership to the UN Country Team, which is composed of the UN agencies, funds, and programs present in the country in question. The function of direct authority vis-à-vis the UN resident coordinator, who has responsibility for all development activities undertaken by UN agencies in a country, and vis-à-vis the UN humanitarian coordinator, who has responsibility for all humanitarian activities undertaken by UN entities in a country, as well as coordinating with other humanitarian actors, was diminished and delegated to UN HQ, where decisions would be taken on a case-by-case basis: "The RC/HC will, whenever feasible, serve as Deputy Special Representative/Representative of the Secretary-General, on the basis of a decision at UN Headquarters" (UNSG 2000, 2). As a general guideline, the RC should "keep the SRSG/RSG informed . . . information-sharing among the SRSG/RSG and the RC/HC is essential" (ibid., 1).

98   *Linked ecologies and revolving doors*

With these rather loose and ad-hoc guidelines, integration of UN activities on the country level assumed many different forms in the ensuing years. Some observers have noted that the idea was perhaps turned into policy too fast: "At some point the idea of IM [integrated missions] was moved to OO [Office of Operations] before the idea had been experimented and tried out – it became doctrine. In peacekeeping, things leap from concept to doctrine very fast" (interview with UN official, October 2, 2012, Oslo).

The issuance of the guidance coincided with the second large expansion of UN peacekeeping operations after the Cold War. From 1999 and onward, the UN deployed new missions to countries like Timor Leste, Sierra Leone, Sudan, Haiti, Liberia, and others. By 2004, troop deployment numbers had regained the previous high of the 1990s and kept climbing. By 2006, there were twenty DPKO-led operations in progress around the world, with more than 100,000 troops and civilians deployed.

According to Espen Barth Eide, who was one of the two lead authors of the *Report on Integrated Missions*, the work "started with the reform agenda of Kofi Annan in 1997 and it coincided with the broader system-wide coherence reform agenda during 2000s" (interview with Espen Barth Eide, June 20, 2011, Oslo).[2] Jan Egeland, the UN under-secretary-general for the Office for the Coordination of Humanitarian Affairs (OCHA) at the time, says that the integrated missions concept was based on the Brahimi Report, whose recommendations were in the process of being turned into active policy (interview with Jan Egeland, May 29, 2011, Oslo). The Brahimi Report, issued in 2000, became the main reference for the reform process for peacekeeping operations during the next decade. While the report did not mention integrated missions as such, it underscored the need to harness all the resources of the UN to consolidate peace and re-establish stable and legitimate governments capable of providing the essential services to their populations (UN 2000a, 12). Egeland feels there was deep common agreement within the UN that the "UN pulled in too many directions and the result was unclear" (ibid.). The integrated missions concept was

> in the extension of the One UN concept, where the RC and HC should have a stronger role and the UN should be co-located. The SRSG should coordinate military, political, development and humanitarian efforts. Opposed to integration were first and foremost some of the development agencies, and even more strongly some NGOs. The most fundamental criticism came from the IASC [Inter-agency Standing Committee] where the NGO alliance was deeply opposed. MSF [Médecins Sans Frontières] said that they would break off contact with the UN if integration went too far.
>
> (ibid.)

From 2003, all missions were to be integrated in the field, but, according to Egeland, "this was a controversial move by the SG" (ibid.). In the organization, it was felt that "one of the problems was that it was a DPKO-focused perspective" (interview with think tank official, May 26, 2011, Oslo). The report was thus

Linked ecologies and revolving doors 99

initiated as a way of consulting with the other agencies as well as field operations, so as to reach a common understanding of the concept. On the ground, integration was interpreted in many different ways: a team that could consult with the organizations and document the practices that had evolved could also help inform the policy debate in New York and Geneva as well as ground it in field-level realities. Eide explained that they "found that the practices on the ground in many cases were far more advanced than the policy debate in New York" (interview with Espen Barth Eide). However, they also saw that there

> was a tension between the 'old' and 'new' UN, i.e. the existing funds, agencies and programmes on the ground and a peacekeeping mission. The 'old' often have a closer relationship to the host government, while the peacekeeping mission comes in with a lot of resources and insists on impartiality.
>
> (ibid.)

Practices in the field varied widely, perhaps due to the loose guidance on the topic. For example, both Egeland and Eide mentioned the discrepancies between the neighboring countries of Sierra Leone and Liberia. In Sierra Leone, SRSG Alan Doss was seen as able to achieve more integration and to set an example for other countries, whereas SRSG Klein in Liberia had great difficulties in achieving integration with the humanitarian organizations (ibid.).

While some of the reasons for the lack of integration were substantive, such as the fear among humanitarian actors of losing their impartiality, others were rooted in internal UN politics and turf battles. This came to the fore not only in the field (ibid.), but also at headquarters:

> Both mission and UNCT [United Nations Country Team] personnel pointed out to the Study Team that some of the limitations to integration in the field actually flowed from the fact that headquarters itself remain fragmented. Frequent turf battles in HQ were an example cited by many as a constraint on more effective integration, beginning with the prospect of system-wide planning processes. It was argued that the actors in the field couldn't be expected to solve these issues on their own while receiving contradictory signals from their respective headquarters.
>
> (Eide et al. 2005, 18)

A research team was compiled in 2003/2004. According to Eide, the initiative for undertaking the study and embarking on a process on this topic started following a personal initiative taken by Jean-Marie Guéhenno (head of UN DPKO from 2000–8), Jan Egeland (head of UN OCHA 2003–6), and the UN Development Group under the leadership of Mark Malloch Brown, head of UNDP (ibid.). Team members were selected by David Harland, who was the head of the Peacekeeping Doctrine and Best Practices Unit at UN DPKO, and Mark Bowden, the head of policy at UN OCHA. According to Egeland, it was mainly these two who proposed the involvement of the Norwegian Institute of International Affairs (NUPI) (ibid.).

100 *Linked ecologies and revolving doors*

The team was led by Espen Barth Eide, who was then director of the UN Programme at NUPI and a former deputy minister of foreign affairs, and Randolph Kent, a former UN humanitarian coordinator in Somalia. The study was an instrument intended to "flesh out the SG guide on SRSGs" and was based on two individuals – "Randolph Kent had been an HC, and academically engaged, and DPKO nominated Espen [Barth Eide] because of his academic track record" (telephone interview with senior UN official, September 3, 2012). Not surprisingly, some of these individuals were already acquainted. Mark Bowden and David Harland had previously worked with each other in Geneva, and Randolph Kent "had known Mark since the mid-80s since the Ethiopian crisis. Mark was with Save the Children when I was the UN, and we kept bumping into each other, for example in Rwanda" (telephone interview with Randolph Kent, September 7, 2012, London). Randolph Kent notes that he "knew Harland as well, I was in New York after Rwanda in 1996–7, and I met David then when he was with peacekeeping" (ibid.). Eide had a long series of publications on peacekeeping and had worked on the research team that provided input to the secretary-general's High-Level Panel on Threats, Challenges and Change from 2003–4 (Ministry of Foreign Affairs [MFA] Norway 2012). He thus had frequent contact with UN officials in various parts of the organization, as well as with other researchers working on these topics.

The team visited five countries in 2004 to assess how integration was working in practice and to record challenges and best practices: Burundi, Côte d'Ivoire, the Democratic Republic of Congo (DRC), Liberia, and Sierra Leone. The other countries with peacekeeping missions was covered by desk studies and interviews (Eide et al. 2005, 47). The findings of the team were presented at a conference in Oslo in May 2005 (MFA Norway 2008).

Gradually, the resistance to integration subsided somewhat. Today it is generally accepted that a peacekeeping operation or special political mission is integrated with the other UN entities, the level of such integration depending on the political situation in the country. Egeland argues that he and OCHA managed to establish some principles – "OCHA fought through a few principles – and one of these I fought through: more violence and war – less integration, and more peacebuilding – more integration" (interview with Jan Egeland, May 29, 2011, Oslo). In practice this has meant that there has been less integration in countries like Afghanistan and Iraq, where the UN is supporting the extension of state authority of a host government that is perceived as a party to an ongoing war and has become one of the main targets of violence, and OCHA has developed specific guidance on this (Metcalfe et al. 2011, OCHA 2011, 2012). The situation is similar in DRC and the Sudan.

The follow-up process to the report on integrated missions

The report showed the wide range of practices in the field with regard to integration and how it was implemented; it noted some of the challenges as well as best practices; and it offered various recommendations. In terms of achieving the

Linked ecologies and revolving doors 101

policy goal of establishing integrated missions as the default option there was, however, still far to go. Norway decided to support a follow-up of the report and funded regional consultations in Beijing, Addis Ababa, Geneva, New York, Johannesburg, and Brussels during 2006 and 2007. These consultations ended with a two-day conference in Oslo in 2007, "Multidimensional and Integrated Peace Operations: Trends and Challenges" (MFA Norway 2008).

Throughout the process, Norway chose to engage in an informal manner and arranged consultations and workshops in all the regions of the world. This enabled states to discuss the issues in unceremonious settings and share their experiences. The consultation in Beijing yielded one somewhat surprising result: China could share its experiences in integrated responses to domestic natural crises, emphasizing the importance of integration in the domestic context (interview with Jostein Leiro, June 27, 2011, Oslo). Establishing buy-in to the concept of integration on the regional level before starting the policy debate at UN HQ in New York was essential to the success of the process, according to the interviewees.

Were the report and the follow-up process a success?

According to Espen Barth Eide and Jostein Leiro (the latter headed the UN Section at the Norwegian Ministry of Foreign Affairs during the follow-up process and was thus involved in the financial backing), the follow-up process was a resounding success. Leiro explained that there are only a few countries that are interested in conceptual change in the UN system and have diverted resources to build up knowledge about the organization in house as well as supporting research institutes and think tanks (ibid.). The continued engagement gave Norway the necessary know-how; that, combined with Norway's relatively large financial contributions to various UN entities, and perception as a relatively impartial state, left Norway well positioned to engage itself in policy change processes within the UN. Other countries have since launched similar policy processes with peacekeeping operations as the main focus, but these have been more formal than the follow-up process on integrated missions, according to Leiro (ibid.). For example the UK and France launched the "New Horizon" process in July 2009, suggesting areas for reform of UN peacekeeping operations (UN 2012).

The integrated missions concept was a clear and simple idea, Leiro explained, and while there was a considerable need and willingness to discuss the issue, there were relatively few arenas where the issue could be discussed in an open and informal manner. During the consultations, participation was at times surprisingly high and from a variety of backgrounds, which could indicate that the issue filled a vacuum. Concurrently with the consultations, the UN was drafting its doctrine for UN peacekeeping operations, and there was significant interest in the integrated missions concept within the UN as part of this policy reform process. However, internal processes at the UN often encounter various obstacles – turf battles, sticking to established positions, and so forth – so it was an advantage that

102 *Linked ecologies and revolving doors*

the integrated missions discussions took place outside the UN and in an informal setting.

Leiro also noted the need for a good network that could draw upon the various actors who are engaged in the issue and who need to contribute to and own the solution (interview with Jostein Leiro). Engaging these actors and involving them throughout the process will strengthen their ownership. Policy, practice, and academia should be involved and may contribute to connecting experiences and knowledge from different institutional backgrounds.

Another important factor mentioned by several of my respondents was the close relationship that had been established over time between the working-level staff in the various organizations. According to Egeland, it was David Harland (then head of DPKO Peacekeeping Doctrine and Best Practices Unit) and Mark Bowden (who held the equivalent position at UN OCHA Policy Development and Studies Branch) who suggested that Espen Barth Eide at NUPI and Randolph Kent be the main authors of the report (interview with Jan Egeland). The main authors were supported by Anja Kaspersen from NUPI and Karin von Hippel, who had worked with the UN and EU in Somalia and Kosovo. Eide was, as mentioned, then the head of the UN Programme at NUPI and had authored several publications on peacekeeping operations and other UN-related topics. Kent had served as the HC in Somalia, Kosovo, and Rwanda. With these backgrounds, they were able to identify other individuals who enjoyed credibility among the stakeholders and were seen as being open to taking the views of all the actors into consideration.

Norway played a significant role in the institutionalization of the integrated missions concept, taking part in the writing of the *Report on Integrated Missions* with two previous deputy ministers of foreign affairs in key positions – Espen Barth Eide as one of the key authors and Jan Egeland as the USG for OCHA at the time. Furthermore, Norway funded the follow-up process, which built more ownership for the concept among member states; among practitioners from the humanitarian, development, and peacekeeping domains; and among academic institutions and think tanks. But Norway could not succeed in institutionalizing the concept without building a policy alliance with the other stakeholders. A two-step process was devised: first, establishing working-level cooperation with the relevant UN organizations, research institutions, and UN missions in the field, and subsequently arranging regional consultations to ensure that sufficient know-how as well as ownership were established among all stakeholders.

However, others have held that, although the integrated missions concept now is a staple ingredient in most peacekeeping missions, the swift move from idea to doctrine without firm guidance on how the idea should be spelled out in practice resulted in a check-list approach. According to one respondent, "It went from a nice idea to a checklist SOP [standard operating procedure] and was caught in the HQ loop, dumbed down to what HQ departments can deal with" (interview with UN official, October 2, 2012, Oslo). This interviewee does not deny that there has "been some evolution after that in the field" but holds that "the structural re-engineering is sadly probably the most enduring feature of PKOs" after the establishment of the integrated missions concept (ibid.).

Linked ecologies and revolving doors   103

Norway as a norm entrepreneur for 'integrated missions'?

Again, it could be useful to revert back to Finnemore and Sikkink and see whether their concept of norm entrepreneur can be useful when analyzing the role of Norway in the integrated missions process. Using the analytical framework developed by Finnemore and Sikkink, one can argue that Norway has played a significant role in the institutionalization of the integrated missions concept – being involved in the *Report on Integrated Missions* with one of the key authors; having Jan Egeland as the USG for OCHA at the time; and funding the follow-up process, which built more ownership for the concept among member states; practitioners from the humanitarian, development, and peacekeeping domains; and academic institutions and think tanks.

According to Finnemore and Sikkink, powerful states are particularly important in the process of a norm's adoption and dissemination – something they term as a "norm cascade" (1998, 895). If accepted as a new norm, the norm will, through the 'cascade' stage, become institutionalized and codified through establishment of best practices, rules, and soft or hard law. However, the integration missions process falls outside the categories of Finnemore and Sikkink. On the one hand, it could be considered as a norm at the 'emergence' stage, being actively promoted and debated. On the other hand, since it has been adopted and put into practice by the UN, one could argue that the norm has reached the 'cascade' stage. Nevertheless, the concept is still vigorously discussed and has remained extremely controversial in some circles, within the International Committee of the Red Cross and Médecins Sans Frontières in particular. Including OCHA as one of the main sponsors of the process and of the report, and making an effort to consult with humanitarian actors, can be seen as efforts to co-opt these actors into accepting the integrated missions concept. The co-optation strategy also depended on scholars and independent studies to lend weight to the process.

Linked ecologies and revolving doors

Only slowly has UN peacekeeping developed in-house capacity to formulate policy guidance. For decades, Ralph Bunche, Brian Urquhart, and the other 'old boys' in UN peacekeeping were the "living institutional memory of peacekeeping" (Benner et al. 2011, 3). When Jean-Marie Guéhenno took over at the helm of UN DPKO, there was an almost complete lack of standard operating procedures and other features of a modern bureaucracy. Guéhenno headed the DPKO from 2000 to 2008, a period that coincided with a period of extensive development of the policy framework for UN peacekeeping.

The Brahimi Report had lamented the lack of a learning cycle in UN peacekeeping (UN 2000a, 39) and had recommended that the "Lessons Learned Unit should be strengthened and moved into the DPKO Office of Operations" (UN 2000a, xiii). Some months later, Kofi Annan appointed Guéhenno and asked member states for additional financing for the new Peacekeeping Doctrine and Best Practices Unit but kept the unit in the office of Guéhenno so that he could

104 *Linked ecologies and revolving doors*

"personally oversee its development" (UN 2000b, 25). This new unit had an additional five positions and was expected to develop generic guidelines as well as support operations with new guidelines responding to specific needs:

> Greater emphasis would be placed on the development of a multidimensional doctrine and guidelines that field operations and Headquarters task forces could draw upon to solve problems, to adopt best practices and to avoid repeating past mistakes. The Unit must also be able to respond to the needs of peacekeeping missions in areas where new guidelines are required and to ensure that best-practice innovations developed in one mission are transferred to other comparable operations.
>
> (UN 2000b, 25)

Guéhenno secured additional funds for the unit from several member states, including the UK, Canada, and Norway (Benner et al. 2011, 41), and appointed David Harland as the head of the new unit. Harland had been a co-author of the 1999 Srebrenica report together with Salman Ahmed, who "became Guéhenno's Special Assistant and a key figure in the implementation of reform" (Benner et al. 2011).

Linked ecologies

The integrated missions report was commissioned at a time when UN engagement with the external environments of think tanks, NGOs, research institutes, and academia was at a high point. The reform agenda under Secretary-General Kofi Annan was achieving momentum, and the High-Level Panel on Threats, Challenges and Change submitted its report, *A More Secure World: Our Shared Responsibility*, in December 2004 (UN 2004). In parallel, the Millennium Project, led by Jeffrey Sachs at Columbia University, submitted *Investing in Development: A Practical Plan to Achieve the Millennium Development Goals* in January 2005 (Millennium Project 2005). The team for the integrated missions report was hired in October 2004 (Eide 2006).

David Harland was seen as the 'brain' behind Best Practices and the man "who breathed life into the unit and reached outside the organization" (interview with UN official, October 2, 2012, Oslo). In addition, Guéhenno was positive to engaging with actors outside the UN: "Guéhenno was very much about the broader policy environment, ever since then it has been chipped away at" (ibid.). Linking up with academia and other actors outside of the UN was part of a "larger initiative driven from Secretary-General Annan's office who successively retained high-profile academics such as Andrew Mack (1998–2001) and Michal Doyle (2001–3) as Research Directors in his Executive Office" (Benner et al. 2011, 42).

Also Kieran Prendergast, the USG at UN Department of Political Affairs, was open toward the academic community. He was a central figure under Secretary-General Kofi Annan, leading the reform process: "Kieran Prendergast was quite helpful. Had a USG who was interested in policy and we could reach outside. Prendergast was the head of the whole reform process, it was quite a different approach to policy development then than now" (telephone interview with senior UN official, September 3, 2012).

Under Harland, "lower levels of doctrine development were outsourced to NGOs and think tanks" (interview with UN official, October 2, 2012, Oslo). One example of these issues was what kind of impact UN peacekeeping operations were making on local economies. The NGO Peace Dividend Trust was tasked with exploring this issue – "It concluded that PKOs added to inflationary pressures, but only in a very narrow sense" (ibid.).

In this book, I argue that an important dimension in developing policy guidance has been the interaction with member states, think tanks, academic institutes, NGOs, and international non-governmental organizations (INGOs). This interaction is most frequent on the working level, and the case study has shown that the working level indeed is particularly important (see also da Costa and Karlsrud 2013, Schia and Karlsrud 2013). Individuals on working levels such as David Harland establish connections with colleagues in other ecologies. This has increasingly been a feature of DPKO. During the integrated missions process, as well as other policy development processes, the DPKO Policy and Best Practices Service (PBPS) has frequently joined forces with think tanks, academia, and NGOs as well as member-state officials.

Interaction between different ecologies can open up for different perspectives, stimulate the policy debate, and expand the knowledge base that gradually progresses up to the member-state level over time. As explained by one officer in DPKO PBPS:

> Academics can analyze issues much more frankly, which allows for provocativeness and frankness. This is helpful for us – it is easier for someone external to say something, and this can be used to start a broader policy dialogue"
> (interview with UN DPKO officer, June 17, 2011, New York.).

Driving change from the working level up

The working-level participation ensured informed discussions and helped prevent the discussions from reverting to political and principled positions:

> It is crucial for the success of a policy process that long-term relationships are built with people in working level positions. In the case of the integrated missions process, David Harland, as head of the Best Practices section, Salman Ahmed and David Haeri were key interlocutors at the UN. Traditional politics often focus at the top level, but these individuals seldom have all the knowledge needed to understand the issues and will revert to political positions.
> (interview with Espen Barth Eide, June 20, 2011, Oslo)

Working-level engagement is important because it can help prevent the debate from circling back to principled positions. Participants can share their experiences and help conceptualize these together with others who have similar experiences. Further,

106 *Linked ecologies and revolving doors*

if there is agreement on pursuing a consultation process, it is the working-level officials, practitioners, and researchers who will follow up and do the legwork, in terms of providing input and, even more importantly, in terms of keeping in touch with the other ecologies and exchanging drafts. Third, working-level participants may eye opportunities for being noticed in their organizations and beyond for the input they provide to the consultation process. I return to this point in connection with the use of high-level panels and research directorates in UN reform processes, as with the work of the ICISS and the Threats, Challenges and Change process.

Testing ideas

Combining the interaction with other environments with informal meetings that also bring in member-state officials can be a good way to inform the policy debate. As an example, the biannual informal discussions convened by NUPI on peacekeeping issues serve as an informal platform where working-level officials can meet and discuss issues. During these meetings, participants take stock of the various issues, including debates on matters like robust peacekeeping, host-state consent, development of peacekeeping doctrine, and the use of civilian capacities. Participants from think tanks and academic institutions have the opportunity to test some of their hypotheses and get a reality check with peacekeeping officials.[3]

> Some of these institutions have the convening power to bring actors together in an informal setting, with Chatham House rules. They can link academic, member states and the UN Secretariat. The yearly meeting that NUPI arranges is a good arena for this kind of informal policy discussions. It combines the external analytical perspective and the convening power of UN DPKO PBPS. That it is outside New York is also helpful, as it avoids some of the entrenched positions that prevail there and opens up for a constructive debate. It is very valuable that the Global South and others are included so that they feel that they are included and that the consultations are not happening behind closed doors.
> (interview with UN DPKO officer, June 17, 2011, New York.)

One key challenge identified during the process was the resistance to integration among many of the humanitarian NGOs (interview with Jan Egeland, May 29, 2011, Oslo). This also shows the importance of the NGO community as actors in UN norm change processes and the need to build support and ownership among these for new concepts and norms, but it could also be seen as an example of an attempt of co-optation.

When questioned on the impact think tanks, research institutes, and academics can have, one interviewee replied that they can be considered "policy entrepreneurs outside the UN. . . [they] can highlight new topics such as transnational organized crime, possible terror/narcotics link. These institutes are preparing the ground – DPKO is fairly cautious in moving on an issue" (interview with UN official, October 2, 2012, Oslo). It then becomes an "iterative process – often a lot more to it than inside process. As long as there is some feedback loop it works." The process also functions as a way of making an idea familiar to the various constituencies, and especially to member states: "you have to 'socialize an idea'" (ibid.). The team should go out and tell people what the idea is about and get feedback, making the process "interactive" – think tanks and research institutes can "put out a stronger statement just to see what will draw fire or little support" (ibid.).

Revolving doors

People change jobs, some more frequently than others. Over the years the same individual may have worked in a think tank, for the UN, and in government. In each place relationships and networks are established that may prove useful later on. In the integrated missions process, many of the people already knew each other, having worked together in some capacity, on the same topic, or on some project. This has been a common feature as regards many of those involved in norm change processes in the area of peacekeeping and in the UN in general. Thus, "the distinction between outsiders and insiders can blur in the case of many prominent individuals who move in and out of institutions through a 'revolving door'" (Weiss et al. 2009, 128).

> A revolving door turns as academics and national political actors move inside to take staff positions in UN secretariats, or UN staff members leave to join NGOs, universities, or national office and subsequently engage from outside, but are informed by experience inside. Primary loyalties to, or location in, one of the three UNs provide strategic and tactical advantages and disadvantages, which give these analytical distinctions their importance.
>
> (ibid., 129)

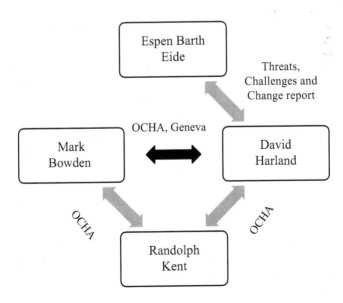

Figure 5.2 Relationships between key actors in the integrated missions process

108   *Linked ecologies and revolving doors*

Also within the UN, this 'revolving door' phenomenon is clearly discernible. People move from headquarters to the field, and vice versa, and also between organizations. Particularly the latter was an important factor in the integrated missions process: "People who have been in a mission together create informal networks that share a worldview that is cemented. These networks can be very influential over time" (interview with UN official, October 2, 2012, Oslo).

In the integrated missions process, most of the key actors knew each other from earlier assignments. The exception was Espen Barth Eide, who had only worked with David Harland previously.

Using expert teams and eminent persons

The interaction with think tanks and academic institutions can be seen as an attempt to augment the knowledge base on a particular issue. However, there are also more instrumental reasons for this engagement. As noted, the process of establishing the integrated missions concept was met with skepticism and resistance within the humanitarian community. From a DPKO point of view, the academic products and the reports should explore the difficult issues, but also advance the aim of greater integration in peacekeeping:

> Frankly, from a DPKO perspective, every IM [integrated mission] study was mobilized with a bureaucratic aim at heart – [we] needed a report in the bureaucratic turf war. [We] knew where we wanted to go and what we wanted to do with integrated missions, just needed a report that could confirm this.
>
> (ibid.)

DPKO attempted to control the process and the products through a detailed Terms of Reference (ToR) and feedback on drafts, even though the former were co-drafted with OCHA: "If you read the ToR closely at the end of the IM study, you can find clear guidance on what the outcome should be" (ibid.). This was a clear attempt at co-opting the humanitarian part of the UN – OCHA – and the humanitarian community into accepting the integrated missions concept. However, here DPKO faced a subtle challenge – having tasked the research team to do the study, they then had only limited control over the output, as the team was composed of senior researchers and staff. This is also the case in other instances where the UN links up with academic institutions and think tanks. Thus it is important to be fairly sure about the general direction the team is likely to take the process, as they become semi-autonomous once they start their work and will insist on their academic integrity and independence. This intricate dance involving academic institutions, think tanks, and the UN is a continuous one and necessitates some kind of tacit agreement on the outcome ahead of the inception of a process. That this is commonplace was also confirmed by one respondent who regularly interacts with the academic community in such processes: "It was the same thing with the . . . study from . . ." (ibid.).[4]

Linked ecologies and revolving doors   109

But it is not only the UN that depends on scholars and independent studies to lend weight to its own norm development processes. The UN controls access to field operations and to UN headquarters, which is crucial for think tanks and academics, as they can get data for projects and improve the possibilities of policy impact, which in turn increases the chances for funding for further projects. There are thus also incentives for scholars to engage with the UN on policy development processes.

During the process of advancing the integrated missions concept, government officials, international diplomats, and staff of think tanks and academic institutions outside the UN were crucial. The UN used an expert team to draft a policy report that could explore the issue and inform member states, and, in the follow-up process, Norway sought to build support through regional consultations, also involving members of academia, think tanks, and internal UN staff. Academic and think tank scholars can bring knowledge, new ideas, and legitimacy to policy development processes and in exchange gain access to data, people, and the possibility of advancing their own understanding of particular issues and advancing possible solutions and ideas.

Regional consultations

Regional consultations have become a staple ingredient in norm and policy change processes and were also central in the follow-up to the *Report on Integrated Missions*. Regional consultations can give content to the often-heard statement that the " 'Global South has a lot to offer,' without spelling out what it means. In the consultation process one goes out to Indonesia and other places and finds out what that actually means" (ibid.).

Eide highlighted the importance of working-level participation with regard to the consultation arranged in Beijing: "Nationally, China had strong integration of their support systems and operations for natural disasters, and they could bring this thinking to the table, especially since they brought working-level staff" (interview with Espen Barth Eide, June 20, 2011, Oslo). Regional consultations also offer an important venue for engaging with MFA officials from various countries. These engagements can develop over time and often contribute to the substantive strengthening of capacity on a particular issue, which in turn can increase the leverage of member states' MFAs vis-à-vis the delegation in New York. If there is no instruction from the MFA to the delegation on a particular issue, it is quite likely that the delegation will use its positioning on the issue as a bargaining tool to advance what they may think are more important issues, for example, reform of the UN Security Council or increasing aid to developing countries.

Role of the donor country

While Canada funded the *Report on Integrated Missions*, Norway funded the follow-up process to the report. According to one interviewee, the influence

110 *Linked ecologies and revolving doors*

Norway can wield on policy processes and norm change processes in the UN is due to its long-term engagement and investment in establishing networks and relationships with working-level officials, its expertise on the nitty-gritty functioning of the UN, and its funding of policy research in think tanks that have a proven track record of influencing policy processes:

> There are few academic networks within the area of peacekeeping. Norway is engaged and knows who the important actors are. The Norwegian MFA spends a lot of money on think tanks in the US, where policy often originates. In the US, think tanks play a major role as agenda setters as there is a tradition of a leaner government sector. It is also very important to anchor the process solidly in the UN: the process needs to be with them and for them, not against them, to be allied to make the UN better. Through such partnerships Norway has the ability to shape UN processes.
>
> (interview with Espen Barth Eide, June 20, 2011, Oslo)

This view is supported by practitioners inside the UN: "Very few governments issue a white paper on the UN. Norway puts a lot of resources into knowledge on the UN, both in the MFA and through support to research institutions such as NUPI, CIC [Center on International Cooperation], and others" (interview with UN official, October 2, 2012, Oslo).

Another important factor is that Norway is encumbered with little negative political ballast. It is generally perceived as a neutral and impartial actor that seeks to improve how the UN works on the ground. In a norm or policy change process, the question of legitimacy is always present and is often dealt with through regional consultations where member states can share their views in informal settings and through involving working-level staff to ensure that discussions remain substantive, without reverting to political positions.

In the process of advancing the integrated missions concept, Norwegian diplomats stressed, they were successful because Norway, as one of a handful of states, had invested time and resources in acquiring knowledge about the UN as an organization and wanted to improve its functioning by means of relatively low-profile reform efforts, thus avoiding politicizing the subject:

> There are about fifteen countries in the world that have a continuing and substantive debate about the UN at the domestic level. For other countries it is the delegation to the UN and the MFA that sets the agenda, and often substantive issues will be secondary to other political objectives that the countries want to achieve or espouse at the UN.
>
> (interview with Espen Barth Eide, June 20, 2011, Oslo)

This quote also supports the previous point about the importance of regional dialogues to strengthen the capitals' influence on a member state's stance on a given subject.

Ripeness

Eide explains that the timing of furthering a new norm is key to success – there has to be a certain ripeness for the issue to remain on the agenda and become accepted by the stakeholders: "The timeliness of the initiative was important, there was ripeness in terms of most actors seeing a need for change in the UN system. Norway worked into this stream and tried to steer it rather than opposing it" (ibid.).Without timeliness and ripeness, the counter-pressures can prove strong enough to silence and stop the progress of a new norm.

Conclusions

The main rationale behind the integrated missions norm process and the policy alliance driving this process was to enable the UN to deliver more efficiently and effectively to the countries hosting peacekeeping missions. Member states were a further set of constituents, and those from the South were perhaps more concerned with whether this process was something imposed by the West. Regional consultations provided for a better anchoring of the concept in national ministries of foreign affairs before moving to discussions between member states at UN headquarters in New York and implementation in the field. The humanitarian community was uneasy about the potential securitization and politicization of humanitarian aid that could follow from integrating the management of humanitarian, peacekeeping, and development pillars; these concerns needed to be heard and accounted for in the process. The legitimacy of the process must be evaluated from the viewpoints of all these groups, so consulting these various constituencies was a key part of the process.

The integrated missions report had established that there was a wide range of practices in the field concerning 'integration' and its implementation. In terms of achieving the policy goal of establishing integrated missions as the default option, this was, however, still only one step along the way, as micro-politics, bureaucratic turf battles, and political horse-trading could impede change, even if there was support in principle.

The process of establishing the integrated missions concept was fraught with many challenges. First of all, many member states did not really understand what the reform fuss was all about – "isn't that what the UN should be doing anyway?" (interview with UN official, October 2, 2012, Oslo). That the UN should be coordinated and under single control in the field seemed self-evident to most member states.

Second, the fact that integrated missions continue to be run along three separate funding schemes even when they are integrated limits the level of actual integration that can be achieved in the field. While a formal integrated structure can be put in place, the reality is that humanitarian agencies still obtain their funding through core funding and pledges to the Consolidated Appeals Process (CAP); development agencies have their separate funding arrangements; and the

112 *Linked ecologies and revolving doors*

peacekeeping mission has its budget from the assessed budget of the UN Secretariat. Some mitigating factors are the establishment of the UN Peacebuilding Fund and the pledge to fund gaps identified between these actors through the Integrated Strategic Framework, but these sources are small compared to the regular funding streams of humanitarian and development actors.

Third, the actual implementation of the concept on the ground has never managed to realize the spirit of the underlying intentions. As noted, according to one respondent, it "went from a nice idea to a checklist SOP and was caught in the HQ loop, dumbed down to what HQ departments can deal with" (ibid.). Although 'integrated planning' in principle sounds very good to all involved, it can easily become a rather pointless and demanding exercise if there is no funding attached to the planning. In recent years, with the implementation of the Integrated Strategic Framework planning process, efforts have been made to link the planning process with funding, creating some incentives to get involved in the planning process. There have been some changes in how operations are structured, but, for the aforementioned reasons, these are often only skin deep.

Even though this case study has exposed significant challenges involved in establishing and implementing the integrated missions concept, I would maintain that it also provides a wealth of material for the study of how norm processes in the UN in general, and UN peacekeeping in particular, proceeded in the period from 2003 to 2007 and has continued today. The key features highlighted here are common to most processes and can provide a fruitful framework for analyzing other process of norm change.

We have identified at least eight key elements of such a process. First, and most important, is the link between the UN and other actors, or 'ecologies,' to expand the knowledge base and create informal alliances of the UN, interested member states, think tanks/research institutes, NGOs, and other concerned actors. Second, in this process, the working level is particularly important, as it is here that the UN bureaucracy links up with external actors who actually drive the process forward. Third, think tanks, research institutes, and NGOs that develop concepts and ideas together with the UN can test out ideas with various constituencies in a way that the UN – vulnerable to member-state sensitivities – cannot. In this manner they can also serve as useful intermediary tools for co-optation of activist groups. Fourth, the 'revolving doors' phenomenon, of staff moving between the different ecologies throughout their careers, creates networks of actors that can ensure speedy transmission and discussion of ideas across ecologies, preparing the ground for informal policy alliances or linked ecologies to be formed and ideas to be developed. Fifth, and closely related to several of the earlier points, the use of expert teams and high-level panels that has come to characterize most norm change processes over the past decade has mainstreamed and institutionalized the linking of ecologies, on both working and senior levels, and has become a staple ingredient of such processes. Sixth, regional consultations are essential for grounding ideas and feeding best practices, inputs, and viewpoints from various regions and countries into the process: this can improve the chances that the norm in question will not fall victim to political bargaining in New York and can increase the buy-in for the substantive arguments for a particular norm. Seventh, donor countries remain important drivers of norm change processes because of the funding they provide as well as the institutional and substantive capacity they can often bring to bear on a particular issue. Eighth – and this is an enduring point – the environment must be ripe for a norm to proceed, and often there may be only a temporary window of opportunity.

The role of working-level officials, practitioners, and researchers who link up and exchange views on an issue is under-researched and under-theorized. Various theory approaches have investigated the role of NGOs, but without systematically identifying how several other classes of actors also engage in norm change processes and how these ecologies interact with each other, particularly at the working level.

The chapter has confirmed my second hypothesis, emphasizing the role of external actors when implementation of mandates is ambiguous or grundnorms clash. In this case both elements were clearly discernible – the integrated missions concept was ambiguous, and there was a clear contestation between the norm of impartiality versus integrating and subsuming all parts of the UN under one leadership to gain efficiency, in effect politicizing humanitarian action.

The chapter has also shown how current constructivist theory has significant shortcomings in grasping how anomalous behavior can be theorized and how norms are formed in the international system. In the area of peacekeeping and peacebuilding, the UN is not one unitary actor, but rather has several centers of agenda and agency. The sociology of professions can augment constructivist theory to account for how other actors affect norm formation in organizations, and a practice-oriented approach can be useful for grasping the norm change at the 'coal face.'

The UN relies on donors, think tanks, and academic institutions to develop policy and analysis capacity. This gives these actors a role in the processes of norm evolution and codification in the UN that is more central than previously argued. Linked ecologies, often through the working level, act as powerful drivers of change in the UN system.

Various factors together are important for the success of a policy process – consultations with substantive input and discussion, ripeness of the topic, political and personal contacts. And here, human agency should not be underestimated.

In sum, we need a more pluralistic and complex understanding of norm development in IOs. While there are clearly many examples of dysfunctions, pathologies, and organized hypocrisy, there are also instances of practical innovation to overcome challenges and rule-bending in order to achieve a positive impact and improve the lives of others. States are not the only actors: NGOs, academic institutions, think tanks, sections within the UN, and powerful individuals are active constituents and guardians of the values of the world organization.

114 *Linked ecologies and revolving doors*

Notes

1 This chapter draws upon empirical material that was published as Karlsrud, John (2014) 'Multiple Actors and Centres of Agency? Examining the UN as Competitive Arena for Normative Change', *Journal of International Organization Studies*, 4 (1), pp. 85–97. The material is reprinted with permission from *Journal of International Organization Studies*/United Nations Studies Association. Copyright 2014 by the United Nations Studies Association.
2 Eide was Norwegian minister of foreign affairs from 2012 to 2013. When interviewed for this book, he was the deputy minister of foreign affairs, and he also served as deputy minister and minister of defense in the interim.
3 NUPI is only one of several research institutions and think tanks that are active in this area; others include NYU's Center on International Cooperation (CIC), the Geneva Centre for Security Policy, and the Folke Bernadotte Academy and its International Forum for the Challenges of Peace Operations.
4 To protect the interviewee, I have chosen to anonymize the process and actors the interviewee is referring to.

References

Benner, Thorsten, Andrea Binder and Philipp Rotmann (2007) 'Learning to Build Peace? United Nations Peacebuilding and Organizational Learning: Developing a Research Framework', *GPPi Research Paper Series No. 7*. Berlin: Global Public Policy Institute.
Benner, Thorsten, Stephan Mergenthaler and Philipp Rotmann (2011) *The New World of UN Peace Operations: Learning to Build Peace?* Oxford: Oxford University Press.
Benner, Thorsten and Philipp Rotmann (2008) 'Learning to Learn? UN Peacebuilding and the Challenges of Building a Learning Organization', *Journal of Intervention and State-building*, 2 (1), pp. 43–62.
da Costa, Diana F. and John Karlsrud (2013) 'Bending the Rules': The Space between HQ Policy and Local Action in UN Civilian Peacekeeping', *Journal of International Peace-keeping*, 17 (3–4), pp. 293–312.
Eide, Espen Barth (2006) 'Curriculum Vitae Espen Barth Eide', Norwegian Ministry of Foreign Affairs, www.regjeringen.no/upload/UD/Vedlegg/cveide.pdf. Accessed October 12, 2010.
Eide, Espen Barth, Anja Therese Kaspersen, Randolph Kent and Karen von Hippel (2005) *Report on Integrated Missions: Practical Perspectives and Recommendations*. New York: UN ECHA Core Group.
Finnemore, Martha and Kathryn Sikkink (1998) 'International Norm Dynamics and Political Change', *International Organization*, 52 (4), pp. 887–917.
Karlsrud, John (2014) 'Multiple Actors and Centres of Agency? Examining the UN as Competitive Arena for Normative Change', *Journal of International Organization Studies*, 4 (1), pp. 85–97.
Metcalfe, Victoria, Alison Giffen and Samir Elhawary (2011) *UN Integration and Humanitarian Space*. London; Washington, DC: Overseas Development Institute; Stimson Center.
Ministry of Foreign Affairs (MFA) Norway (2008) 'Multidimensional and Integrated Peace Operations', Norwegian Ministry of Foreign Affairs, www.regjeringen.no/nb/dep/ud/tema/fn/integratedmissions.html?id=465886. Accessed August 29, 2012.
Ministry of Foreign Affairs (MFA) Norway (2012) 'Utenriksminister Espen Barth Eide', Norwegian Ministry of Foreign Affairs, www.regjeringen.no/nb/dep/ud/dep/ebe.html?id=699545. Accessed September 27, 2012.

Millennium Project (2005) *Investing in Development: A Practical Plan to Achieve the Millennium Development Goals.* New York: Millennium Project.

Office for the Coordination of Humanitarian Affairs (OCHA) (2011) *Policy Instruction: OCHA's Structural Relationships within an Integrated UN Presence.* Geneva: OCHA.

Office for the Coordination of Humanitarian Affairs (OCHA) (2012) *OCHA on Message: Integration: Structural Arrangements.* Geneva: OCHA.

Schia, Niels N. and John Karlsrud (2013) ' "Where the Rubber Meets the Road": Everyday Friction and Local Level Peacebuilding in South Sudan, Liberia and Haiti', *International Peacekeeping,* 20 (2), pp. 233–48.

UN (1997) *A/51/950. Renewing the United Nations: A Programme for Reform. Report of the Secretary General, 14 July 1997.* New York: United Nations.

UN (2000a) *Report of the Panel on United Nations Peace Operations.* New York: United Nations.

UN (2000b) *A/55/502. Report of the Secretary-General on the Implementation of the Report of the Panel on United Nations Peace Operations. 20 October 2000.* New York: United Nations.

UN (2004) *A More Secure World: Our Shared Responsibility: Report of the High-Level Panel on Threats, Challenges and Change.* New York: United Nations.

UN (2005) *A/59/2005. In Larger Freedom: Towards Development, Security and Human Rights for All. Report of the Secretary-General, 25 March 2005.* New York: United Nations.

UN (2012) 'The "New Horizon" Process', United Nations, www.un.org/en/peacekeeping/operations/newhorizon.shtml. Accessed August 29, 2012.

United Nations Secretary-General (UNSG) (2000) 'Note of Guidance on Relations between Representatives of the Secretary-General, Resident Coordinators and Humanitarian Coordinators', United Nations, http://reliefweb.int/node/22011. Accessed August 17, 2011.

Weiss, Thomas G., Tatiana Carayannis and Richard Jolly (2009) 'The "Third" United Nations', *Global Governance,* 15 (1), pp. 123–42.

6   The United Nations as a competitive arena for norm change

Introduction

In the area of peacekeeping, the UN is the primary arena for advancing norms. Previous chapters have shown that, aside from members states, various levels at the UN, think tanks, and academic institutions are important actors in norm change processes. This expands the understanding of agency in norm change in international organizations (IOs). To analyze the interaction of these ecologies further, this chapter uses the concept of 'arena,' a concept used primarily by neo-realists and rational institutionalists. Here I employ it somewhat differently, viewing the UN as a *competitive arena* for linked ecologies or informal norm change alliances.[1] I outline two understandings of arena – a wide and a narrow sense. In the narrow sense, member states come together in the UN, discuss matters of common concern, and establish regimes, along the lines described by rational institutionalism. In a wider sense, member states, along with many other actors, pursue policy agendas and prepare their arguments outside of the 'official' UN, with the ultimate aim of advancing norms inside the UN. Linked ecologies compete to frame issues and build support for new norms, concepts, and rules. These may be advanced on altruistic grounds, to increase the efficiency and effectiveness of the organization, or to strengthen the sovereignty of member states.

Processes of norm change in the UN often encounter obstacles in the form of political bargaining and horse-trading, turf battles between UN entities, and bureaucratic resistance to implement change. This chapter examines the UN as a competitive arena on two levels – one formal and one informal – where states, think tanks, academia, and non-governmental organizations (NGOs) try to avoid internal UN spoiling, turf battles, and political tugs-of-war by often forming informal policy alliances to further norm goals.

As mentioned, the 'arena' concept has traditionally been used by neorealists and rational institutionalist in international relations theory. According to Mearsheimer, neorealists view the international system as a "brutal arena where states look for opportunities to take advantage of each other . . . International relations is not a constant state of war, but is a state of relentless security competition" (Mearsheimer 1994, 9). Principal-agent theory sees the UN as an arena where the member states (principals) delegate authority to the UN (agent) or where the UN, acting as a second-level principal, delegates some tasks to other actors, like NGOs, think tanks, and academia.

Dijkstra argues that "to efficiently handle these increasing demands of peacekeeping, states have delegated planning and conduct functions to the Secretariat" and "weigh anticipated efficiency gains against sovereignty loss" (2012, 581–82).

However, it seems clear that the interaction the UN has with think tanks, academia, and NGOs goes beyond delegation of simple tasks. In the processes detailed so far in this book, the UN has been engaged in informal policy alliances to achieve change, change that some member states have seen as being against their interests or where interests of member states have been redefined in the course of the process.

In the following, I outline two understandings of the arena concept – a narrow and a wide one – and then examine the role of the 'Third UN' in the wide understanding of the arena concept. We begin with a closer look at how Norway has used the arena concept in its UN policy. Small states such as the Nordic countries, as well as the Netherlands and Canada, are known for the close relationship between advocacy actors, think tanks, and the government in policy processes and have actively pursued policies that in Lawler's words could allow them to be described as 'good states' – or states committed to an internationalist and normative agenda (Lawler 2005, 441–7).

Taking inspiration from the Norwegian case, the chapter moves on to expand on the two understandings of the arena concept. We then turn to the UN and policy development in the Secretariat under Kofi Annan. Second, to broaden the scope and see whether this understanding of arena and interaction between policymakers and think tanks in policy formulation could apply to other member states, the chapter examines the role of think tanks and the academic community in policy formation on peace and security issues in Brazil, Indonesia, South Africa, and Turkey, arguing that there is increasing participation on these issues from member states that have not traditionally acted as norm entrepreneurs. 'Good states' are trying to find entry points to engage with the BRICS countries (Brazil, Russia, India, China, and South Africa) on various policy issues, and in many cases the think tank sector provides an entry point for informal engagement. This chapter then analyses the role that think tanks and academic communities play in these countries, finding that informal policy alliances and linked ecologies are not a solely Western phenomenon, but are common to many member states and their engagement in norm processes at the UN. Finally, the chapter underscores the need for further research in this area.

Building policy alliances for norm change: Norway

Norway views the UN "as the world's central norm-setter, an arena for drawing up rules that many are bound by" (Johansen 2009). Norway believes that the UN can check the influence of great states, in fact, even asserting:

> In our view, the supremacy of the great powers is an illusion. Reality is that there can be no permanent solution to common challenges unless the UN's norms and arena functions are used to bring states and *actors* together.
>
> (ibid., emphasis added)

118 *The UN as a competitive arena*

Based on the history of Norway's involvement in various norm change processes, such as the Mine Ban Convention and advancing the integrated missions concept, 'actors' here denote civil society, international non-governmental organizations (INGOs), the research community, and other classes of actors with whom Norway works together in seeking trying to advance norms on the agenda of the UN. According to Dryzek et al., Norwegian NGOs in the environmental arena pursue "highly co-operative relationships with government" (Dryzek et al. 2003, 18), and, in Norway, "such groups can end up as arms of the state" (ibid., 3).

The Norwegian understanding of the arena concept merits deeper exploration. Does it diverge from traditional understandings, and if so, how? At first glance, there appears to be a wider understanding of the arena concept than that held by neorealists, but it converges quite nicely with the principal-agent understanding of the arena concept. However, the involvement of other (undefined) classes of actors calls for a closer exploration.

Involvement of actors other than states in global agenda setting is pointing us to the general direction of constructivist theory. However – as noted earlier in this book – while there has been some constructivist theory that examines the role that civil society, or social activists, can play, the interaction between different classes of actors, also involving think tanks and academia, remains under-researched.

The understanding of the UN conveyed here is not unique to Norway, but rather is shared by many other small and medium-sized states. In previous chapters we have seen how Canada funded the *Report on Integrated Missions* (Eide et al. 2005) and was one of the key supporters during the Responsibility to Protect (R2P) process. But is this also a trend outside the Western world? In the final section of this chapter we look more closely at interaction with think tanks, academia, and civil society in Brazil, Indonesia, South Africa, and Turkey.

Two understandings of the UN as an arena

In the narrow understanding of the UN as an arena, we have seen how the UN is understood as either a "brutal arena" where states compete with each other (Mearsheimer 1994, 9) or as an arena where states agree on regimes that are in their mutual interest. According to Nielson et al., constructivists argue that

> institutional change will most likely occur when the proposed changes dovetail cleanly with the existing organizational norms in a way that modifies without critically challenging cultural ideologies and norms. *From this insight of organizational theory, the following constructivist hypothesis flows: gaps between principals' preferences and agent behaviour will shrink to the degree that new norms and ideas are 'adjacent' to the prevailing culture.*
>
> (Nielson et al. 2006, 113, italics in original)

In the cases examined in previous chapters, change seems to have occurred because the norms have been advanced outside the organization. However, that does not necessarily conflict with the aforementioned thesis: it might also be a solution to

The UN as a competitive arena   119

the same challenge. If it is commonly known that the UN has great difficulty in reforming itself, then a logical step may be to start developing change processes outside the UN and then move a process to center stage once momentum has been gained and resistance to change has become more costly, in terms of reputation. This hypothesis also converges with how the UN secretary-general often uses high-level panels to advise on particular issues, to strengthen the empirical arguments for change, and to draw on the legitimacy of various actors, as described in the chapter on R2P. Taking a policy discussion out of the UN and into the informal arena can thus be part of a strategy to avoid substantive issues falling prey to turf battles between different UN departments, funds, and agencies.

Wide understanding of the UN as an arena

In recent years there has been a "growing body of work that calls for a conception of 'multiple multilateralisms'" in global governance (Weiss et al. 2009, 124). When taking up the editorship of *Global Governance* in 2006, Barry Carin and his team encouraged scholars studying global governance to look beyond "conventional international intergovernmental organizations" to "address the full range of global governance," underscoring that "the various transworld regulatory institutions and structures are intimately interlinked with other governance apparatuses that are based in local, country and regional spheres" (Carin et al. 2006, 3). Second, emphasizing the need for the journal to be policy relevant, the editors also showed an understanding of the role the scholarly community could and should play: "If successful, our editorship will generate publications and stimulate debates that people ten to fifteen years hence will identify as having been influential catalysts to key developments in global public policy" (ibid., 2).

Expanding the view of who can be said to be part of global governance also has implications for our understanding of authority and agency in global governance. Avant and colleagues have taken agency in global governance as a starting point and have examined who and what classes of actors can be considered "global governors" (Avant et al. 2010, 2). They define global governors as "authorities who exercise power across borders for the purpose of affecting policy" (ibid., 2) and include NGOs, private companies, states, and international organizations among these authorities. Examining the legitimacy upon which the authority of these actors rests, they find that authority generally has several components, including institutional, delegated, expert, principled, and capacity-based authority (ibid., 11–14). In general, I agree with this classification of various types of authority that global governors can draw upon, but I would add that authority is heavily dependent on the constituencies that global governors communicate with and are accountable to – and these constituencies are multiple and diverse in their nature.

The United Nations has two main functions – it is an arena where member states meet and establish regimes for global governance, and it is an actor (indeed, several actors) that implements the tasks entrusted to it by member states. As one of these member states, Norway is explicit as to its view of the organization as an arena where norms are formed and the responsibility of the organization to further

120 *The UN as a competitive arena*

these norms: "A UN-led world order is in the interests of Norway. We need a UN that functions as a global arena, norm-setter and executive body" (Ministry of Foreign Affairs [MFA] Norway 2012).

Consultation processes can support the development of capacity and knowledge on policy issues in capitals around the world. When ministries of foreign affairs participate in regional consultations, they prepare for the meetings to provide relevant input. Concept notes and relevant reports, research, and other substantive material are usually shared well in advance. During the meeting the subject will be discussed at length, and there is a reasonable chance that the meeting will end with a consensus-based declaration by the chair or the host country. In this way, consultative processes contribute to build knowledge and capacity on an issue area in the capitals of the countries participating in regional consultations. This can enable the MFA of the particular country to better prepare when the issue is formally discussed in the General Assembly or other multilateral forums. If the permanent representatives of member states at the UN in New York have received guidance on how to relate to a particular issue area from their capitals, there is also less chance that the issue will fall victim to political bargaining in the General Assembly.

Infusing the UN with intellectuals – strategic planning at the UN

Kofi Annan infused the UN with a culture where engagement with academic circles and think tanks was supported and stimulated. Early on in his tenure, Annan brought on board such prominent academics as John Ruggie, Andrew Mack, and Ramesh Thakur. According to Thakur, "Kofi surrounded himself with intellectually impressive people . . . Ruggie, Mack and me were known as the three professors" (interview with Ramesh Thakur, November 15, 2012, Oslo). Thakur held a post as vice rector (peace and governance), at the United Nations University (UNU) in Tokyo and was thus somewhat removed from the action in New York. John Ruggie is a very well-known scholar, with key and frequently cited academic articles on international relations (see e.g. 1992, 1993, 1998). He was engaged as the first UN assistant secretary-general (ASG) for strategic planning from 1997 to 2001, "a post created specifically for him by then Secretary-General Kofi Annan" (Ruggie 2012).[2] The Strategic Planning Unit (SPU) in the Executive Office of the Secretary-General (EOSG) was set up by Kofi Annan as part of his reform efforts when taking up the post in 1997, asking for funds from member states to support the unit (UN 1997, 17). Since Ruggie first took up the post, three others have served as ASGs for strategic planning. Andrew Mack was the director of the SPU from 1998 to 2001. Previous to that he had been a colleague to Ramesh Thakur at Australia National University, and he spent one year at Harvard University immediately after his assignment at the UN. Mack since established the Human Security Report Project at University of British Columbia (Mack 2012).

Other staff members in the close circles around Annan were also known for their intellectual capacity and academic experience. Michael Doyle, a professor at

The UN as a competitive arena 121

Princeton before taking up his post as ASG for strategic planning (2001–3), later moved to Columbia University (Doyle 2012). He has made important contributions to the literature on UN peacekeeping, including *Making War and Building Peace: United Nations Peace Operations* (2006). Robert C. Orr has filled the post since 2004. He also had a long and distinguished academic career, having served as executive director of the Belfer Center for Science and International Affairs at the Kennedy School of Government at Harvard University and director of the Council on Foreign Relations in Washington, DC (Orr 2012). We should also note Abiodun Williams, who came from a background as a lecturer at various US universities and who was the director of strategic planning in the Office of the United Nations Secretary-General from 2001 to 2007, later the senior vice president at the Center for Conflict Management at the United States Institute of Peace, and at the time of writing president at the Hague Institute for Global Justice. Detailing the history of the SPU, he underscores the importance of the contributions from the academic community, NGOs, and others to strategic planning and development at the UN. Preparing the agenda for the second term of Kofi Annan,

> the SPU organized a strategic planning meeting at the UN with over thirty academics, policy advisers, leaders of nongovernmental organizations (NGOs), and journalists from around the world in order to advise Annan on the priority issues for his second term.
>
> (Williams 2010, 441)

According to Williams, the discussion was structured in four working groups along the four main priority areas that Annan had set for his second term: 1) extreme poverty; 2) sustainable development; 3) conflict prevention; and 4) peacebuilding and democratization. However, "no overarching framework was imposed on the working groups; the intention was to encourage unrestricted reflection and discussion" (ibid., 442), and their recommendations "were later discussed in the SMG [Senior Management Group]" (ibid., 442). Based on the discussions in the SMG, the SPU then drafted the recommended priorities under each main priority area.

The SPU also initiated and got the secretary-general's backing for a colloquia series "for the EOSG and related staff" (ibid., 444). The series aimed to bring in scholars with expertise on the main priority areas detailed earlier "to engage staff members in the latest academic and policy debates in these and related fields, thereby enhancing the analytic and policy work of the EOSG" (ibid., 444). The funding was provided by the John D. and Catherine T. MacArthur Foundation (ibid., 449, endnote 25).

The practice of bringing in academic scholars also inspired a culture of reaching outside the organization during reform and change processes on lower levels, as we have seen in the example of the integrated missions process. Kieran Prendergast, under-secretary-general (USG) for the Department of Political Affairs (DPA), was the focal point for the secretariat of the High-Level Panel on Threats, Challenges and Change (Myint-U and Scott 2007, 112) and led the reform process leading up to the World Summit in 2005 (telephone interview with senior UN

122 *The UN as a competitive arena*

official, September 3, 2012). He, as well as other key leaders of other departments in the UN Secretariat such as Guéhenno and Egeland, was open to engagement with the academic community and think tanks in the period under Annan (ibid.).

As regards funding, the SPU had three core staff from the beginning, expanded to five in 2005 in connection with the reform process leading up to the World Summit (Williams 2010, 436). In addition, six staff members on short-term contracts or secondment from other UN departments were brought on board (ibid.). Some of these short-term contracts were awarded to senior scholars such as Bruce Jones, as noted in the chapter on the R2P process. This was a way of bolstering the capacity of the unit during intense periods like the run-up to the World Summit, and I would argue that it also increased the influence of academic scholars and think tanks on the policy-making process in the organization. For the World Summit,

> the SPU established a "2005 Team" composed of staff members of the SPU, the Deputy Secretary-General's office, and the High-Level Panel secretariat to work jointly on the report. In addition, the SPU established informal brainstorming groups for further contributions by experts inside and outside of the UN system.
>
> (ibid., 444–5)

Their work fed into the *In Larger Freedom* report (2005) released in March 2005, preparing the ground for the World Summit in September 2005.

Not only was the Strategic Planning Unit built up and staffed with academic scholars who were exchanged and who walked through revolving doors on a regular basis, it also had an explicit strategy of having a "close relationship with the scholarly community" (ibid., 446). Williams argues that the UNU and other UN research institutes lacked the in-house capacity to provide the policy analysis needed by the UN, so the SPU, together with the Peace and Governance Program led by Ramesh Thakur, worked "to enhance cooperation between producers of research in the institutes and potential consumers in the operational parts of the UN system" (ibid., 446). According to Williams, the scholarly community in academic institutions and think tanks "contributed to the strategic thinking of the Secretary-General in five ways": 1) Intellectual input to secretary-general reports such as the Annual Report, the Millennium Report, and *In Larger Freedom*; 2) reports on specific issues – for instance, the InterAcademy Council produced a report on African agriculture published in June 2004; 3) policy papers and studies; 4) SPU-sponsored lectures and colloquia; and 5) training for UN staff (ibid., 446–7).

Current situation

This trend has continued today – as one interviewee in the UN explains:

> We are just so thin and small so that we cannot play the role of think tank ourselves, but we can bring in think tanks and that's what is expected of us.

The UN as a competitive arena   123

We tap in the best brains there are on this issue and convene them and *use their analysis for our own conclusions.*

(telephone interview with senior UN official,
December 13, 2012, emphasis added)

Another UN interviewee has argued that the UN needs the "intellectual and experiential contribution [that think tanks can make], you have to have global inputs, people sharing their experience, gaps, analysis" (interview with senior UN official, November 14, 2012, Oslo).

Advancing reform through inclusive and consultative processes

The period under Kofi Annan – with various consultative processes ongoing, specifically related to peacekeeping, but also on larger reform issues – was perhaps the high-water mark of interaction between the UN and think tanks, civil society, and academic institutions (telephone interview with senior UN official, September 3, 2012; see also Weiss 2011).

Among these processes was the review of peacekeeping resulting in the *Report of the Panel on United Nations Peacekeeping Operations* (UN 2000), widely known as the Brahimi Report after its head, former minister of foreign affairs of Algeria and long-time UN diplomat Lakhdar Brahimi. The panel was composed of eight men and two women, who with some relevant experience, whether as diplomats working with the UN or working directly with the North Atlantic Treaty Organisation (NATO), Organization of American States (OAS), Organization for Security and Co-operation in Europe (OSCE), or UN peacekeeping operations; there was also a representative of the International Committee of the Red Cross (ICRC). The panel was supported by a research team of three persons based at the Stimson Center, a US think tank, and two UN officials. The team at the Stimson Center was led by Dr. William Durch, who had already published widely on UN peacekeeping, starting with *Keeping the Peace: The United Nations in the Emerging World Order* in 1992. According to the Brahimi Report:

> Producing a review and recommendations for reform of a system with the scope and complexity of United Nations peace operations, in only four months, was a daunting task. It would have been impossible but for the dedication and hard work of Dr. William Durch (with support from staff at the Stimson Center), Mr. Salman Ahmed of the United Nations and the willingness of United Nations officials throughout the system, including serving heads of mission, to share their insights both in interviews and in often comprehensive critiques of their own organizations and experiences. Former heads of peace operations and force commanders, academics and representatives of non-governmental organizations were equally helpful.
>
> (ibid., iii)

124 *The UN as a competitive arena*

I have previously described the process of establishing R2P as a norm, so here I will recapitulate only briefly. The International Commission on Intervention and State Sovereignty (ICISS) was set up by Canada to help the secretary-general reflect on if, when, and how the international community should respond to situations that shocked the conscience of the world to ensure that civilians were protected by their governments or by the international community. The Commission was composed of a blend of statesmen, senior UN officers, and international scholars and was supported by a research directorate. They coined the term 'Responsibility to Protect,' and their work was taken up by Kofi Annan in his further efforts to get member states to adopt this concept. The Commission engaged in numerous consultations around the world, as did the Research Directorate. This consultation process helped allay fears that the norm was a cover for regime change and ensured a broad support base when the discussion eventually advanced to the General Assembly.

The High-Level Panel on Threats, Challenges and Change has also been mentioned. Its report, commissioned by Kofi Annan, resulted in *A More Secure World: Our Shared Responsibility* (UN 2004), outlining the broad areas for reform and recommendations for these for the UN 2005 World Summit. This panel was supported by a research team, headed by Stephen J. Stedman, professor at the Center for International Security and Cooperation at Stanford University, and Bruce Jones from the Center on International Cooperation at New York University. After his assignment as research director for the High-Level Panel, Stedman served as

> Assistant Secretary-General and Special Advisor to the Secretary-General of the United Nations, with responsibility for working with governments to adopt the Panel's recommendations for strengthening collective security and for implementing changes within the United Nations Secretariat, including the creation of a Peacebuilding Support Office, a Counter Terrorism Task Force, and a Policy Committee to act as a cabinet to the Secretary-General.
>
> (Stedman 2012)

The years of Kofi Annan seem to have been a period of very active interaction between the UN, member states, think tanks, academia, and civil society. In part, this was thanks to the interest that senior leadership showed in engaging with external actors:

> A lot of this depended on senior leadership interest and support for engagement with academic institutions and they had their own academic links. Guéhenno and Egeland and Prendergast were engaging more with academics and intellectuals. I don't get the same impressions of the UN today. More of a culture than it is now, and the UN tends to be more inward looking.
>
> (telephone interview with senior UN official, September 3, 2012)

All the same, there are also several reforms ongoing today, and they too include think tanks, academic institutions, and civil society in the discussions and consultations held prior to and on the margins of the General Assembly.

The UN as a competitive arena   125

According to a senior UN official working in the office of the secretary-general, informal regional consultations, often funded by traditional donor states willing to support change processes, are central to the efforts of furthering change at the UN: "We can't live without them. We would not have the broad-based political support without the regional consultations. We wouldn't have come where we have without them" (interview with senior UN official, November 14, 2012, Oslo).

According to this interviewee, the Mediation Support Unit at the Department of Political Affairs would not have existed without regional consultations. In regional consultation processes,

> you learn and educate, so it's a mutual learning process. So this is how you can address this problem in this framework. Once we learn from each other we can talk together. Member states will support issues because it resonates with them . . . The informal part is 90% of the battle. If you haven't done that negotiations won't succeed . . . The regional consultations help prepare formal negotiations and decision-making at the UN in New York, and can bring alternative sources of information to draw on besides the SG Report.
>
> (ibid.)

Western dominance of think tanks influencing the UN?

Some trends emerge when we examine this picture. Most of the scholars who move through the revolving doors of the UN, providing input to the strategic thinking and development at the UN, hail from Western universities, in particular from the Ivy League institutions of the US East Coast. Geographic proximity is important; we have also noted the importance of the Center of International Cooperation at New York University, the International Peace Institute, and other institutions based in New York or the immediate vicinity. Most often these scholars continue to work on related topics after their UN assignment and can enjoy privileged access to the senior decision-makers there. It should also be noted that in the United States there is an established culture of revolving doors between government and think tanks: fairly large parts of the bureaucracy are government appointed and thus change when the government changes (see e.g. Abelson 2002). The Democratic and Republican parties have their 'own' think tanks and supporting institutions, which provide key support in formulating policies that are later implemented if the party wins the election. The fact that many of the scholars who have been moving through the revolving doors of the UN are from or are living in the United States makes it only natural for them to contribute to the development of UN policy from their position in the scholarly community, occasionally moving inside the organization to take up a post for a shorter or longer duration.

Think tanks providing a neutral space?

Several interviewees mentioned that think tanks can provide a neutral space where one can discuss issues more freely, without having to stick to established positions. Heiko Nitzschke and David Malone argue that think tanks can offer a space

126 *The UN as a competitive arena*

where key decision-makers from the UN can meet with scholars, policy analysts, and practitioners to engage in frank discussion and exchange ideas and criticism. They note, the "key to the success of these meetings is that comments made are generally non-attributable ('Chatham House Rules'), a particularly helpful approach given the highly politicized UN-context" (Nitzschke and Malone 2004). They were at the time affiliated with the International Peace Academy (IPA, now International Peace Institute, IPI), which, in addition to arranging policy discussions, also held a training seminar for new members of the Security Council on the formal and informal working methods and procedures of the Council, prior to the term beginning in 2004. The informal atmosphere provided by IPA at the time, and the fact that Malone was a former deputy permanent representative of Canada at the United Nations (1990–4) and on the Security Council (1992–4) and had written several accounts on decision-making in the Council (1998, 2004), contributed to the amicable atmosphere at the training seminar:

> It is startling to witness the extent to which an informal, private setting and the company of some eminent expert personalities can help senior officials shed their official personas and engage in genuine give and take on issues that are often hyper-sensitive for them in their official capacities.
>
> (ibid., 23)

This example is indicative of the importance of geographical proximity as well as personal relationships and the phenomenon of revolving doors in the UN–think tank nexus: "Central to such interaction is a relationship of trust between those organizing these events and their participants, trust often based on long acquaintanceship" (ibid.). Being able to establish close relationships with the representatives of newly elected members of the Security Council prior to the start of their term also means IPA could enjoy privileged access to key decision-makers among member states, a point that also the UN was probably quick to notice. Malone served as the president of IPA from 1998 to 2004, served as head of the International Development Research Centre (IDRC) from 2008 until 2013, and became the new rector of the United Nations University on March 1, 2013 (UN 2012).

Another interviewee emphasized the background of the head of the UN Department of Peacekeeping Operations (DPKO), Hervé Ladsous, with experience from the Situation Centre in the French Foreign Ministry and the former head of UN DPA; B. Lynn Pascoe, with experience from the US State Department, as decisive when the UN finally moved to set up a joint UN Operations and Crisis Centre at the end of 2012 (interview with senior UN official, August 23, 2012, New York).

Think tanks and the African Union

The trend of engaging with and at times relying on think tanks during policy development processes applies not only to the UN: in addition, the African Union has relied on the support of think tanks in the formulation of key policy documents (interview with African Union official, November 23, 2012, Zurich; interview

The UN as a competitive arena   127

with think tank official, February 7, 2013, Oslo). The practice of using outside experts began already with the Organization of African Unity (OAU) during the 1990s (ibid.) and has continued until today. During the review of the vision and doctrine for the African Standby Force (ASF), the AU invited the Institute for Security Studies (ISS) from South Africa to undertake the doctrine review; the Institute for Peace and Security Studies (IPSS) at Addis Ababa University did the review of the ASF vision (interview with African Union official, November 23, 2012, Zurich). The African Centre for the Constructive Resolution of Disputes (ACCORD) has worked with the AU to strengthen the mediation support capacity of the AU (ACCORD 2012). In 2013, the AU planned to review strategic and operational standard operating procedures (SOPs) for Peace Support Operations and intended to bring in the African Peace Support Trainers' Association (APSTA) to this endeavor (interview with African Union official, November 23, 2012, Zurich).

The use of think tanks in formulating policy is motivated by several factors: first, it is seen as a "benefit that we have an external view on the issue" (ibid.). Second, the AU is moving from pure military operations to bring in more civilians, and this change entails a need to change the leadership culture, from seeing peace operations as a military endeavor to a more multi-dimensional one: "No more military-led but civilian-led" (ibid.). Third, bringing in think tanks and institutes enables the AU to get "more buy-in, by having external organizations helping to develop doctrine" (ibid.). Finally, involving think tanks and institutions based in key member states impacts on the funding and political support that the AU receives: "We can get more financial and political support from the member states" (ibid.). To ensure ownership by member states, the documents prepared by think tanks and academic institutions are discussed in consultative meetings with the regional blocs, the Regional Economic Communities (RECs): "Before we submit the document we arrange consultative meeting with all the RECs together to see what the institute has done, get comments, make some changes and then submit it to the Special Technical Committee on Defense, Safety and Security" (ibid.), where member states then adopt the document.

Think tanks and policy formulation in member states

So far I have focused on the role of scholars in the formulation of policy and reform processes in the UN, but policy formulation is also heavily dependent on whether member states have a vibrant academic community and engage with this community. After all, it is the member states that discuss, decide, and agree in international organizations. Various scholars have examined the role that NGOs can play in shaping and framing domestic politics to achieve change in international forums (Keck and Sikkink 1998, Risse et al. 1999, Djelic and Quack 2011). The Ottawa or Mine Ban Treaty is one key example. Weiss argues that in this process "a transnational coalition successfully imbued the domestic politics of a sufficient number of states with enough humanitarian concern to redefine state interests in a way that led to a treaty" (2000, 16, see also Hubert 2000). Similarly,

128 *The UN as a competitive arena*

Kathryn Sikkink has underscored how a shift in the definition of state interests is needed to achieve change on the global level: "The adoption of human rights policies represented not the neglect of national interests but a fundamental shift in the perception of long-term national interests" (Sikkink 1993, 140, cited in Weiss 2000, 19).

Thus, state involvement and the formulation or reformulation of policy on particular issues are necessary to achieve change on an international level. Think tanks play an important and perhaps under-emphasized role in the formulation of policy and in framing and shifting what are perceived as national interests. However, there are some thorny issues involved in assessing how much influence think tanks have in different political systems. For example, the relative proximity between the think tank and the government may mean greater ability to influence an agenda, but it can also reduce independence and the ability to come up with new ideas, depending on the country and political system (see e.g. Stone and Denham 2004, 10–15). There has been a strong dominance of Western views in norm development processes:

> Scholarship to date on global norms remains largely tied to Western-centric, unidirectional and linear-teleological models of norm diffusion and stops short of analyzing conflictive, non-linear interactions between increasingly assertive powers.
>
> (Global Public Policy Institute [GPPi] 2012a)

However, this Western-dominated understanding of global norm change is being challenged by the increasing assertiveness of emerging powers in the BRICS grouping as well as other rapidly developing states like Indonesia and Turkey, and scholarship is paying more attention to the role these states play in the formation of global norms. In the following I briefly explore the role that academic community and think tanks play in the processes of developing norms on peace and security in these countries.

Brazil

The think tank sector on peace and security issues in Brazil is developing. According to one senior government representative, think tanks and civil society have not traditionally been active with regard to policy, but this is changing rapidly (interview with senior government official, November 28, 2012, Brasilia). He argues that the peace and security sector has lagged behind, as academia and civil society have not really been interested in peace and security issues. This is due to the historical stigma attached to the military since the period when Brazil was led by a military regime. There was "a stigma on academics dealing with military issues, and that lowers civilian competence" (interview with academic scholar based in Brazil, November 24, 2012, Zurich). Another problem has been the general trend of a critical theory approach among academics so that scholarly production has generally been viewed as perhaps too critical and not relevant to policy-making (interview with AU official, November 23, 2012; and telephone interview with senior UN official, November 28, 2012). This statement could also be interpreted to support a conclusion that co-optation has been more difficult in Brazil due to the critical tradition of the academic community.

Exceptions here are the Igarapé Institute, the Group of Analysis on International Conflict Prevention (GAPCon), and some university institutes, according to the ministry official: "Igarapé is filling a void in Brazil, to my knowledge it is only one other organization GAPCon that is interested. These are the only two. Then you have the university" (interview with senior government official, November 28, 2012, Brasilia). An interviewee from a Brazilian university agrees that the MFA is now opening up: "[The] foreign ministry has traditionally been extremely closed towards civil society and academic community, which has very recently started to open" (interview with academic scholar, November 24, 2012, Zurich). The Ministry of Defense appointed Antônio Jorge Ramalho, a professor in international relations at the University of Brasilia, as special advisor to the Brazilian Ministry of Defense and in charge of creating a think tank, Instituto Pandiá Calógeras, located at Escola Superior de Guerra, the Brazilian War College. The think tank will bring together civilian experts on defense and security issues to advise the Ministry of Defense (interview with think tank official, November 29, 2012, and personal communication on December 5, 2012). At the Ministry of Foreign Affairs,

> there is an permanent interest in engaging with these kinds of groups and entities . . . Brazil [Ministry of Foreign Affairs] has two academic arms – one is the IPRI Instituto de Pesquisa de Relações Internacionais [Institute of Research of International Relations] and FUNAG – Fundação Alexandre de Gusmão.
> (interview with senior government official,
> November 28, 2012, Brasilia)

Opening up to think tanks and civil society is due to the ministry moving into new areas where it has little expertise, one interviewee maintained: "As they are moving into areas where they don't have so much expertise they are opening up more" (interview with academic scholar based in Brazil, November 24, 2012, Zurich). He also asserted that the Brazilian MFA still is elite oriented and staffed mainly with classical diplomats who are generalists. This has led to a lack of specialists in substantive areas.

The senior government representative stressed that the previous minister of external relations, Antonio Patriota, understood the value of interacting with civil society, including think tanks and NGOs: "The minister is personally a 'UN man' – he was in the UN mission, he is very used to the dialog between government and think tanks, NGOs, academia, etc." (interview with senior government official, November 28, 2012, Brasilia). This interviewee also mentioned a conference he would attend, where one of the main questions would be how "to stimulate engagement between the government and think thank NGOs" (ibid.).

130 The UN as a competitive arena

As an upcoming initiative, the government intends to discuss the issue of Security Council reform with civil society organizations in Brazil, he added.

A challenge this respondent noted was the need to develop distinctly Brazilian views on issues (ibid.). An example could be the Responsibility while Protecting (RwP) concept. Efforts to establish and deepen the concept of responsibility by Brazilian think tanks and academic community are interesting. Given the failures of the UN in Rwanda and Bosnia, there was a clear sense of urgency among member states for taking swift and determined action in Libya in 2011. But in the aftermath, many of the states that voted for United Nations Security Council Resolutions (UN SCRs) 1970 and 1973 have criticized the manner in which the alliance of states implemented them, accusing them of overstepping their mandates. Since 2011, R2P has come to a standstill, and the international community has again become deeply divided. Brazil has attempted to build a bridge between supporters and opponents of the principle by launching the Responsibility while Protecting.

RwP was launched by Brazilian president Dilma Rousseff after the intervention in Libya by NATO states and partners from the Arab World (Rousseff 2011) in an attempt to strengthen the accountability framework not only for the country where an intervention takes place, but also for those intervening, ensuring that the protection of civilians is maintained as the primary goal, and not instrumentalized as a way to achieve regime change. RwP thus seeks to balance the responsibility to protect by the host state and the responsibility of intervening actors. Oliver Stuenkel has argued that this is an attempt by Brazil to "play the role as a mediator between the United States and Europe (which tend to be quick to recommend military intervention) on the one hand and reluctant BRICS members, such as Russia and China on the other" (Stuenkel 2012).

Several Brazilian scholars have since written about the concept and also engaged with the international scholarly and policy community. On November 9, 2011, the UN arranged an informal discussion on the topic, also inviting members of civil society. Brazil presented a concept note, outlining the concept in more detail (UN 2011):

> Multiple speakers urged Brazil and other actors to provide clarification on how such mechanisms could be developed as well as their practical implications, noting that these discussions would be appropriate in future debates on Security Council working methods and reform.
>
> (International Coalition for the Responsibility
to Protect [ICRtoP] 2012)

According to one Brazilian scholar in the field of peace and security studies, the first draft of RwP was developed and written by young staff at the Ministry of Foreign Affairs, with full support from the top: "Patriota himself was heavily involved" (interview with academic scholar based in Brazil, November 24, 2012, Zurich). Several Brazilian think tanks and research institutes have since been working on the concept. To continue the discussion and deepen the concept, the

The UN as a competitive arena   131

Center for International Relations at Fundação Getulio Vargas, Global Centre for the Responsibility to Protect (GCR2P), and the Stanley Foundation arranged the workshop "Responsibility While Protecting: What Is Next?" on August 23, 2012 (GPPi 2012b), and Igarapé Institute and Centro Brasileiro de Relações Internacionais (CEBRI) arranged the seminar "Implementing the Responsibility to Protect: New Directions for Peace and Security," held on November 21–2, 2012 (Igarapé Institute 2012).

At both workshops, international scholars were brought in, as well as the aforementioned Foreign Minister Patriota. The idea was to "take this RwP further, but it didn't happen" (interview with academic scholar based in Brazil, November 24, 2012, Zurich). However, it still seems to be the only alternative to R2P; as Brazil has managed to draw significant attention to the concept, and many view it as a possible bridge between supporters of R2P and those weary of Western states using R2P for regime change, it is likely to be part of the debate on where to take R2P in the future. Some have argued that Brazil here is attempting to act as a norm entrepreneur, which is encountering significant resistance from Western states accustomed to their virtual monopoly on being able to develop, codify, and disseminate new global norms (Benner 2012, 254).

Indonesia

Also in Indonesia, the government is increasingly interacting with think tanks. As one senior government representative noted, "conversations with NGOs, academics and think tanks [are] necessary. They are an important for the formulation of our policy . . . Their opinion and input are important" (interview with senior government official, November 29, 2012, Brasilia). A researcher at one key think tank in Indonesia argued that informal relations are essential. The director of the think tank is "a friend of the minister of the Ministry of Foreign Affairs and high officials. They went to the same university in the same class" (interview with think tank official, November 28, 2012, Brasilia). This is of course not unique to Indonesia: it is common in developed as well as developing countries. Indonesian government officials were also keen to point out that think tanks can provide a channel for more informal track-two mediation initiatives – for example, in the conflict in the Philippines:

> In Indonesia we have certain NGOs who are very advanced in the involvement in the mediation process, conflict and reconstruction, post-disaster reconstruction and so forth. I think the government in this case needs to learn and base their policy based on their experience. I can mention one example – the NGO Muhamadiyah's involvement in mediation process in the South Philippines between the Moro Islamic Liberation Front and the Government of Philippines. That involvement is their initiative, their program, not the government's. They are part of the negotiation mediation consultative group. That initiative has been initiated, proposed and executed by the Muhamadiyah. And it works, and the government in this case supports it. It is not a new

132 *The UN as a competitive arena*

policy as such, but we certainly support any initiative that is good. It is good for the region and good for Indonesia.

(interview with senior government official, November 29, 2012, Brasilia)

It was emphasized that a think tank should play a subtle role, providing recommendations for the Ministry of Foreign Affairs. When Indonesia hosted the Association of Southeast Asian Nations (ASEAN) summit in November 2012, "the ministry came to the institute and asked for what kind of issues they should bring up in the meeting" (interview with think tank official, November 28, 2012, Brasilia). But the think tank must take care not take credit for policies it may have suggested, as that would damage the relationship with the government:

> If our recommendations are well taken they [the government] can shift policies and that would be good for us. We have to play some kind of subtle role, the government would not be pleased to see that our initiative becomes the policy of the government, so we cannot take credit for what was our policy at the beginning. That can be a disadvantage for us as a think tank although our points are well taken.
>
> (ibid.)

Think tanks can also act as brokers between civil society and the government in sensitive areas. During the November 2012 ASEAN Summit, a think tank arranged a meeting between permanent representatives of ASEAN member states and think tanks and NGOs from Southeast Asia on the human rights architecture in the region. According to an interviewee, the meeting was very productive and was conducted in an atmosphere of mutual respect and openness for suggestions and criticism: "We could see how people from the think tanks reformulate and present points from NGOs to government and the government take the points better – tend to be more respective in responding to those suggestions and critics from the NGOs" (ibid.). The think tank was seen as a door opener by members from the civil society – "ASEAN Secretariat, ASEAN PRs [permanent representatives], they tend to value it highly when they invite invitations from us," and the think tank additionally could act as a broker between activists and practitioners: "we as a think tank combine between practice on the ground and theory" (ibid.).

Another example of the rising influence and prominence of think tanks in Asia is the establishment of the ASEAN Institute for Peace and Reconciliation (AIPR) at the ASEAN Summit in November 2012. As described by Indonesian foreign minister Marty Natalegawa, "the institute would comprise think-tanks or second-track institutions across the Southeast Asia region . . . [and] the institute will allow a process where any conflict can be responded to through non-state mechanisms" (Alexandra 2012). According to Lina A. Alexandra, a researcher at one of the participating think tanks, "the institution is very much expected to play a significant role in preventing disputes turning into armed conflicts and to

The UN as a competitive arena   133

build national and regional capacities to address conflicts in a constructive manner" (2012).

South Africa

A high-level government official in South Africa reports that the government is making use of think tanks in developing and formulating policies related to the UN:

> Basically, think tanks [are] the backbone of our policymaking. We use them as a soundboard; they are trendy in terms of their networks. They host workshops and meetings and we consult them when we need to get some views . . . It makes it easier when you put the policy in the public, because by and large the gaps that may be there are closed during such interactions.
>
> (interview with senior government official,
> November 29, 2012, Brasilia)

As examples of such processes, the interviewee highlighted that the relationship is open for suggestion from both sides – most often the government has a general policy but would like to deepen it; on other occasions, think tanks and other institutions may highlight a topic or a particular concern (ibid.). According to another interviewee, think tanks were used more actively in the 1990s but experienced a dip after the new government took office at the end of that decade (interview with think tank official, February 7, 2013, Oslo).

However, South Africa has not been using think tanks actively to frame and develop policies and further change in international organizations in the way we have seen Norway and other states engaging with think tanks, academia, and NGOs. In South Africa, it is more a matter of responding to calls from think tanks than actively using them in policy formulation and agenda setting (ibid.).

Turkey

As regards Turkey, Toktaş and Aras divide think tanks in the security sector in five categories: "a) autonomous and semi-autonomous, b) state-sponsored, c) university-sponsored, d) sponsored by a political party, and e) local branches of foreign think tanks" (2012, 255). Think tank staff "perceived themselves as contributive actors in the formulation of security policy and culture" (ibid., 257) and believed that they had influence on Turkish security policy. The rising influence of think tanks in Turkey also has implications for the understanding of authority in international relations, according to these authors.

> [It] marks a deviation from the systemic analysis of Neo-Realism on a single type actor-structure. The rise of think tanks, both in numbers and in impact, reveals *a multilevel, multi-actor and multifaceted arena* of security in which

134 *The UN as a competitive arena*

representatives of the state and military are not the sole determinants, as a result of the trend towards civilianization in culture of national security.

(ibid., 259–60, emphasis added).

A leader of one prominent security-sector think tank in Turkey argues that the space for think tanks in Turkey has opened up only quite recently due to the democratization process:

> Some of these think tanks are close to policymakers – similar to the Brookings Institution and the Democratic Party [in the United States], and the others are more critical think tanks. When you look at the policies you see that they play an influential role on the development of policies. To what extent are they influencing policy? Turkey's Iraq policy – one think tank has been very influential. On democratization another think tank has been very influential.
>
> (interview with senior Turkish think-tank official,
November 29, 2012, Brasilia)

Not many Turkish think tanks focus on peacekeeping, which falls mostly under the Center for Strategic Studies housed in the Ministry of Foreign Affairs (ibid.).

Government and independent think tanks

In the course of the interviews conducted for this book, two main types of think tanks and academic institutions emerged. The first is the independent or semi-independent think tank, located outside of a country's ministry of foreign affairs both physically and institutionally, sometimes part of a university and sometimes not. Think tanks of the second type are part of the country's ministry of foreign affairs and are designed to feed research and knowledge into policy-making processes, but much less independent and expected not to diverge too much from the 'party line.'

The potential that think tanks in member states have in influencing member-state policy development and interest formulation is also recognized by private foundations and other member states that provide direct or indirect financial support to these institutions. Several Western states have been providing direct funding to think tanks based in the developing world as a way of strengthening civil society and independent research in these countries, but also as a means of forming policy positions on particular issues. One example is the IDRC, led by the earlier mentioned David Malone. It has a Think Tank Initiative that provides funding to fifty-one think tanks in the developing world to "support public accountability by helping researchers and policy research institutions to participate in local, national, and international policy debates" (IDRC 2012a, IDRC 2012b).

Northern member states, think tanks, and universities still dominate the UN peacekeeping debate, for several reasons. First, engagement in these processes requires both human and financial resources. These resources should be present in the MFA of the respective countries, enabling the development of expertise on particular issue areas. Academia and think tanks play an important function in providing background information, undertaking research and analysis, and serving as a venue for informal discussions – but, to undertake these activities, human and financial resources are required as well. If funding comes from the North, this is likely to steer the development of the discourse in a particular direction. Risse and colleagues have argued for the existence of a "boomerang" effect when national advocacy groups link up with international advocacy networks that can help them put pressure on the government on specific issues (Risse et al. 1999, 18).

Common to scholars from academia and think tanks in both hemispheres is the implicit or explicit acceptance of a trade-off between access to data, people, and the ability to access funding due to relevance and being to some degree co-opted into legitimizing a policy process. When ecologies link up in a balanced manner, these relationships are symbiotic, but they can also result in skewed relationships where either the international organization is gaining too much leverage over research findings or where scholars are able to set the agenda to the detriment of the influence of the main constituents of these processes, namely member states themselves. Finally, participation in processes of norm change requires time and patience and, thus, long-term funding. For many institutions, engagement in the R2P process has lasted for more than a decade, and there is still considerable debate around the norm.

Linked ecologies: contributions to norm change

Taking into account the relatively small number of actors involved in the processes described here, we must ask: are these norm development processes in fact legitimate? Avant and colleagues have taken agency in global governance as a starting point, examining who and what classes of actors can be considered "global governors" (Avant et al. 2010). Our analysis in the previous section points to the uneven access to these processes, given that time, funding, and human resources are vital for engaging and sustaining participation in a norm change process.

Linked ecologies have an ability to frame, interpret, and reinterpret global norms. In the case studies, we have seen how informal alliances between the UN, member states, scholars, and NGOs have been decisive in defining issue areas and coming up with suggestions for solutions through the development of new concepts, principles, and norms. While these may relate to existing grundnorms for UN peacekeeping, seen in the case of R2P and the case of integrated missions, linked ecologies can revive old debates by reframing them and finding ways to avoid politicization of a debate at a an early stage.

Together with NGOs and advocacy networks, linked ecologies can rally support and engage stakeholders from local, national, regional, and global constituencies, but they may also act as gatekeepers, partially managing access to a particular debate. The debate on R2P can again serve as an example, as most of the think tanks involved were from the North. In the case of integrated missions, very few in the member states understood what the issue actually was about, seeing it as an

136 *The UN as a competitive arena*

internal UN issue of little concern to member states and others (interview with UN official, October 2, 2012, Oslo); it was assumed the UN would handle it internally.

To compensate for the dominance of northern-based think tanks, linked ecologies can strengthen the legitimacy and ownership of emerging norms through regional consultations, engagement, and funding of research in the Global South. Regional consultations are now a staple ingredient in most processes of norm change, aimed at building understanding, support, and ownership. They can also function as a way of informally conveying more information on a specific issue to member states and other actors, bringing in scholars to provide substantive inputs to debates, to avoid a politicized debate, and to steer the discussion in a particular direction. Although the goal of a policy-change process often is to improve the effectiveness of the organization, the question of legitimacy is always present. And despite attempts to address the legitimacy gap through regional consultations where member states can share their opinions in informal settings, this remains a lacuna in these processes. Basically, regional consultations have a partially instrumental purpose, involving working-level staff in these discussions in order to ensure that discussions remain substantive and do not revert to political positions and to help the MFAs in the South develop substantive positions that they can then share with their delegation in New York, avoiding political horse-trading in official debates.

The informal arenas that are created may be permanent or semi-permanent to enable discussion of evolving norms and may include a mix of actors, from international organizations, member states, academia, think tanks, and NGOs/CSOs. Finally, linked ecologies can contribute to the development and implementation of follow-up mechanisms, provide sanctioning and control, and serve as guardians of norms.

Diane Stone and Christopher Wright have showed how the World Bank gradually has opened up to outside actors and became a "forum for conflicting ideas and sources of knowledge to confront each other, which has increased scrutiny of the Bank's own development policy prescriptions" (2009, 1). However, they also find that while the Bank is "increasingly permeable" to outside groups, the interaction with these groups is based on

> prior assumptions of professional expertise in development, scholarly credentials and master of technical codes among participants in dialogues. Those without a Western doctoral degree or institutional affiliation can avail themselves of the Bank-sponsored training networks and capacity-networks.
>
> (ibid., 10)

In this chapter we have seen that there are only a handful of think tanks from the non-Western world that have developed capacity on issues pertaining to UN peacekeeping or are in the process of doing so. In practice, entry into the policy arena requires achieving a certain level as regards the topics and discussions. The example of RwP is perhaps one of the few instances of a policy debate driven by a member state in the South, Brazil.

Conclusions

The United Nations has two main functions – it is an arena where member states meet and establish regimes for global governance, and it is an actor (or indeed several actors) that implement the various tasks entrusted to it by member states. This chapter has sought to nuance and deepen our understanding of the concept of 'arena' in international relations by showing how linked ecologies are formed to further change in the UN. Further, noting the emerging literature on this subject, I have tried to deepen the theoretical understanding of the interaction between the UN and the 'Third UN' by launching the idea of the UN as a *competitive arena* for norm change. Having shown how, in particular, Secretary-General Kofi Annan opened up the organization to academic scholars, I have continued the exploration of the role of academic institutions and think tanks in processes of norm change.

Shifting the focus to what degree these processes can be said to be representative, I have emphasized the importance of regional consultations to enable knowledge sharing, debate, and buy-in by member states in norm change processes. Such regional consultations allow for the framing and reframing of the issue area, building knowledge and ownership. This improves the chances that a given issue or norm will be advanced on the more formal arena involving member states at the UN in New York, where states formally discuss issues of common concern and establish and modify rules guiding the operations of the world organization. In the example of integrated missions, we have also seen how taking the issue 'out' of New York can be a strategy for avoiding internal turf battles between UN agencies and political horse-trading between member states. This is a very real problem that can block change if member states rally to support various UN agencies.

In this way, the chapter has also added conceptual depth to the arena concept as understood in international relations. Furthermore, the chapter has showed that this 'arena' function is not a phenomenon unique to the UN as an international organization or to Western states, academic institutions, and think tanks. Examining policy processes related to peacekeeping at the African Union and in Brazil, Indonesia, South Africa, and Turkey, the chapter identified similar patterns in organizations and countries traditionally not among those that have most vigorously advocated change at the UN as norm entrepreneurs.

The chapter, and indeed the entire book, has stressed that norm change can be achieved only through processes and, further, that there are important elements in these processes that must be in place for a process to succeed, such as the regional consultations. This also reverberates with the methodological and theoretical choices of the book, using practice theory to grasp the social practices that linked ecologies represent.

The production and dissemination of knowledge on an issue area, and anchoring this knowledge in the regional and local context, thus serve at least four critical purposes in international and multilateral norm change processes. First, it builds capacity to engage on the topic at hand, at national and regional levels, including in regional organizations such as the African Union, the League of Arab States, the Association of Southeast Asian Nations, and the Organization of American

138 *The UN as a competitive arena*

States. Second, it contributes to the level of ownership a given country can have. Third, it can open up a political process to the inclusion of other voices and inputs from civil society organizations, NGOs, think tanks, and academia, expanding the knowledge base and the options available to policy-makers. Fourth, the process may help to 'save' an issue from falling victim to political bargaining between member states at UN headquarters.

In short, engaging with concerned member states, the academic community, think tanks, and NGOs often stems from the desire to avoid spoiling; avoid bureaucratic turf battles between various UN entities at UN HQ in New York, in Geneva, and elsewhere; and build knowledge and consensus with member states to avoid political horse-trading where substantive issues may well fall prey to political positions. In this understanding of norm change processes, the UN is seen as a competitive arena where there are tried and tested strategies for advancing a given norm or issue.

The chapter has explored the role of think tanks and academic institutions in establishing competence and knowledge in the African Union as well as in Brazil, Indonesia, South Africa, and Turkey. While there is considerable variation among the countries, the linked ecologies phenomenon is clearly discernible here as well. As such, using the sociology of professions as a tool to look at the relationship between norms, practices, and competence has proved useful. The chapter has supported the second hypothesis and shown that external actors indeed can and have influence on policy development processes in the area of UN peacekeeping, not only at the UN, but also in other regional organizations such as the AU and in national policy development processes on topics pertinent to UN peacekeeping.

This chapter has also discussed the issue of legitimacy, as this view on norm development and change involves informal policy alliances that advance their ideas partially outside of the UN, and these involve actors still based mainly in the North. The need for regional consultations has been mentioned; a further important element is timeliness. The timing in promoting a new norm is crucial to success – there has to be certain ripeness for the issue to stay on the agenda and be accepted by the stakeholders. If the timeliness and ripeness are not in place, counter-pressures may be sufficiently strong to silence and stop the advancement of a new norm.

Notes

1   Previous versions of the discussion on the UN as a competitive arena appeared in two incarnations: 1) Karlsrud, John (2014) 'Multiple Actors and Centres of Agency? Examining the UN as Competitive Arena for Normative Change', *Journal of International Organization Studies*, 4 (1), pp. 85–97. The material is reprinted with permission from *Journal of International Organization Studies*/United Nations Studies Association. Copyright 2014 by the United Nations Studies Association; and 2) Karlsrud, John (2013) 'UN as a Competitive Arena for Linked Ecologies: The Case of UN Peacekeeping', *Political Perspectives*, 7 (1), pp. 6–25. The material is reprinted with permission from *Political Perspectives*.
2   He has since held a professorship at Harvard University while also serving as the UN SRSG for business and human rights since 2005.

References

Abelson, Donald E. (2002) *Do Think Tanks Matter?: Assessing the Impact of Public Policy Institutes*. Quebec: McGill-Queen's University Press.

African Centre for the Constructive Resolution of Disputes (ACCORD) (2012) 'African Union Mediation Support Capacity Project', ACCORD, www.accord.org.za/our-work/peacemaking/au-mediation-support-project. Accessed December 30, 2012.

Alexandra, Lina A. (2012) 'Bringing Peace and Reconciliation to ASEAN', *Jakarta Post*, www2.thejakartapost.com/news/2011/05/31/bringing-peace-and-reconciliation-asean.html. Accessed December 31, 2012.

Avant, Deborah D., Martha Finnemore and Susan K. Sell (2010) *Who Governs the Globe?* Cambridge: Cambridge University Press.

Benner, Thorsten (2012) 'Brasilien als Normunternehmer. Die "Responsibility While Protecting"', *Vereinte Nationen*, 6, pp. 251–56.

Carin, Barry, Richard Higgott, Jan Aart Scholte and Diane Stone (2006) 'Global Governance: Looking Ahead, 2006–2010', *Global Governance*, 12 (1), pp. 1–6.

Dijkstra, Hylke (2012) 'Efficiency versus Sovereignty: Delegation to the UN Secretariat in Peacekeeping', *International Peacekeeping*, 19 (5), pp. 581–96.

Djelic, Marie-Laure and Sigrid Quack (2011) 'The Power of "Limited Liability" – Transnational Communities and Cross-Border Governance,' in Marquis, Christopher, Michael Lounsbury and Royston Greenwood eds., *Communities and Organizations (Research in the Sociology of Organizations)*, 33, pp. 73–109.

Doyle, Michael W. (2012) 'Michael Doyle', Columbia University, www.law.columbia.edu/law_school/communications/reports/fall2003/mdoyle. Accessed December 29 2012.

Doyle, Michael W. and Nicholas Sambanis (2006) *Making War and Building Peace: United Nations Peace Operations*. Princeton, NJ: Princeton University Press.

Dryzek, John S., David Downes, Christian Hunold, David Schlosberg and Hans K. Hernes (2003) *Green States and Social Movements: Environmentalism in the United States, United Kingdom, Germany, and Norway: Environmentalism in the United States, United Kingdom, Germany, and Norway*. Oxford: Oxford University Press.

Eide, Espen Barth, Anja Therese Kaspersen, Randolph Kent and Karen von Hippel (2005) *Report on Integrated Missions: Practical Perspectives and Recommendations*. New York: UN ECHA Core Group.

Global Public Policy Institute (GPPi) (2012a) 'Global Norm Evolution and the Responsibility to Protect', Global Public Policy Institute, www.globalnorms.net/approach/research/global_norm_evolution/welcome/. Accessed January 21, 2013.

Global Public Policy Institute (GPPi) (2012b) 'GPPi Contributes to Workshop on Responsibility While Protecting', Global Public Policy Institute, www.gppi.net/news/news_item/article/gppi-contributes-to-workshop-on-responsibility-while-protecting/. Accessed January 18, 2013.

Hubert, Don (2000) *The Landmine Ban: A Case Study in Humanitarian Advocacy*. Providence, RI: Thomas J. Watson Jr. Institute for International Studies.

Igarapé Institute (2012) 'Implementing the Responsibility to Protect: New Directions for Peace and Security', Igarapé Institute, http://pt.igarape.org.br/event-bsb/. Accessed January 18, 2013.

International Commission on Intervention and State Sovereignty (ICISS) (2001) *The Responsibility to Protect: Report of the International Commission on Intervention and State Sovereignty*. Ottawa: International Development Research Centre.

140 *The UN as a competitive arena*

International Coalition for the Responsibility to Protect (ICRtoP) (2012) 'United Nations Informal Discussion on "Responsibility While Protecting". 21 February 2012', International Coalition for the Responsibility to Protect, www.responsibilitytoprotect.org/index.php/component/content/article/35-r2pcs-topics/4002-informal-discussion-on-brazils-concept-of-responsibility-while-protecting. Accessed January 1, 2013.

International Development Research Centre (IDRC) (2012a) *2010–2011 Think Tank Initiative Annual Report.* Ottawa: International Development Research Centre.

International Development Research Centre (IDRC) (2012b) 'Social and Economic Policy', International Development Research Centre, www.idrc.ca/EN/Programs/Social_and_Economic_Policy/Pages/default.aspx. Accessed December 30, 2012.

Johansen, Raymond (2009) 'Do We Need the United Nations? Address at ISFiT Conference, Trondheim, 27 February 2009', Norwegian Ministry of Foreign Affairs, www.regjeringen.no/nb/dep/ud/aktuelt/taler_artikler/taler_og_artikler_av_ovrig_politisk_lede/tidligere-statssekretaer-johansen/2009/isfit_un.html?id=547873.   Accessed September 16, 2012.

Karlsrud, John (2013) 'UN as a Competitive Arena for Linked Ecologies: The Case of UN Peacekeeping', *Political Perspectives*, 7 (1), pp. 6–25.

Karlsrud, John (2014) 'Multiple Actors and Centres of Agency? Examining the UN as Competitive Arena for Normative Change', *Journal of International Organization Studies*, 4 (1), pp. 85–97.

Keck, Margaret E. and Kathryn Sikkink (1998) *Activists Beyond Borders: Advocacy Networks in International Politics.* Ithaca, NY: Cornell University Press.

Lawler, Peter (2005) 'The Good State: In Praise of "Classical" Internationalism', *Review of International Studies*, 31 (3), pp. 427–49.

Mack, Andrew (2012) 'Andrew Mack', Human Security Report Project, www.hsrgroup.org/about-hsrp/OurPeople/Andrew_Mack.aspx. Accessed December 29, 2012.

Malone, David (1998) *Decision-making in the UN Security Council: the case of Haiti, 1990–1997.* Oxford: Oxford University Press.

Malone, David (2004) *The UN Security Council: from the Cold War to the 21st century.* Boulder, Colorado: Lynne Rienner.

Mearsheimer, John J. (1994) 'The False Promise of International Institutions', *International Security*, 19 (3), pp. 5–49.

Ministry of Foreign Affairs (MFA) Norway (2012) 'Norway and the UN', Norwegian Ministry of Foreign Affairs, www.norway.or.kr/aboutnorway/government-and-policy/peace/un/. Accessed April 28, 2012.

Myint-U, Thant and Amy Scott (2007) *The UN Secretariat: A Brief History (1945–2006).* New York: International Peace Academy.

Nielson, Daniel L., Michael J. Tierney and Catherine E. Weaver (2006) 'Bridging the Rationalist–Constructivist Divide: Re-Engineering the Culture of the World Bank', *Journal of International Relations and Development*, 9, pp. 107–39.

Nitzschke, Heiko, and David M. Malone (2004) 'Friends and Critics: Think Tanks and the United Nations', *Development & Cooperation*, 31, pp. 20–3.

Orr, Robert C. (2012) 'Robert C. Orr, Assistant Secretary-General for Policy Coordination and Strategic Planning', www.un.org/sg/management/senstaff_details.asp?smgID=134. Accessed December 29, 2012.

Risse, Thomas, Stephen C. Rapp and Kathryn Sikkink (1999) *The Power of Human Rights: International Norms and Domestic Change.* New York: Cambridge University Press.

Rousseff, Dilma (2011) 'Statement by H.E. Dilma Rousseff, President of the Federative Republic of Brazil at the Opening of the General Debate of the 66th Session of the

United Nations General Assembly. New York, 21 September 2011', http://gadebate.un.org/sites/default/files/gastatements/66/BR_en_0.pdf. Accessed October 10, 2012.

Ruggie, John G. (1992) 'Multilateralism – the Anatomy of an Institution', *International Organization*, 46, pp. 561–98.

Ruggie, John G. (1993) 'Wandering in the Void – Charting the UN's New Strategic Role', *Foreign Affairs*, 72, pp. 26–31.

Ruggie, John G. (1998) 'What Makes the World Hang Together? Neo-Utilitarianism and the Social Constructivist Challenge', *International Organization*, 52, pp. 855–85.

Ruggie, John G. (2012) 'John Ruggie', Harvard University, www.hks.harvard.edu/about/faculty-staff-directory/john-ruggie. Accessed December 29, 2012.

Stedman, Stephen J. (2012) 'Profile: Stephen J. Stedman', Stanford University, http://cisac.stanford.edu/people/stephenjstedman/. Accessed February 29, 2012.

Stone, Diane and Andrew Denham (2004) *Think Tank Traditions: Policy Analysis Across Nations*. Manchester, UK: Manchester University Press.

Stone, Diane and Christopher Wright (eds.) (2009) *The World Bank and Governance: A Decade of Reform and Reaction*. Oxon, UK: Routledge.

Stuenkel, Oliver (2012) 'BRICS and the "Responsibility while Protecting" Concept', *Hindu*, www.thehindu.com/opinion/op-ed/article2985190.ece. Accessed January 1, 2013.

Toktaş, Şule and Bülent Aras (2012) 'National Security Culture in Turkey: A Qualitative Study on Think Tanks', *Bilig: Journal of Social Sciences of the Turkish World*, 61, pp. 245–62.

UN (1997) *A/51/950. Renewing the United Nations: A Programme for Reform. Report of the Secretary General, 14 July 1997*. New York: United Nations.

UN (2000) *Report of the Panel on United Nations Peace Operations*. New York: United Nations.

UN (2004) *A More Secure World: Our Shared Responsibility: Report of the High-Level Panel on Threats, Challenges and Change*. New York: United Nations.

UN (2005) *A/59/2005. In Larger Freedom: Towards Development, Security and Human Rights for All. Report of the Secretary-General, 25 March 2005*. New York: United Nations.

UN (2011) *A/66/551–S/2011/701. Letter Dated 9 November 2011 from the Permanent Representative of Brazil to the United Nations Addressed to the Secretary-General*. New York: United Nations.

UN (2012) 'Secretary-General Appoints David M. Malone of Canada as Rector of United Nations University', United Nations, www.un.org/News/Press/docs/2012/sga1376.doc.htm. Accessed December 30, 2012.

Weiss, Thomas G. (2000) 'The Politics of Humanitarian Ideas', *Security Dialogue*, 31 (1), pp. 11–23.

Weiss, Thomas G. (2011) *Thinking about Global Governance: Why People and Ideas Matter*. New York: Routledge.

Weiss, Thomas G., Tatiana Carayannis and Richard Jolly (2009) 'The "Third" United Nations', *Global Governance*, 15 (1), pp. 123–42.

Williams, Abiodun (2010) 'Strategic Planning in the Executive Office of the UN Secretary-General', *Global Governance*, 16 (4), 435–49.

7 Linked ecologies in international relations

The beginning and end of all literary activity is the reproduction of the world that surrounds me by means of the world that is in me, all things being grasped, related, re-created, molded, and reconstructed in a personal form and original manner.

Johann Wolfgang von Goethe quoted by
Edward Hopper (O'Doherty 1982, 14)

But in what sense can a person ever leave a previous community (so to speak) completely behind (Beer 1989)? To the extent that knowledge is embedded in what they do, it will in turn show traces of their training, occupation and the contexts in which they have used it. *Persons ferry knowledge about*, drawing on different aspects of their own biographies . . .

Marilyn Strathern (2004, 23–5, my emphasis)

Introduction

UN peacekeeping is not mentioned in the UN Charter, and yet it has become one of the most characteristic, versatile, well-known, and oft-used features of the world organization. The development of UN peacekeeping has been inductive, according to evolving needs, and reliant upon strong leadership on the ground. UN peacekeeping developed rapidly, from non-existent in the 1945 Charter to the UN mission in Congo (1960–4), where the tension between humanitarian intervention and sovereignty first came to the fore. The rapid development was halted and reversed with the untimely death of Secretary-General Dag Hammarskjöld in 1961 and for the remainder of the Cold War remained limited to monitoring peace agreements. Then, with the missions in Namibia (1989–90) and Cambodia (1991–3), and even more so with the missions to the former Yugoslavia, peacekeeping developed anew and took on civilian roles. The tension between the grundnorms of core human rights and sovereignty was still there, however, and resurfaced with the failures of the UN to prevent and respond to the atrocities in Bosnia and in Rwanda.

Since the end of the Cold War, UN peace operations have continued to change, and quite significantly so. Peacekeeping missions have expanded and assumed civilian peacebuilding and statebuilding tasks to prevent the reoccurrence of

Linked ecologies in IR 143

violent conflict and promote "action to identify and support structures which will tend to strengthen and solidify peace in order to avoid a relapse into conflict" (Boutros-Ghali 1992, 3) Since Secretary-General Boutros Boutros-Ghali issued *An Agenda for Peace*, UN peacekeeping operations have increasingly taken on civilian tasks. In the UN there is an evolving understanding that 'peacekeepers are peacebuilders' and should implement early peacebuilding tasks (UN 2010a, UN 2010b, UN 2012). In 2014, Secretary-General Ban Ki-moon nominated a high-level panel on peace operations in order to provide recommendations on how peace operations should adapt to new threats and tasks on the ground (see also Karlsrud 2015). The panel delivered its report in June 2015, recommending that the UN should adapt financing to include funding from the assessed budget for special political missions and only take on peace enforcement tasks for limited durations (Ramos-Horta et al. 2015). Change has thus been a core feature of UN peacekeeping since its inception until today, and there has been a continuous tension between the grundnorms of sovereignty and the need for intervention to prevent and respond to violations of core humanitarian principles and human rights.

The core norms of peacekeeping – consent of main parties, non-use of force, and impartiality, resting on the grundnorm of sovereignty in the international system – were challenged when the world witnessed UN inaction to the war crimes in Bosnia and the genocide in Rwanda. While everyone could agree that the protection of civilians should be central, the normative framework guiding peacekeeping still emphasized the traditional core norms. A rebalancing was necessary, between the core norms of consent, non-use of force, and impartiality on the one side and protection of civilians on the other. This required reinterpreting what sovereignty means in the international system and underscoring that impartiality does not mean indifference. The norm change processes that followed, concomitant with the return to an upsurge of peacekeeping operations in the late 1990s, have been the main study of this book.

Main findings of the book

As the two quotes by Edward Hopper and Marilyn Strathern opening this chapter eloquently display, people bring with them their prior experiences and values when moving from one job to another. They "ferry knowledge about" and bring with them networks and knowledge (Strathern 2004, 25), but also reconstruct and remold that knowledge according to their personal beliefs and values to fit their new environment. This book has aimed to contribute to the understanding of how norms guiding UN peacekeeping change and who the important actors are in these processes, thereby contributing to the wider literature on norm change in international organizations (IOs). In terms of theory, I have drawn attention to the role of practices on the ground and how these may create a bottom-up influence on norm change in UN peacekeeping and the complex interplay between government and UN officials, applied and academic researchers, and civil society activists in processes of norm change.

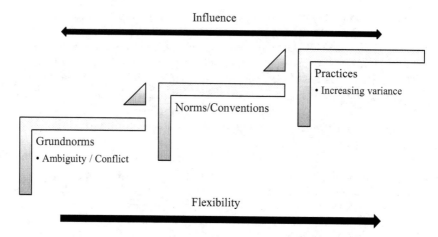

Figure 7.1 Grundnorms, norms/conventions, and practices in UN peacekeeping

To analyze norm change processes in UN peacekeeping, I have further developed constructivist theoretical and methodological tools. I have introduced the concept of grundnorms, adopted from Hans Kelsen. The concept of grundnorms has been employed as an analytic rather than ontological tool, to better understand how core norms are in constant contestation with each other in the field of UN peacekeeping. Drawing upon constructivism, practice theory, and the sociology of professions, this book has showed a certain level of analytic eclecticism (Sil and Katzenstein, 2010). Analytic eclecticism as an approach does not mean that theory and methodology are being adapted to achieve a certain set of findings, but instead are reflecting the need to adapt to the phenomena in question and be flexible to change while maintaining methodological and analytical rigor. Certain problems require certain methods, and to better understand and analyze individual and social practices in the area of UN peacekeeping and the potential impact these may have on norm change in the field, these methodological and theoretical choices have enabled me to develop tools to study these practices, both at the field level and the social practices that linked ecologies produce.

My theoretical and methodological choices are related to ongoing developments in the study of norm change in IOs, and other studies employing similar methods include Seabrooke and Tsingou (2009, 2015), Stone (2013), and Seabrooke and Nilsson (2015). In the following, I summarize the findings and offer a few final observations and recommendations for further research and for policy-makers.

Epistemologically, the thesis has shown how norm change can be explored through the study of competent practices drawing upon the sociology of professions, both in UN field operations and in the formation of linked ecologies for norm change. The concept of linked ecologies has proven to be a useful analytical concept principally for three reasons: First, the ecologies concept helps describe various heterogeneous groups, focusing on their common aspects rather than what divides them. Within ecologies there is competition between coalitions

Linked ecologies in IR 145

who fight over control over how an issue should be defined and how it should be solved. Coalitions in one ecology can reach out to actors in other ecologies to form linked ecologies to gain strength and achieve change in areas formally outside their remit. By this linked ecologies are formed. Second, linked ecologies can be formed as informal and formal alliances. Ecologies may be linked up through individuals who move through revolving doors, but this is not a necessary feature for linked ecologies to occur. Third, the linked ecologies concept improves our understanding of how change can be achieved in international organizations by taking a process-oriented view. It balances between structural and individual understandings of agency and change and emphasizes the role of individuals as carriers of knowledge, ideas, methods, and skills who can form bridges from one ecology to another.

Ambiguity is deep-seated in UN peacekeeping, as the grundnorms and norms guiding peacekeeping are not in concordance. This highlights the role of practices and how senior professionals deliberate and weigh the conflicting norms applicable to particular situations. Thus, the book argues for the role of practices informing the development of new norms. The evolving concepts of modern-day peacekeeping have a significant impact on how the UN operates in post-conflict states. First, the book investigates the role that practices of the special envoys and representatives of the secretary-general (SRSGs) have in norm change processes. I have argued that practices from the field, crystallized through the actions of special envoys and representatives, provide a potential a bottom-up source of influence on process of norm change in the UN. SRSGs, often coming from diplomatic careers and/or enjoying relative autonomy and interpretation of what the UN is and what it stands for, wield this influence, thanks to the decentralized authority and their own personal prestige.

The book has explored the practices of SRSGs in the UN missions in Afghanistan and Côte d'Ivoire, as well as the sources of authority that decision-makers in the UN draw upon, and added *prestige* as an important source of authority. An SRSG can make controversial decisions and may lose prestige in one setting, or 'ecology,' but gain prestige in another and use this as an exit strategy. Here the 'revolving doors' phenomenon between linked ecologies becomes particularly prominent.

The book has found that individuals matter – and not only when they have positions of authority such as the secretary-general or SRSGs. I have highlighted the role of *working-level officials* as the actual contact points when linking up with other ecologies, as seen in the case studies of Responsibility to Protect (R2P) and integrated missions, and when looking at how norms form and change in the AU, Brazil, Indonesia, Norway, South Africa, and Turkey. Individuals contribute to the shaping and reshaping of the organization in more ways than normally recognized. The impact of the social practices of linked ecologies goes beyond that of dysfunctional behavior, pathologies, and organized hypocrisy and can include instances of norm change where the relationship between existing norms is rebalanced.

Decisions on the ground in UN peacekeeping are often taken by individuals and cannot be seen as solely the collective output of the organization. Analyzing the

146 *Linked ecologies in IR*

engagement through a practice-oriented approach, the book has shown that within the UN several parallel sets of norms, rules, and practices coexist, which may be at odds or indeed mutually contradictory to each other, and that SRSGs can arbitrate between these norms. The literature has dealt with these contradictions only in a simplistic manner; the real world is more complex and differentiated. Using a practice-oriented method, I have shown that senior managers in the field rely on various sources of authority when they perform actions that are seemingly in contradiction to established norms and rules. Thus, practices evolve at the field level in advance of codification of these practices into doctrine at HQ.

In turn, this means that there is a spatio-temporal lag between practice and theory in the formation of UN guidelines on peacekeeping – as a function of the lack of capacity, but also because of the silent acceptance by member states of informal practices and norms in the UN at field level. The gap between theory and practice should not necessarily be characterized as organized hypocrisy or a 'pathology,' but could be a functional expression of the temporal lag of norm formation in the organization. Practices can be seen to evolve both at the top and ground level, and norms trickle both up and down in the system. The acceptance of parallel norms, rules, cultures, and practices indicates what could be termed *pragmatic hypocrisy* or *functional disharmony* in peacekeeping.

Second, the book has combined practice theory with the theory framework of the sociology of professions to theorize the cooperation between the UN, donor governments, and think tanks in processes of norm change. This harkens back to the origins of constructivism where sociology played a central role; the use of the sociology of professions theory greatly strengthens the explanatory power of constructivism in this specific setting. The case studies on R2P and the integrated missions concept have shown how professionals frequently spend time as actors in different sectors – donor governments, academia, and think tanks – constituting a 'revolving door' phenomenon (see also Abbott 2005, Fourcade 2006, Seabrooke and Tsingou 2009, Kittikhoun and Weiss 2011, Seabrooke and Nilsson 2015, Seabrooke and Tsingou 2015). Through this revolving door phenomenon, ecologies link up to form informal policy alliances to achieve norm change in peacekeeping. Individuals at the top as well as on the working levels move between various ecologies, bringing knowledge, connections, and networks from one ecology to the other. These linked ecologies and their actions have been examined as social practices that advance particular sets of ideas in the international arena.

Third, the arena concept has been explored in a wide sense, including other actors than member states. This has enabled a better understanding of how the concepts, rules, and norms of peacekeeping develop through interaction between these ecologies. As a formal arena, the United Nations is a meeting place for member states to discuss and agree on issues – for instance, on the norms for UN peacekeeping. But the UN is also an important informal arena for other actors, such as think tanks, academic institutions, non-governmental organizations (NGOs), and private corporations. These represent various ecologies that can link up in norm development processes to form new norms.

Linked ecologies in IR 147

Linked ecologies have the ability to frame, interpret, and reinterpret global norms. Together with NGOs and advocacy networks, they can rally support and engage stakeholders from local, national, regional, and global constituencies (as with R2P), but can also act as gatekeepers, partially managing access to a particular debate. Linked ecologies can create informal arenas for discussion of evolving norms, including actors ranging from international organizations, member states, academia, think tanks, and NGOs/CSOs. Linked ecologies can strengthen the legitimacy and ownership of emerging norms through regional consultations, engagement, and funding research in the Global South. Finally, linked ecologies can develop and implement follow-up mechanisms, providing sanctioning and control and serving as guardians of norms.

Drawing on the empirical case studies of the R2P and integrated missions norm processes, the book has argued that the UN can be seen as a competitive arena in a wide and a narrow sense, where linked ecologies take hold of issues and put forward ideas on how to resolve these issues. In a wide sense, informal alliances are formed around issues of common concern; with the monetary support of donor states, and the knowledge production of think tanks, academia, and the working level of the UN, ownership among member states gets built into consultative processes. At a certain stage, these processes end up in more formal negotiations in the UN, where think tanks, academia, and civil society take a supportive, background role. This is the *narrow* understanding of the UN as a competitive arena.

The book shows that the norm change processes investigated in the book can signify three different drivers of norm change. In chapter 3, looking at how SRSG are interposed between conflicting normative pressures, we have seen how the SRSG may rebalance the relationship between norms through practice and how this practice can feed into the overall discussion at UN headquarters and among actors engaged and involved in the global discussion on norms guiding UN peacekeeping missions. In chapter 4, the focus shifted to the R2P norm process, which was, and is, perceived to be much more controversial, involving various member states, statesmen, high-level officials, and so forth. In chapter 5, looking at the development and operationalization of the integrated missions concept, the underlying grundnorms gave material for continued conflict between those promoting and those resisting the concept, but member states perceived it to be more of a bureaucratic turf fight than a struggle worth engaging in.

While there clearly are varying levels of engagement in these three processes, I have shown that all of them were based on key grundnorms guiding the international system. However, while the R2P process could be seen as an effort of a linked ecology to strengthen a new norm and redefine the understanding of what sovereignty means, the other processes in this chapter have been cases of rebalancing between norms that have been somewhat less conflictual and thus considered less significant by member states and other actors.

The book deepens and widens the understanding of who has authority and agency in international relations – deepens by showing the relevance and importance of practices on the ground, as exemplified by the actions of SRSGs in Afghanistan and Côte d'Ivoire, and widens by including academic institutions

148 *Linked ecologies in IR*

and think tanks in the analysis. The interactions emerging from informal alliances for norm change constitute practices that impact on norm change processes in international organizations.

The book also advances our understanding of how norms change in international relations, what role practices in the field can play, and who can be considered as agents in informal and formal processes of norm change. It has shown how think tanks and academia have, together with member states and UN officials, and through practices in the field, formed informal policy alliances to establish new norms, principles, and concepts such as 'integrated missions' and 'responsibility to protect,' thereby constituting and driving norm change in the international system. With this contribution, the study expands our understanding of which actors have agency and what sources of authority they draw on in processes of norm change in international organizations.

Final observations and recommendations

This book has sought to shed light on processes of norm change in UN peacekeeping. For practitioners, the results of the study may not appear surprising. As Giddens noted, "the 'findings' of social sciences, as I have emphasized, are not necessarily news to those whom the findings are about" (Giddens 1984, 335).

The UN must rely on cooperation with member states, the academic community, think tanks, and NGOs to develop its capacity for policy and analysis. At times the UN also seeks to co-opt these actors to achieve a controlled knowledge production that suit the goals of the organization. Usually, academic and think tank scholars are aware of this danger, but choose to engage nevertheless, as access to data, people, and the opportunity to influence policy most often outweigh the potential costs of engagement.

The considerable requirements as to human and financial resources, time, and commitment posed by norm change processes give an advantage to those member states that are able and willing to commit such resources and to support processes and other members of linked ecologies when it comes to norm change in the UN. However, we have also seen that emerging economies are increasingly engaging with think tanks, academic communities, and other ecologies in policy formulation and norm processes, helping balance the picture. The near monopoly of Western states on norm entrepreneurship has ended, and other states are engaging in global norm development processes. This should be explored further. The book has shown that local think tanks and scholars are part of this process, confirming that the linking of ecologies to achieve norm change is becoming a global phenomenon.

However, most UN member states still have limited capacity, in the state apparatus and among NGOs, to engage in the wide range of issues being discussed in a myriad of international organizations. When it comes to the ability to influence global norm change processes, there remains a considerable imbalance between high- and medium-income states on the one hand and lower-income countries on the other. A possible exception is the g7+ coalition of states emerging from conflict, whose Peacebuilding and Statebuilding Goals were released at the Fourth High-Level Forum on Aid Effectiveness in Busan in 2011 (g7+ 2011). This grouping has been able to speak with a coherent voice on issues concerning states in the aftermath of conflict – although the considerable support from Organisation for Economic Co-operation and Development (OECD) countries should be noted here. The influence on the agenda that the g7+ are championing remains to be seen and should be subjected to further study.

Leonard Seabrooke and Lasse Folke Henriksen have launched the term 'issue professionals' to refer to professionals in areas such as peacekeeping, humanitarian action, and development work. In the area of peacekeeping, economists, sociologists, anthropologists, international relations (IR) theorists and practitioners, think tank experts, government officials, diplomats, and practitioners from widely differing formal backgrounds and experience are engaging in practices that are driving the debate on what peacekeeping is and for what purpose (Seabrooke and Henriksen forthcoming 2016). Alongside the focus on peacekeeping during the last twenty years, ecologies of many fields have developed 'peacekeeping' offshoots. In the academic world, there are pure peacekeeping courses drawing upon a range of schools and theories, as well as courses hosted within traditionally relevant academic departments such as international relations. Peacekeeping has become an 'issue profession' that is defined more by its tasks than by the professional backgrounds of its members. This, too, is an area that merits further work, and further studies of the humanitarian and the development field as 'issue professions' could be undertaken (Mühlen-Schulte and Karlsrud forthcoming 2016). The tools that I have developed here are well suited to conduct such studies and can help increase the understanding of how norm change is coming about in these fields as well.

Finally, seeing the processes of norm change in a conflictual space where grundnorms collide shows that norm change processes are never unilinear: they continue to ebb and flow, depending on external circumstances and events, as well as the interest of the main supporters among member states to keep advocating for a particular norm. Practices and linked ecologies together form constitutive pillars for a new understanding of how norms, principles, and concepts evolve in international organizations.

References

Abbott, Andrew D. (2005) 'Linked Ecologies: States and Universities as Environments for Professions', *Sociological Theory*, 23 (3), pp. 245–74.

Boutros-Ghali, Boutros (1992) *An Agenda for Peace: Preventive Diplomacy, Peacemaking, and Peace-Keeping: Report of the Secretary-General Pursuant to the Statement Adopted by the Summit Meeting of the Security Council on 31 January 1992.* New York: United Nations.

Fourcade, Marion (2006) 'The Construction of a Global Profession: The Transnationalization of Economics', *American Journal of Sociology*, 112 (1), pp. 145–94.

g7+ (2011) *A New Deal for Engagement in Fragile States.* Paris: International Dialogue for Engagement in Fragile States, Organisation for Economic Co-operation and Development (OECD).

150 *Linked ecologies in IR*

Giddens, Anthony (1984) *The Constitution of Society: Outline of the Theory of Structuration.* Cambridge: Polity Press.

Karlsrud, John (2015) 'The UN at War: Examining the Consequences of Peace Enforcement Mandates for the UN Peacekeeping Operations in the CAR, the DRC and Mali', *Third World Quarterly*, 36 (1), pp. 40–54.

Kittikhoun, Anoulak and Thomas G. Weiss (2011) 'The Myth of Scholarly Irrelevance for the United Nations', *International Studies Review*, 13 (1), pp. 18–23.

Mühlen-Schulte, Arthur and Karlsrud, John (forthcoming 2016) 'Quasi-Professionals in the Organisation of Transnational Crisis Mapping', in Seabrooke, Leonard and Lasse F. Henriksen eds., *Professions and Organizations in Transnational Governance.* Cambridge: Cambridge University Press.

O'Doherty, Brian (1982) *American Masters: The Voice and the Myth.* New York: Random House.

Ramos-Horta, José et al. (2015) *Uniting Our Strengths for Peace – Politics, Partnership and People: Report of the High-Level Independent Panel on United Nations Peace Operations.* New York: United Nations.

Seabrooke, Leonard and Lasse F. Henriksen (forthcoming 2016) 'Issue Control in Transnational Professional Networks and Organizations,' in Seabrooke, Leonard and Lasse F. Henriksen eds., *Professional Networks in Transnational Governance.* Cambridge: Cambridge University Press.

Seabrooke, Leonard and Emelie R. Nilsson (2015) 'Professional Skills in International Financial Surveillance: Assessing Change in IMF Policy Teams', *Governance*, 28 (2), pp. 267–54.

Seabrooke, Leonard and Eleni Tsingou (2009) *Revolving Doors and Linked Ecologies in the World Economy: Policy Locations and the Practice of International Financial Reform.* Warwick: University of Warwick, CSGR Working Papers.

Seabrooke, Leonard and Eleni Tsingou (2015) 'Professional Emergence on Transnational Issues: Linked Ecologies on Demographic Change', *Journal of Professions and Organization*, 2 (1), pp. 1–18.

Sil, Rudra and Katzenstein, Peter (2010) *Beyond Paradigms: Analytic Eclecticism in the Study of World Politics.* Basingstoke, UK: Palgrave Macmillan.

Stone, Diane (2013) '"Shades of Grey": The World Bank, Knowledge Networks and Linked Ecologies of Academic Engagement', *Global Networks*, 13 (2), pp. 241–60.

Strathern, Marilyn (2004) 'Working Paper One: Knowledge on Its Travels: Dispersal and Divergence in the Make-up of Communities,' in Strathern, Marilyn ed., *Commons and Borderlands:Working Papers on Interdisciplinarity, Accountability and the Flow of Knowledge.* Oxon, UK: Sean Kingston Publishing.

UN (2010a) *S/2010/386. Progress Report of the Secretary-General on Peacebuilding in the Immediate Aftermath of Cconflict, 16 July 2010.* New York: United Nations.

UN (2010b) 'Secretary-General's Remarks to Security Council Open Debate on Post-Conflict Peacebuilding', United Nations, www.un.org/sg/statements/?nid=4495. Accessed September 16, 2012.

UN (2012) *Peace: Keep It. Build It. The Contribution of United Nations Peacekeeping to Early Peacebuilding: Strategy.* New York: United Nations Department of Peacekeeping Operations and Department of Field Support.

Index

Analytic eclecticism, 144
Annan, Kofi, 18, 25, 58, 72, 74–75,
   77–79, 83, 85–86, 95–98, 104,
   120–124, 137
Afghanistan, 43, 52–56
   War on Terror, 53
   Taliban, 53–56
African Union, 84, 126–127, 137, 138
Authority
   Bureaucratic authority, 24
   Charismatic authority, 60
   Delegated authority, 44, 58–59, 62,
   Expert authority, 29, 59, 87
   Moral authority, 56, 59–60, 61, 62
   Prestige or revolving doors authority,
     13, 44, 56, 60–61, 64–66, 145
Agency
   Multiple sources, 1, 7, 25
   Working level, 1–2, 15, 95, 102,
     105–106, 109–113, 136, 145–147
   SRSGs, 25, 56–61
ASEAN, 132
Axworthy, Lloyd, 79, 81

Boutros-Ghali, Boutros
Brazil, 46, 76, 83, 88, 117, 118,
   128–131, 136, 137, 138, 145

Canada, 32, 74, 77, 79, 81, 83, 84,
   85, 95, 104, 109, 117, 118, 124, 126
Choi, Young-jin, 12–13, 30, 43, 45,
   49–51, 63
Cohen, Alberta, 74, 79–81, 84–85
Côte d'Ivoire, 43, 48–52

Deng, Francis, 74, 79–81, 84–85
Doyle, Michael, 104, 120–121

Eide, Espen Barth, 98–102, 105, 107,
   108–110

Eide, Kai, 12, 28, 43, 53–56, 59, 63
EU, 54, 102
Evans, Gareth, 79, 80, 83, 86

France, 101

Harland, David, 99–100, 102, 104–105,
   107, 108
Hubert, Don, 81

IASC, 98
Indonesia, 109, 117, 118, 128, 131–133,
   137, 138, 145
Insider ethnography, 9

Jones, Bruce, 79, 80, 83, 88, 122, 124

Malone, David N., 126, 134
MINURCAT, 5
MINUSMA, 5
MINUSTAH, 5, 46
MONUC, 46, 57
MONUSCO, 5

NATO, 59, 76, 79, 123, 130
Norms
   Ambiguity, 8, 145
   Basic norms / Grundnorms, 1, 7, 8–9,
     18–20, 43, 74, 143
   Bureaucracies, 24–26
   Civil society, 7, 31, 36–37, 81, 83–85,
     118, 123–124, 128–130, 132, 134,
     138, 143, 147
   Organizational culture, 22–24
   Definition of, 4
   Epistemic communities, 1, 20–21,
     32–33
   Generative ambiguity, 44, 64–65
   Integrated missions, 2, 6, 9, 14, 20, 36,
     38, 62, 94–113

152 Index

Lessons learned and best practices, 4
Logic of Appropriateness, 20–22
NGOs, 1, 9, 23, 31–37, 44, 60–61,
  81–83, 88, 95, 98, 104–107,
  112–113, 116–121, 127, 129,
  131–138, 146–148
Norm arbitrators, 62–63
Norm entrepreneurs, 25, 44, 62, 85, 87,
  95, 103, 106, 117, 131, 137, 148
  Academics and statesmen; 79–80
  Secretary-General, 25, 44, 62,
    77–78, 85
  SRSGs
Peacebuilding, 2–3, 12, 16, 18, 20,
  22–23, 30, 38, 82, 100, 112–113,
  121, 124, 142–143, 149
Think tanks, 1–2, 8–15, 22, 32–38,
  79–88, 95, 101–113, 116, 118–138,
  146–148
Norway, 32, 36, 82, 83, 85, 95, 96, 101,
  102, 103–104, 109–111, 117–118, 119,
  120, 133, 145
Kent, Randolph, 100, 102, 107
Ki-moon, Ban, 6, 18, 72, 75, 143
Linked ecologies
  Academia and think tanks, 78, 79–83
  Civil society, 83
  Competitive arena, 35–37, 116–141
  Definition of, 6–7
  Informal alliances, 1, 32–35
  Member states, 83–84
  Revolving doors, 31–32, 81,
    86–88, 95
  Transnational advocacy networks, 83
Luck, Edward C., 79, 80, 84–85
Mack, Andrew, 104, 120
Malone, David M., 126, 134

Observant participation, 9–10
ONUC, 76–77
Orr, Robert C., 121
OSCE, 123

Peacekeeping
  History after the Cold War, 2–7, 12, 32,
    64, 74, 95, 97–98, 142
  Linked ecologies, 6–7
  Peace enforcement, 4–6, 47,
    50–52, 143
  Principles, 4, 44, 56, 143
  Professionalization of, 6
  Protection of Civilians, 45,
  Robust peacekeeping, 45–52, 106

Use of force, 4–6, 44–47, 50–52, 72,
    106, 143
Practices, 4, 76–77
  Background knowledge, 10, 27–28,
    61, 65
  Bourdieu, 27, 28, 39
  Informal alliances, 28–29
  Methodology, 9–10
  Practice theory, 26–29
  SRSGs, 2, 45, 65–66
Prendergast, Kieran, 104, 124

R2P
  AU Constitutive Act, 84
  Côte d'Ivoire, 48–52
  Evolution, 73–75
  ICISS, 74–77, 79–84, 86, 106, 124,
  Linked ecologies, 86–87
  Libya, 75
  Responsibility while Protecting, 76, 88,
    130–131, 136
Ramos-Horta, José, 6, 12, 143
Ruggie, John, 4, 120

Sociology of professions, 29–31
  Fiduciary responsibility, 29–30, 87–88
  Issue profession, 15, 29, 31, 38, 149
  Jurisdictional control, 29, 76, 87
  Revolving doors, 31–32, 86–88, 95
South Africa, 118, 127, 133, 137, 138, 145
SRSGs
  Norm entrepreneurs, 25, 44, 62
  Norm arbitrators, 62–63
Stedman, Stephen J., 79, 80, 124

Thakur, Ramesh, 79–80, 81, 83, 84, 85,
    86, 120, 122
Turkey, 118, 128, 133–134, 137, 117,
    138, 145

UNAMA, 43, 52–56, 59
UNAMID, 5
UNEF, 77
UNMISS, 5
United Kingdom, 32, 43, 54, 77, 82, 83,
    95, 101, 104
United States, 3, 25, 52–55, 83, 125, 130, 134
UNPROFOR, 4
UNOCI, 5, 30, 43, 45–52
UNTSO, 2

Weiss, Thomas G., 78, 81, 85
Williams, Abiodun, 121